READING
ROMANS
IN CONTEXT

FOREWORD BY FRANCIS WATSON

READING ROMANS
IN CONTEXT

PAUL AND SECOND TEMPLE JUDAISM

BEN C. BLACKWELL, JOHN K. GOODRICH,
& JASON MASTON, EDITORS

ZONDERVAN

Reading Romans in Context
Copyright © 2015 by Ben C. Blackwell, John K. Goodrich, and Jason Maston

This title is also available as a Zondervan ebook.
Visit www.zondervan.com/ebooks.

Requests for information should be addressed to:
Zondervan, 3900 *Sparks Dr. SE, Grand Rapids, Michigan 49546*

Library of Congress Cataloging-in-Publication Data

    Reading Romans in context : Paul and Second Temple Judaism / edited by Ben C. Blackwell,
John K. Goodrich, and Jason Maston.
      pages cm.
    Includes indexes.
    ISBN 978-0-310-51795-5 (softcover)
    1. Bible. Romans – Criticism, interpretation, etc. 2. Bible. Apocrypha – Criticism, interpretation,
etc. 3. Judaism – History – Post-exilic period, 586 B.C.–210 A.D. I. Blackwell, Ben C., 1974- editor.
BS2665.52.R377 2015
227'.106 – dc23   2014049415

Cover design: W Design Company
Cover photo: © Kip Lee Jones, LLC
Interior design: Denise Froehlich

Printed in the United States of America

15 16 17 18 19 20 21 22 /DCI/ 20 19 18 17 16 15 14 13 12 11 10 9 8 7 6 5 4 3 2 1

To John Barclay and Francis Watson,
who taught us the value of reading Paul in context

Contents

—⚬⚬⚬—

Abbreviations

OLD TESTAMENT, NEW TESTAMENT, APOCRYPHA

Gen	Genesis	Matt	Matthew
Exod	Exodus	Rom	Romans
Lev	Leviticus	1–2 Cor	1–2 Corinthians
Num	Numbers	Gal	Galatians
Deut	Deuteronomy	Eph	Ephesians
Judg	Judges	Phil	Philippians
2 Sam	2 Samuel	Col	Colossians
1–2 Kgs	1–2 Kings	1 Thess	1 Thessalonians
1–2 Chr	1–2 Chronicles	1–2 Tim	1–2 Timothy
Neh	Nehemiah	Heb	Hebrews
Ps/Pss	Psalm/Psalms	Jas	James
Prov	Proverbs	1 Pet	1 Peter
Isa	Isaiah	Rev	Revelation
Jer	Jeremiah	Bar	Baruch
Ezek	Ezekiel	1–2 Macc	1–2 Maccabees
Dan	Daniel	Sir	Sirach/Ecclesiasticus
Hos	Hosea	Tob	Tobit
Hag	Haggai	Wis	Wisdom of Solomon
Mal	Malachi		

DEAD SEA SCROLLS

1QapGen	*Genesis Apocryphon*
1QH	*Hodayot* or *Thanksgiving Hymns*
1QM	*Milhamah* or *War Scroll*
1QpHab	*Pesher Habakkuk*
1QS	*Serek Hayyahad* or *Rule of the Community* (also *Community Rule*)
4QFlor	*Florilegium*
4QpGen	*Pesher Genesis*
4QpIsa	*Isaiah Pesher*
4QMMT	*Some Works of the Law*
4Q246	*Apocryphon of Daniel*
CD	Cairo Genizah copy of the *Damascus Document*

OTHER ANCIENT TEXTS

Ag. Ap.	*Against Apion* (Josephus)
Ant.	*Jewish Antiquities* (Josephus)
1 En.	*1 Enoch*
Gen. Rab.	*Genesis Rabbah*
GLAE	*Greek Life of Adam and Eve (Apocalypse of Moses)*
IPriene	*Priene inscription*
J.W.	*Jewish War* (Josephus)
Jub.	*Jubilees*
Life	*The Life* (Josephus)
Leg.	*Legum allegoriae/Allegorical Interpretation* (Philo)
m. Qidd.	*Qiddushin* (Mishnah)
Opif.	*De opificio mundi/On the Creation of the World* (Philo)
Pss. Sol.	*Psalms of Solomon*
QG	*Questions and Answers on Genesis* (Philo)
Spec.	*De specialibus legibus/On the Special Laws* (Philo)
Virt.	*De virtutibus/On the Virtues* (Philo)

JOURNALS, PERIODICALS, REFERENCE WORKS, SERIES

AB	Anchor Bible
AJEC	Ancient Judaism and Early Christianity
AYBC	Anchor Yale Bible Commentary
AnBib	Analecta Biblica
BJS	Brown Judaic Studies
BJRL	*Bulletin of the John Rylands University Library of Manchester*
BZNW	Beihefte zur Zeitschrift für die neutestamentliche Wissenschaft
CBQ	*Catholic Biblical Quarterly*
CEJL	Commentaries on Early Jewish Literature
CII	*Corpus inscriptionum iudaicarum.* Edited by Jean-Baptiste Frey. 2 vols. Rome, 1936–1952.
ConBNT	Coniectanea biblica: New Testament Series
CSCO	Corpus scriptorum christianorum orientalium. Edited by I. B. Chabot et al. Paris, 1903–.
DSD	*Dead Sea Discoveries*
DJD	Discoveries in the Judaean Desert

ECC	Early Christianity in Context
ESV	English Standard Version
FSBP	Fontes et Subsidia ad Bibliam pertinentes
GAP	Guides to the Apocrypha and Pseudepigrapha
IJST	*International Journal of Systematic Theology*
JBL	*Journal of Biblical Literature*
JETS	*Journal of the Evangelical Theological Society*
JSJSup	Supplements to the Journal for the Study of Judaism
JSNT	*Journal for the Study of the New Testament*
JSNTSup	Journal for the Study of the New Testament: Supplement Series
JSPSup	Journal for the Study of the Pseudepigrapha: Supplement Series
JTS	*Journal of Theological Studies*
LCL	Loeb Classical Library
LNTS	Library of New Testament Studies
LSTS	Library of Second Temple Studies
LW	Martin Luther, *Luther's Works*. American Edition. 55 vols. St. Louis and Philadelphia: Concordia and Fortress, 1958–1986.
NETS	New English Translation of the Septuagint
NSBT	New Studies in Biblical Theology
NTM	New Testament Monographs
NTS	*New Testament Studies*
OTL	Old Testament Library
PACS	Philo of Alexandria Commentary Series
ProEccl	*Pro ecclesia*
PVTG	Pseudepigrapha Veteris Testamenti Graece
SHBC	Smyth & Helwys Biblical Commentary
SBLDS	Society of Biblical Literature Dissertation Series
SBLEJL	Society of Biblical Literature Early Judaism and Its Literature
SNTSMS	Society for New Testament Studies Monograph Series
NovTSup	Supplements to Novum Testamentum
STDJ	Studies on the Texts of the Desert of Judah
TUGAL	Texte und Untersuchungen zur Geschichte der altchristlichen Literatur
UPATS	University of Pennsylvania Armenian Texts and Studies
WUNT	Wissenschaftliche Untersuchungen zum Neuen Testament
ZECNT	Zondervan Exegetical Commentary on the New Testament

GENERAL

AD	*anno Domini* (in the year of [our] Lord)
BC	before Christ
c.	*circa* (about, around, approximately)
cf.	confer, compare
ch(s).	chapter(s)
ed(s).	editor(s), edited by, edition
e.g.	*exempli gratia*, for example
esp.	especially
et al.	*et alii*, and others
idem	the same
i.e.	*id est*, that is
p.	page
repr.	reprinted
rev.	revised
trans.	translator, translated by
vol(s).	volume(s)

Foreword

It is easy to suppose that the books that make up the Bible are set apart from all other books and that they relate only to each other. The biblical writings are typically contained within the confines of a single volume, identified as "Holy Bible" and marked out from other books even by its physical appearance: leather covers, perhaps, or gilded page edges or specially fine quality paper or a double-column format. Yet the familiar single-volume Bible is far more characteristic of the second Christian millennium than of the first. In the early church there was no Bible—only "Scriptures" or "writings" occurring individually (as with most of the oldest gospel manuscripts) or in collections such as the Pauline letters. There is little or nothing in the physical appearance of the scriptural books to differentiate them from other books. It is true that early copies of the Christian Scriptures are normally codices (like a modern printed book) rather than scrolls. But the codex was originally the equivalent of a modern notebook or exercise book and had no association with sanctity. During the first Christian centuries, the codex format was increasingly extended to secular books as well.

In one sense, these early Christian scriptural texts were already set apart, in their usage if not in their appearance. They can be referred to as the *Holy Scriptures*—holy writings—and there was much debate about which texts qualified for canonical status and which did not. Most of their early interpreters move freely between one scriptural writing and another but are less likely to seek connections with texts outside the canonical boundary. Yet users of the Christian Scriptures also read and valued other texts. We know this because so much of the surviving Jewish literature from the Second Temple period was preserved within Christian rather than Jewish communities. Some of the most important of these texts have survived only because they were thought worthy of translation into languages such as Armenian, Church Slavonic, or Ethiopic (Ge'ez), in the expectation that Christian readers would benefit from reading them alongside the canonical literature.

These texts are highly diverse, catering to all theological tastes and abilities. For the Christian intellectual, the philosophical theology of Philo of Alexandria revealed unsuspected depths beneath the simple surface of

Genesis or the rest of the Pentateuch. The writings of Josephus provided a wealth of historical information about the Jewish context of Jesus and the early Christians. Texts attributed to Enoch, Ezra, and Baruch stirred the imagination of the apocalyptically inclined, helping them to view the present world in the light of its unseen but greater heavenly counterpart. A great store of practical advice for Christian living could be found in the Book of the All-Virtuous Wisdom of Ben Sira, commonly called Sirach. The Book of Tobit provided both edification and entertainment. In their different ways, these texts engaged with many, if not all, of the fundamental issues of Christian Scripture. Even though they were not themselves scriptural and their teaching was not regarded as infallible, they were valued for the light they could shed on the canonical texts. No one seems to have worried that the holiness of the Holy Scriptures is compromised when they are read alongside nonscriptural texts that share a concern with the scriptural subject matter.

The present book seeks to foster this ancient practice of reading a scriptural text—here, Paul's letter to the Romans—alongside relevant nonscriptural texts. This should not be dismissed as a purely modern scholarly practice, serving only to distract readers of the Bible from the things that really matter. Contributors to this book are united in the conviction that patient engagement with selected non-Pauline texts enhances and enriches our understanding of Paul himself. Paul presents himself as "set apart for the gospel of God" (Rom 1:1), but that does not mean that his texts must be read in total isolation from nonscriptural counterparts that share his concern with God and humankind, sin and righteousness, Scripture and covenant, creation and salvation. Indeed, Paul's texts will be diminished if we read them in a vacuum. Their Christian radicalism comes to light only if we allow them to converse with related texts that share some of their core concerns but understand them differently.

FRANCIS WATSON, DURHAM UNIVERSITY, UK

Preface

This project was born out of time spent as doctoral students at Durham University. There we had the privilege not only to study under some of today's most respected Pauline theologians, but also to learn alongside many other doctoral students who were researching topics closely related to our own. A fruit of our time in Durham, beyond the writing projects we originally went there to complete, was a network of great friendships centered on a shared commitment to serve the church through academic ministry as well as a common interest in studying the intersection between the thought world of ancient Judaism and the apostle Paul. Fascinated by what our peers at Durham and other institutions were investigating, we eventually caught a vision for bringing together these and a few other scholarly contributions into a single volume that would allow us to distill our technical research for a student audience and thus demonstrate for nonspecialists the benefit of studying Scripture alongside extrabiblical texts.

We soon came to learn that producing a collection of short essays is quite challenging, and this volume could not have come to fruition without the support of many people. The editors want to thank all the contributors for enthusiastically catching the vision of the project and for effectively articulating their ideas in a readable and accessible format. We are very appreciative of Katya Covrett, executive editor at Zondervan Academic, who served as our primary contact with the publisher from day one. Her keen editorial eye and endless wit made this project both possible and enjoyable. We cannot thank our families enough (Heather, Elam, and Silas Blackwell; Christin and Justin Goodrich; and Erin, Andrew, Kate, and Iain Maston) for supporting our love for theological studies and for tolerating our many late nights of writing, editing, and emailing. A huge thanks is also owed to Joshua Bremerman (Moody Bible Institute) for compiling the indexes. Finally, we are grateful to our respective institutions (Houston Baptist University, Moody Bible Institute, and Highland Theological College) for allowing us to teach this material on a regular basis and to our students, who regularly impress us by their desire to know, love, and serve the Lord Jesus Christ.

Ben C. Blackwell, John K. Goodrich,
and Jason Maston, October 2014

Introduction

BEN C. BLACKWELL, JOHN K. GOODRICH, AND JASON MASTON

The text lives only by coming into contact with another text (with context). Only at the point of this contact between texts does a light flash, illuminating both the posterior and anterior, joining a given text to a dialogue.

M. M. Bakhtin

Paul's letter to the Romans is widely celebrated as the apostle's clearest and fullest exposition of the good news concerning Jesus Christ. As William Tyndale lauded, "[It] is the principal and most excellent part of the New Testament, and the most pure Euangelion, that is to say glad tidings and that we call gospel."[1]

Writing from Corinth toward the end of his third missionary journey in AD 57, Paul wrote Romans in part to win support for his anticipated mission to Spain. To that end, he aimed in the letter to introduce himself to the believers in Rome, to summarize his theology, and to offer pastoral wisdom to troubled Christians and divided house churches.[2] Over the course of sixteen chapters, Paul incorporates many of his favorite theological themes, including sin, death, law, justification, participation ("in/with Christ"), the Spirit, and ethnic reconciliation. Given its careful argumentation and nearly comprehensive coverage, it is easy to see why Romans has remained at the center of Christian discourse throughout church history and continues to be cherished by believers the world over. As Martin Luther memorably wrote, "It is impossible to read or to meditate on this letter too much or too well."[3]

Not all readings of Romans, however, are equally insightful. Romans, like the rest of the Bible, was written at a time and in a culture quite different from our own. Accordingly, reading Scripture *well*, as most biblical studies students

---

1. William Tyndale, "A Prologue upon the Epistle of St. Paul to the Romans," as quoted by F. F. Bruce, *History of the Bible in English* (Cambridge: Lutterworth, 1979), 45.
2. On the many purposes of Romans, see Richard N. Longenecker, *Introducing Romans: Critical Issues in Paul's Most Famous Letter* (Grand Rapids: Eerdmans, 2011), 92–166.
3. Martin Luther, "Preface to the Letter of St. Paul to the Romans" (1522), in *D. Martin Luther: Die gantze Heilige Schrifft Deudsch 1545 aufs new zuricht* (ed. Hans Volz and Heinz Blanke; trans. Bro. Andrew Thornton; Munich: Roger & Bernhard, 1972), 2:2254–68.

will know, requires careful consideration of a passage's historical-cultural context. The study of Romans is no different. And although it is true that some contextual awareness is better than none, it is also true that not every contextual observation has equal bearing on determining the meaning of a passage.

The History of Religions School of the late nineteenth and early twentieth centuries, for example, exposed an array of parallels between the religious beliefs and practices of various ancient Mediterranean societies and those of the earliest Christian communities.[4] Yet subsequent scholarship has demonstrated the irrelevance of many of those parallels for NT studies in general and the study of Romans in particular, especially relative to the Jewish context of early Christianity. Most notably, Albert Schweitzer argued that Pauline theology—specifically the Pauline doctrine of Christ-mysticism (being "in Christ")—rather than being a product of **Hellenism**, should be studied within the worldview of Jewish **apocalyptic**.[5] Many of Schweitzer's contributions would fail to be accepted in his own day; in fact, most now would agree that he too easily separated Judaism from Hellenism.[6] Nevertheless, influential scholars such as W. D. Davies, Ernst Käsemann, and E. P. Sanders later stood on Schweitzer's shoulders by offering thorough readings of Paul in the light of his Jewish theological context.[7]

The impact of Sanders's *Paul and Palestinian Judaism* has been especially long-standing. While Sanders conceded that identifying parallel motifs in Paul and his Jewish contemporaries can be illuminating, he has been influential in challenging students of Paul to go beyond detecting surface-level similarities to conducting close comparative readings of Jewish and Pauline texts. "What is needed," Sanders insisted, "is a comparison which takes account of both the numerous agreements and the disagreements—not only the disagreements as stated by Paul, but those evident from the Jewish side, the discrepancy between Paul's depiction of Judaism and Judaism as reflected in Jewish

---

4. The History of Religions School (*religionsgeschichtliche Schule*) refers to a group of German Protestant scholars who saw OT/NT communities as religions in their own historical environments and studied them in comparison with other Mediterranean religions of the time. Cf. Richard N. Soulen and R. Kendall Soulen, *Handbook of Biblical Criticism* (4th ed.; Louisville: Westminster John Knox, 2011), 180–81.
5. Albert Schweitzer, *The Mysticism of Paul the Apostle* (trans. W. Montgomery; Baltimore: John Hopkins University Press, 1998), 26–40.
6. See, e.g., Troels Engberg-Pedersen, ed., *Paul beyond the Judaism/Hellenism Divide* (Louisville: Westminster John Knox, 2001).
7. W. D. Davies, *Paul and Rabbinic Judaism: Some Rabbinic Elements in Pauline Theology* (London: SPCK, 1948); Ernst Käsemann, *New Testament Questions of Today* (trans. W. J. Montague; New Testament Library; Philadelphia: Fortress, 1969); idem, *Perspectives on Paul* (trans. M. Kohl; Philadelphia: Fortress, 1971); E. P. Sanders, *Paul and Palestinian Judaism: A Comparison of Patterns of Religion* (Philadelphia: Fortress, 1977).

sources."[8] Sanders's own approach was to conduct a large-scale comparison between early Judaism and Pauline Christianity, tracing especially how Paul and his contemporaries understood "getting in" and "staying in" the people of God. Sanders studied numerous types of Jewish literature and argued that there was a common "pattern of religion" shared by most branches of **Second Temple Judaism**—a pattern that Sanders labeled "**covenantal nomism**" and believed should be differentiated from Paul's own theological framework.[9] Not all of the details of Sanders's readings of Jewish and Pauline texts have been accepted. Nevertheless, as a result of his work, Pauline scholars today are more aware than ever of the importance of interpreting Paul's letters in their **Second Temple Jewish** context and in close relation to contemporary Jewish literature.[10]

Even so, many Christians, especially in the evangelical tradition, remain suspicious of extracanonical literature and its value for biblical interpretation. For some, this is simply a matter of canonicity—those books lying outside of Scripture should not be allowed to influence Christian, especially post-Reformation, theology.[11] For others, it is a matter of utility. John Piper is a case in point. In his widely publicized critique of N. T. Wright's understanding of Pauline theology, Piper directs his initial criticism toward Wright's biblical-theological methodology—namely, his extensive reliance on extra-biblical sources. Rather than encouraging Christians to explore the Bible's theological claims by reading them in the light of early Jewish literature, Piper cautions that "not all biblical-theological methods and categories are illuminating," for "first-century ideas can be used (inadvertently) to distort and silence what the New Testament writers intended to say."[12] According to Piper,

---

8. Sanders, *Paul and Palestinian Judaism*, 12.
9. James D. G. Dunn and others, however, believe that Paul's theological framework fits Sanders's description of covenantal nomism ("The New Perspective on Paul," *BJRL* 65 (1983).: 95–122; reprinted in *The New Perspective on Paul* [rev. ed.; Grand Rapids: Eerdmans, 2008], 99–120).
10. Most scholarly responses to Sanders and the so-called New Perspective on Paul have likewise offered close readings of Jewish texts and comparisons of them with Paul's letters. See, e.g., A. Andrew Das, *Paul, the Law, and the Covenant* (Peabody, MA: Hendrickson, 2001); Simon J. Gathercole, *Where Is Boasting? Early Jewish Soteriology and Paul's Response in Romans 1–5* (Grand Rapids: Eerdmans, 2002); D. A. Carson, Peter T. O'Brien, and Mark A. Seifrid, eds., *Justification and Variegated Nomism: Volume 1—The Complexities of Second Temple Judaism* (Grand Rapids: Baker, 2001); Francis Watson, *Paul and the Hermeneutics of Faith* (London: T&T Clark, 2004); John M. G. Barclay and Simon J. Gathercole, eds., *Divine and Human Agency in Paul and His Cultural Environment* (LNTS 335; EEC; London: T&T Clark, 2007).
11. This reaction goes beyond that of Martin Luther, however, who famously insisted that the books of the Apocrypha "are not held as equal to the sacred Scriptures, and nevertheless are useful and good to read" (cited in *The Apocrypha: The Lutheran Edition with Notes* [St. Louis: Concordia, 2012], xviii).
12. John Piper, *The Future of Justification: A Response to N. T. Wright* (Wheaton, IL: Crossway, 2007), 33–34. See also Piper's video conversation with D. A. Carson, "Mastered by the Book"

such exegetical distortion can occur in at least three ways: "misunderstanding the sources," "assuming agreement with a source when there is no agreement," and "misapplying the meaning of a source."[13] He concludes, "It will be salutary, therefore, for scholars and pastors and laypeople who do not spend much of their time reading first-century literature to have a modest skepticism when an overarching concept or worldview from the first century is used to give 'new' or 'fresh' interpretations to biblical texts that in their own context do not naturally give rise to these interpretations."[14]

While we share Piper's desire to interpret the NT accurately in the service of the church, much contemporary scholarship demonstrates that Piper's misgivings fail to appreciate the many advantages of utilizing Second Temple Jewish literature for illuminating the meaning of the NT. Obviously, misreadings and misapplications of ancient texts remain real dangers in biblical studies; over half a century ago Samuel Sandmel warned the academy against illegitimate uses of background material, such as "parallelomania."[15] Accordingly, the appropriate solution to the misuse of comparative literature is not its outright dismissal, but its responsible handling by students of Scripture. As Wright asserts in response to Piper, "Of course literature like the Dead Sea Scrolls, being only recently discovered, has not been so extensively discussed, and its context remains highly controversial. But to say that we *already* have 'contextual awareness' of the Bible while screening out the literature or culture of the time can only mean that we are going to rely on the 'contextual awareness' of earlier days."[16] Bruce Metzger similarly assessed the importance of early Jewish literature (esp. the **Apocrypha**) for biblical studies over a half century ago:

> Though it would be altogether extravagant to call the Apocrypha the keystone of the two Testaments, it is not too much to regard these

---

(http://thegospelcoalition.org/blogs/tgc/2011/07/25/mastered-by-the-book/). Pauline scholar Tom Holland shares many of the same misgivings as Piper, insisting that the use of Second Temple Jewish sources in NT studies has "polluted the academic process and significantly distorted the conclusions of scholarship by imposing an extraneous and poorly constructed meaning on the New Testament text" (*Contours of Pauline Theology: A Radical New Survey of the Influences on Paul's Biblical Writings* [Fearn, Ross-Shire, Scotland: Mentor, 2004], 51–68, here at 54). Cf. Tom Holland, *Romans: The Divine Marriage—A Biblical Theological Commentary* (Eugene, OR: Pickwick, 2011), 23–26.

13. Piper, *Future of Justification*, 34–36. Importantly, E. P. Sanders warned of a similar danger without dismissing the use of Jewish parallel material altogether: "Parallels *are* often illuminating, as long as one does not jump from 'parallel' to 'influence' to 'identity of thought'" (*Paul and Palestinian Judaism*, 11).

14. Piper, *Future of Justification*, 36.

15. Samuel Sandmel, "Parallelomania," *JBL* 81 (1962): 1–13.

16. N. T. Wright, *Justification: God's Plan and Paul's Vision* (Downers Grove, IL: InterVarsity, 2009), 48.

intertestamental books as an historical hyphen that serves a useful function in bridging what to most readers of the Bible is a blank of several hundred years. To neglect what the Apocrypha have to tell us about the development of Jewish life and thought during those critical times is as foolish as to imagine that one can understand the civilization and culture of America today by passing from colonial days to the twentieth century without taking into account the industrial and social revolution of the intervening centuries.[17]

Piper seems particularly anxious about the illegitimate *imposition* of external meaning onto the biblical text. That is a fair concern. What he fails to realize, however, is that many comparative studies are interested just as much, if not more, in exposing the theological *differences* between texts as observing their *similarities*. To interpret his letters rightly, then, students of Paul must not *ignore* Second Temple Jewish literature, but must *engage* it with frequency, precision, and a willingness to acknowledge theological continuity *and* discontinuity.

But while monographs that situate Paul within Judaism abound, there exist virtually no nontechnical resources for beginning and intermediate students to assist them in seeing firsthand how Paul is similar to and yet different from his Jewish contemporaries. This volume seeks to investigate Paul's relationship with Second Temple Judaism by bringing together a series of accessible essays that compare and contrast the perspectives and hermeneutical practices of Paul and his various kinsmen. Going beyond an introduction that merely surveys historical events and theological themes, this book examines select passages in Second Temple Jewish literature to illuminate the context of Paul's theology and the nuances of his thinking.

To provide focus, the volume concentrates on Paul's letter to the Romans, a suitable target text on numerous counts. As noted above, Romans is Paul's most comprehensive letter, addressing nearly all of the issues that arise elsewhere in the Pauline corpus. Following, then, the progression of Romans, each chapter in the volume (1) pairs a major unit of the letter with one or more sections of a thematically related Jewish text, (2) introduces and explores the theological nuances of the comparator text, and (3) shows how the ideas in the comparator text illuminate those expressed in Romans. The end of each chapter also contains a short list of other thematically relevant Second Temple

---

17.   Bruce M. Metzger, *An Introduction to the Apocrypha* (Oxford: Oxford University Press, 1957), 151–52. See also David A. deSilva, *The Jewish Teachers of Jesus, James, and Jude: What Earliest Christianity Learned from the Apocrypha and Pseudepigrapha* (Oxford: Oxford University Press, 2013).

Jewish texts recommended for additional study and a focused bibliography pointing students to critical editions and higher-level discussions in scholarly literature. Finally, at the end of the book is a glossary where readers will find definitions of important terms. Whether one reads the entire book or only a few essays, it is our hope that readers will gain a new appreciation for extrabiblical Jewish texts, begin to see the many benefits of studying the NT alongside its contemporary literature, and acquire a better understanding of Paul and his letter to the Romans.

Before proceeding to our comparisons, however, it is necessary briefly to survey the events of the **Second Temple Period** and the literature that it produced.

INTRODUCING THE SECOND TEMPLE PERIOD AND EARLY JEWISH LITERATURE
FROM THE FIRST TEMPLE PERIOD TO THE SECOND

In the exodus, a pivotal event in the history of national Israel, Abraham's family was liberated from Pharaoh after nearly four centuries of forced labor. The Israelites were led by God into the desert and given the Mosaic law at Sinai to regulate Hebrew life and religion, with the sacrificial system at the center of their community (Exod 19:1–8). Separated from the nations through their distinctive way of life (Lev 20:22–26), the Israelites were to keep the commandments that God had given them, lest they profane the holy **covenant** and be exiled from the land of promise (Lev 26:14–39; Deut 28:15–68; 30:15–20).

From the conquest of Canaan to the end of the united monarchy, the nation inhabited the land for almost five hundred years. During that era, King Solomon built the first temple in the mid-tenth century, fulfilling David's original aspiration for the project (1 Kgs 6:1–8:66). After Solomon's death, the kingdom divided and, following a series of evil rulers, Israel's northern ten tribes (the kingdom of Israel/Samaria) were captured and exiled by Assyria in 722 BC (2 Kgs 17:1–23; 18:9–12). The southern two tribes (the kingdom of Judah) ultimately fared no better. By the beginning of the sixth century the Babylonians had waged war on Jerusalem, and in 586 BC, King Nebuchadnezzar destroyed the city, including the first temple, and exiled many of its inhabitants (2 Kgs 24:10–25:21; 2 Chr 36:17–21).

The Babylonian captivity marks a low point in Israel's history. The nation had faced the full brunt of the **Deuteronomic** curses as a result of their covenant disobedience. Consequently, the Israelites were without a homeland, just as Yahweh had promised would happen through Moses and the prophets.

But even before their captivity, God had also promised he would return his scattered people to the land and fully restore the nation (Lev 26:40–45; Deut 30:1–10; 32:34–43; Isa 40:1–66:24; Jer 30:1–31:40; Ezek 36:8–37:28). Israel was to experience the glory of its former days, and, as it would turn out, they did not remain under Babylonian rule for long. In 539 BC, Cyrus of Persia conquered Babylon and famously decreed that all exiles could return to their ancestral homelands (2 Chr 36:22–23; Ezra 1:1–4). Many Israelites therefore gradually returned to and rebuilt Jerusalem. Zerubbabel was instrumental in the rebuilding of the temple, while Nehemiah oversaw the construction of the city walls (Ezra 3:8–6:15; Neh 2:9–6:15). It is the building of this second temple in 516 BC that marks the beginning of the Second Temple Period.

The newly renovated city, however, was not what was promised. When Israel's returnees gazed at the new temple's foundation, some celebrated and others cried over its unimpressive stature (Ezra 3:10–13; Hag 2:3). Israel's promised restoration had not arrived at the hands of Ezra and Nehemiah. As the centuries to follow would demonstrate, the peace and prosperity God swore to his people had yet to be realized in the period immediately following the Babylonian exile. Instead, generation after generation witnessed subjugation and suffering at the hands of still other foreign powers—namely, Medo-Persia, Greece, and Rome—and these experiences significantly colored the texts these Jews produced.

Israel survived under the rule of the Medo-Persian Empire from 539 to about 332 BC, when the Greek Empire, led by Alexander the Great, conquered the known world. Alexander's rule would not last long. Following his death in 323 BC, Alexander's territories were partitioned among his military generals, who established their own kingdoms (e.g., the Ptolemaic Kingdom in Egypt and the **Seleucid Kingdom** in Syria) and continued the former emperor's systematic spread of Hellenism, or Greek culture (1 Macc 1:1–9; 2 Macc 4:7–17). These kingdoms, which were often embroiled in war with one another, also created challenges for the Jews, who were positioned geographically between them. The Seleucid Kingdom in particular, under the rule of **Antiochus IV Epiphanes** in 167 BC, raided Jerusalem (1 Macc 1:20–40), desecrated the temple (1:47, 54, 59), outlawed observance of the covenant (1:41–53), and prohibited possession of the Torah (1:56–57). In his pursuit of **Hellenization**, Antiochus banned the Jews' customs (1:41–44) and violently forced their assimilation (1:50, 57–58, 60–64). But Antiochus's persecution was not passively tolerated. The Jewish resistance that arose in response (the **Maccabean Revolt**, 167–142 BC) resulted in the Jews' repossession of the land, rededication of the temple, and institution of the festival of Hanukkah (1 Macc 4:36–59; Josephus, *Ant.* 12.316–325).

With the renewed national sovereignty of the **Hasmoneans** (the family that led the Maccabean Revolt), various groups held differing opinions about how to manage the political and temple leadership of Israel. This infighting eventually led to the weakening of the Jewish national leadership, and Pompey, a Roman general contemporaneous with Julius Caesar, seized control of Israel in 63 BC, making it a territory of the Roman republic. Although Rome largely tolerated Jewish religious practices, pressures leading toward political, cultural, and religious assimilation were ever-present. Eventually, the Zealots (a Jewish resistance group) fomented the hopes of another successful revolt. But the Romans, under the soon-to-be emperor Titus, defeated the Jews and destroyed the second temple in AD 70 (Josephus, *J.W.* 6.220–270), thus bringing an end to the Second Temple Period.

The Second Temple Period (516 BC–AD 70) began with the Jews under the control of the Persians and ended under the control of the Romans. This was, without question, a time of crisis for the Jewish people, and devout men and women reflected on their experiences in a variety of ways. With the pressures from a consecutive transfer of foreign nations pushing the Jews toward assimilation, numerous Second Temple Jewish literary works preserve their thoughts and hopes about God and life in the covenant. These reflections survive in the numerous literary works produced during this period. We turn now to survey these texts.

OVERVIEW OF SECOND TEMPLE JEWISH LITERATURE

The Second Temple Jewish writings were composed by numerous authors in multiple languages over several hundred years. Moreover, they derive from geographical provenances extending over much of the **ancient Near East**. Thus, there is no easy way to characterize or categorize these texts. Still, scholarly surveys of ancient Judaism normally assign individual Second Temple Jewish texts to one of three main literary bodies—the **Septuagint**, the Apocrypha, and the **Pseudepigrapha**—collections that were unrecognized by the original authors, having been determined by later editors and/or scholars. Accordingly, these corpuses overlap in different places.

The Septuagint (abbreviated **LXX**) is a collection of Jewish texts in Greek that includes the Greek translation of the OT, as well as other Jewish writings. It was the most widely used Greek version of Jewish scriptures in antiquity, though other Greek versions also existed. The OT Apocrypha (also called the **deuterocanonical** books) are a subset of the texts found in the Septuagint (though not in the Hebrew Bible) that were accepted as authoritative by patristic (and medieval) Christians and included in the Vulgate (a Latin translation that became the authoritative version for the medieval church).[18] Different Christian groups have variations in their **canonical** lists related to the Apocrypha, but the primary collection includes the books of Tobit, Judith, Additions to Esther, the Wisdom of Solomon, Sirach (Ecclesiasticus), Baruch, Epistle of Jeremiah, Additions to Daniel (the Prayer of Azariah, the Song of the Three Young Men, Susanna, and Bel and the Dragon), and 1 and 2 Maccabees. Certain Christian traditions also afford special status to works such as 1 and 2 Esdras (= "Ezra" in Greek), the Prayer of Manasseh, and Psalm 151. In addition to the Greek translation of the Hebrew Bible and what later became known as the Apocrypha, the LXX also includes, in certain copies, the books of 3 Maccabees, 4 Maccabees, 1 Esdras, *Psalms of Solomon*, and *Odes of Solomon* (including the Prayer of Manasseh).

The OT Pseudepigrapha (meaning "falsely attributed writings") is a diverse body of ancient Jewish works, many of which claim to be authored by famous OT persons, although they did not write them. Some Septuagint works mentioned above are also falsely attributed. For example, neither the Wisdom of Solomon nor *Psalms of Solomon* were authored by Israel's third king, though they bear his name.[19] In distinction to the Septuagint and the Apocrypha as (relatively) fixed bodies of texts, all early Jewish religious literature not considered to be (deutero)canonical is commonly placed in the open category of Pseudepigrapha — aside from **Philo, Josephus**, and the **Dead Sea Scrolls**.[20]

While these classifications (esp. Apocrypha) are widely used and indeed useful for classifying texts that may be considered authoritative in certain religious traditions, an alternative and more descriptive way to group these writings is according to genre. We survey the main early Jewish literary genres below.[21]

The first early Jewish literary genre to be familiar with is *history*. Several works fall into this category, including 1–2 Esdras and 1–2 Maccabees. The

---

18. The canonical status of these texts for patristic Christians is unclear, but they did treat them as authoritative. These texts were later included in the OT by Roman Catholic and Orthodox Christians because of their reception by the church in the patristic period.

19. It is conventional to italicize the titles of noncanonical and nondeuterocanonical works; cf. Patrick H. Alexander et al., eds., *The SBL Handbook of Style: For Ancient Near Eastern, Biblical, and Early Christian Studies* (Peabody, MA: Hendrickson, 1999), 73–81.

20. Loren T. Stuckenbruck, "Apocrypha and Pseudepigrapha," in *Early Judaism: A Comprehensive Overview* (ed. J. J. Collins and D. C. Harlow; Grand Rapids: Eerdmans, 2012), 173–203, at 191–92.

21. Our overview generally follows the categories of James C. VanderKam, *An Introduction to Early Judaism* (Grand Rapids: Eerdmans, 2001), 53–173.

books of 1–2 Esdras (Vulgate) refer to the books of Ezra and Nehemiah and thus report Israel's immediate postexilic history.[22] The books of 1–2 Maccabees chronicle important events between the biblical Testaments, including the Maccabean Revolt. Together, the early Jewish histories are essential for understanding the events, influences, challenges, and commitments of the Second Temple Jewish people.

A second early Jewish literary genre is *tales*. According to James Vander-Kam, these are "stories with no serious claim to historicity but [which] aim to inculcate wise teachings through the stories and the speeches they narrate."[23] To this category belong such books as Tobit, Judith, Susanna, 3 Maccabees, and the *Letter of Aristeas*. These works normally cast important, sometimes heroic, men and women at the center of their narratives in order to model Jewish piety and inspire trust in God's promises.

Our third genre is *rewritten Scripture*. Often books belonging to this group also take a narrative form, since these works typically reproduce, paraphrase, and elaborate on the accounts of specific OT events and characters. To this category belong such books as *Jubilees* (a retelling of the biblical events from creation to Mount Sinai) and the *Genesis Apocryphon* (an expansion of select patriarchal narratives). Also considered by some scholars as rewritten Scripture are the *Life of Adam and Eve* (an account of the advent of death and restoration of life) and the *Testaments of the Twelve Patriarchs* (an elaboration on Jacob's final words to his twelve sons in Gen 49). Works such as these are important for demonstrating how biblical literature was interpreted during the Second Temple Period, when exegetical commentaries were quite rare.[24]

Fourth among the early Jewish literary genres is *apocalypse*, which normally consists of otherworldly visions given to a human recipient (seer) through the mediation of a supernatural, sometimes angelic, being. Most Jewish apocalypses were written during times of great distress—especially during Seleucid oppression and following Rome's destruction of the Jewish temple. Apocalypses therefore seek to bring comfort to suffering Jewish communities by providing a heavenly perspective on past, present, and future events. Often coded in elaborate symbolism, these visions typically anticipate the eventual cessation of evil and political oppression. Early Jewish apocalypses include

22. The contents of 1–2 Esdras differ in the ancient Greek (LXX) and Latin (Vulgate) corpuses in which they were transmitted. The title 2 Esdras, for instance, can refer to the apocalyptic work also known as 4 Ezra; in other cases it refers to the book of Nehemiah (Vulgate), or to the books of Ezra and Nehemiah combined (LXX).
23. VanderKam, *Introduction to Early Judaism*, 69.
24. Cf. Molly M. Zahn, "Rewritten Scripture," in *The Oxford Handbook of the Dead Sea Scrolls* (ed. T. H. Lim and J. J. Collins; Oxford: Oxford University Press, 2010), 323–36.

4 Ezra, the *Sibylline Oracles*, the *Testament of Moses*, and several portions of *1 Enoch*: the *Book of Watchers* (*1 En.* 1–36); the *Similitudes/Parables of Enoch* (*1 En.* 37–71); the *Astronomical Book* (*1 En.* 72–82); the *Book of Dreams* (*1 En.* 83–90); and the *Apocalypse of Weeks* (*1 En.* 93:1–10; 91:11–17).

The fifth and sixth genres, *poetry* and *Wisdom literature*, are similar in both content and style to their antecedent biblical literature (Job, Psalms, Proverbs, Ecclesiastes). Hebrew poems are normally songs of praise and lament utilizing meter and structural parallelism. The songs written during this period of Jewish history commonly entreat the Lord for deliverance from pain and oppression. Examples include the *Psalms of Solomon*, the Prayer of Manasseh, the Prayer of Azariah, and the Song of the Three Young Men. Wisdom literature appeals to common experience in order to instruct people how to live virtuously. Examples include Sirach (Ecclesiasticus), the Wisdom of Solomon, and perhaps Baruch and the *Epistle of Enoch* (*1 En.* 91–108).[25]

Three additional collections deserve special mention, the origins of which we know far more about than the various works previously surveyed. First are the works of Philo (c. 20 BC–AD 50). A Diaspora Jew from Alexandria, Egypt, heavily influenced by **Platonism**, Philo authored numerous philosophical treatises and exegetical studies on the Pentateuch. Second are the books of the historian Josephus (AD 37–c. 100). Once a Jewish Pharisee and military leader, Josephus was taken captive during the Jerusalem War against Rome and eventually became a Roman citizen and dependent of Emperor Vespasian. Josephus's four extant works include a history of the Jewish people (*Jewish Antiquities*), an account of the Jerusalem War (*Jewish War*), a work in defense of Judaism and the Jewish way of life (*Against Apion*), and an autobiography (*The Life*). Third are the Dead Sea Scrolls. Although many of the scrolls discovered near **Qumran** are ancient copies of the OT or versions of apocryphal and pseudepigraphal texts (e.g., Tobit, *1 Enoch, Jubilees*), most are **sectarian** documents—works that describe how the Dead Sea community originated and was organized, and how members of the community should live and worship. These works are labeled by the Qumran cave number in which they were found (1Q, 4Q, etc.) and a cataloging number, though many have other shortened names describing their content (e.g., 1QS = *Rule of the Community*; 1QH = *Hodayot/Thanksgiving Hymns*; 4QMMT = *Some Works of the Law*).

Our goal here has been only to provide a concise overview of certain foundational elements for understanding early Jewish history and literature. For a full account, the reader should consult the resources listed below. Having

---

25. VanderKam, *Introduction to Early Judaism*, 115–24.

oriented ourselves to Paul's Jewish context, we now turn to read Romans in conversation with some of these Second Temple Jewish texts.

FOR FURTHER READING

For the most comprehensive overview of early Jewish literature, see Craig A. Evans, *Ancient Texts for New Testament Studies: A Guide to the Background Literature* (Peabody, MA: Hendrickson, 2005), which summarizes the literature and provides the bibliographic details for critical texts, research tools, and key scholarly works. The volume's appendixes also show how Jewish literature can illuminate the NT. See also David W. Chapman and Andreas J. Köstenberger, "Jewish Intertestamental and Early Rabbinic Literature: An Annotated Bibliographic Resource Updated (Part 1),"*JETS* 55 (2012): 235–72; David W. Chapman and Andreas J. Köstenberger, "Jewish Intertestamental and Early Rabbinic Literature: An Annotated Bibliographic Resource Updated (Part 2)," *JETS* 55 (2012): 457–88.

Standard Translations of Early Jewish Literature

Bauckham, Richard, James R. Davila, and Alexander Panayotov, eds. *Old Testament Pseudepigrapha: More Noncanonical Scriptures*. Grand Rapids: Eerdmans, 2013.

Charlesworth, James H., ed. *The Old Testament Pseudepigrapha*. 2 vols. Garden City, NY: Doubleday, 1983–1985.

Coogan, Michael D., Marc Z. Brettler, Carol Ann Newsom, and Pheme Perkins, eds. *The New Oxford Annotated Apocrypha: New Revised Standard Version*. Rev. 4th ed. Oxford: Oxford University Press, 2010.

García Martínez, Florentino, and Eibert J. C. Tigchelaar, eds. *The Dead Sea Scrolls Study Edition*. 2 vols. Leiden: Brill, 1997–1998.

Pietersma, Albert, and Benjamin G. Wright, eds. *A New English Translation of the Septuagint*. Oxford: Oxford University Press, 2007.

Introductions to Early Jewish Literature

Collins, John J., and Daniel C. Harlow, eds. *Early Judaism: A Comprehensive Overview*. Grand Rapids: Eerdmans, 2012.

deSilva, David A. *Introducing the Apocrypha: Message, Context, and Significance*. Grand Rapids: Baker, 2002.

Helyer, Larry R. *Exploring Jewish Literature of the Second Temple Period: A Guide for New Testament Students*. Downers Grove, IL: InterVarsity Press, 2002.

Kamesar, Adam, ed. *The Cambridge Companion to Philo.* Cambridge: Cambridge University Press, 2009.

Mason, Steve. *Josephus and the New Testament.* 2nd ed. Peabody, MA: Hendrickson, 2002.

Nickelsburg, George W. E. *Jewish Literature between the Bible and the Mishnah: A Historical and Literary Introduction.* 2nd ed. Minneapolis: Fortress, 2011.

VanderKam, James C. *An Introduction to Early Judaism.* Grand Rapids: Eerdmans, 2001.

VanderKam, James C., and Peter Flint. *The Meaning of the Dead Sea Scrolls: Their Significance for Understanding the Bible, Judaism, Jesus, and Christianity.* San Francisco: HarperCollins, 2002.

CHAPTER 1

Psalms of Solomon and Romans 1:1–17: The "Son of God" and the Identity of Jesus

WESLEY HILL

The apostle Paul begins his letter to the Christians in Rome with a brief sketch of the key elements of his gospel. He describes this gospel as originating with God (1:1), foreshadowed in the prophetic writings of Israel's Scriptures (1:2), and, finally, centered on the figure of God's "Son" (1:3, 9). This Son, Paul says, was a Davidic descendant (1:3), raised in power through the action of the Spirit (1:4), and now dispenses grace and commissions certain people—notably Paul himself—to testify to his identity and saving power among all nations (1:5).

Although this summary is sequentially laid out and easy enough to follow, it nonetheless raises some thorny questions. What does it mean, for instance, for the God of Israel to have a "Son"? Does this mean that Paul lends some credence to pagan notions of fertility and procreation in the divine realm itself? And what does Paul mean when he says it was only at the resurrection that this "Son" of God was "declared," or "appointed" (NIV), "Son of God in power"? Might this imply that Paul thought Jesus Christ was *not* the Son of God prior to being raised from the dead?

When asking questions like these, it is vital to keep in mind one of the basic canons, or rules, of biblical interpretation: we must focus not only on what is temporally "in front" of the text, but also on what is contextually "behind" it. In other words, when reading Paul, we must pay attention to the teaching about the "Son of God" that grew out of what Paul wrote—but in doing so, we must not overlook what Paul's contemporary Jews were saying about the title and how that might have influenced the way Paul described Jesus' role in God's purposes.

Paul was not the first Jew of his day to use the term "Son of God."
Already in the OT the term had been used metaphorically to refer to God's
adopted "son," the nation of Israel (Exod 4:22–23; Hos 11:1) and, by ex-
tension, the king of Israel (2 Sam 7:14; Ps 2:7). But in the **Second Temple
Period**, Jewish writers had begun, like accomplished musicians, to play
multiple variations on the theme of God's Son. One example of this "tradi-
tioned improvisation," as we might call it, is found in the *Psalms of Solomon*,
a collection of eighteen poetic texts originally written in Hebrew in the first
century BC and later translated into Greek and included in the **Septuagint**.
This essay will explore Paul's **Christology** in Rom 1 by way of *Psalms of
Solomon* 17.

Psalms of Solomon
"RAISE UP FOR THEM THEIR KING, THE SON OF DAVID"

The *Psalms of Solomon* were probably composed at a time when faithful,
law-upholding Jews felt besieged, both literally and figuratively. In *Psalms
of Solomon* 17, the most prominent of the collection, reference is made to
a warrior who arrives from the west, the land of the Gentiles (17:12–14).
Probably this refers to the Roman general Pompey, who sacked Jerusalem in
63 BC only to die unburied, away from his homeland, in Egypt (cf. 2:26–27).
Pompey's action in the Jerusalem temple following his military conquest of
the city was sacrilegious and elicited a renewed cry from observant Jews for
divine judgment. But this was not the only obstacle faced by the writer(s) of
these psalms.[1] Unfaithful members of their own ranks, **Hasmonean** Saddu-
cees who took control of political and religious functions in Jerusalem (17:6,
45; cf. 1:8), also led the psalmist to view himself and their law-observant way
of life as under threat.

Consequently, the psalmist and his people turned to **eschatology**.
Rather than make peace with Jerusalem's current circumstances, they looked
forward to the future arrival of the eschatological **Messiah**, who would
right these wrongs and undo the present evil. In fact, according to R. B.
Wright, "There is more substance to the ideas concerning the Messiah in the
Psalms of Solomon than in any other extant Jewish writing."[2]

---

1.   Although multiple authors may be responsible for the final form of the psalms, I will from
here on refer to the author in the singular.
2.   R. B. Wright, "*Psalms of Solomon*: A New Translation and Introduction," in *The Old Testament
Pseudepigrapha* (vol. 2; ed. James H. Charlesworth; Garden City, NY: Doubleday, 1985), 639–70, at
643.

The Messiah as Davidic Ruler. The psalmist begins the seventeenth psalm with an affirmation of God's selection of David and David's line for kingship in Israel: "You, Lord, chose David as king over Israel and you swore to him concerning his seed forever, that his kingdom might not fail before you" (17:4). Following this there appears a catalog of all that is wrong with Jerusalem's present plight, focusing on the desecration of the conquering warrior himself (17:5–20). In response to this grim litany, the psalmist entreats God to intervene: "Behold, O Lord, and raise up for them their king, the son of David, at the time you know, O God, to rule over Israel your servant" (17:21).

The Messiah as Eschatological Agent. The kind of intervention the psalmist pleads for is decisive and violent. When the son of David appears, the psalmist hopes that he will both expel the marauding Gentiles from Jerusalem (17:22, 24) and deal with compromised Jews (the "sinners," 17:23, 25). But in the wake of this destructive judgment, the psalmist also hopes that a new reign of righteousness and the cessation of violence will follow. The son of David will lead and judge a renewed Israel (17:26). He will subjugate the Gentiles (17:30), receiving their gifts as tribute (17:31), in much the same way Solomon himself welcomed the homage of the queen of Sheba (1 Kgs 10:1–13; cf. Isa 45:14; 60:10–14). This Davidic heir will be "a righteous king, taught by God, over them, and there will not be unrighteousness in his days among them, for all shall be holy and their king shall be the Lord Messiah [or Messiah of the Lord]" (17:32). This Davidic ruler, now identified as the "Christ," the anointed one or "Messiah," will have the "Lord," the God of Israel, as his king (17:34). As he reigns, he will be sinless (17:36), empowered by the Holy Spirit (17:37), and the giver of eschatological prosperity and blessing to all who submit to his rulership (17:40–46).

In this way, the following picture emerges, according to the seventeenth psalm. There is a present order of things that is out of step with the psalmist's hopes for the future. Externally, God's people face political and military opposition from powerful pagan forces, and internally, they have to confront the compromised, unfaithful members within their own ranks. The solution to these problems is the appearance of the long-awaited descendant of David, the king of Israel's golden age, who will bring the Gentiles into subservience and purge Israel of her own disobedient ones. This messianic figure will be the embodiment of what God himself had pledged in times past to accomplish, and so the psalmist can remain confident in the face of a bleak set of present circumstances.

Romans 1:1–17

"A DESCENDANT OF DAVID ... APPOINTED THE SON OF GOD IN POWER"

The Messiah as Davidic Ruler and Eschatological Agent. Strikingly, Paul agrees with the author of the *Psalms of Solomon* that God's Messiah is the son of David and is marked out for his role in God's eschatological timetable by the action of the Holy Spirit, or "Spirit of holiness,"as Paul calls him.[3] Romans 1:3 is the only place in Paul's undisputed letters that he mentions Jesus' Davidic descent.[4] With this mention, Paul demonstrates that he has in mind traditions such as what we observed above in the *Psalms of Solomon* — that the Messiah would be David's royal heir and the bearer of David's mandate to shepherd and rule the people of Israel.[5] Thus, when Paul calls Jesus the "Son of God in power,"he very likely means to say, "Jesus is the anointed eschatological agent of God's final redemption of his people Israel."

The Messiah's Eternal Sonship. However, Paul makes at least two seismic modifications to the Jewish tradition and the messianic eschatological expecta-tion he inherits. First, although he recognizes God's raising of his Son through the Spirit to be the decisive public announcement of Jesus' messianic identity, Paul makes it equally clear that this moment of messianic installment and acclamation happens to one who is *already* God's Son, prior to his resurrection. Rom 1:3–4 says that Paul's gospel concerns God's "Son ... a descendant of David ... [who was] appointed the Son of God in power."Hence, the one who is appointed "Son"was already, before that appointment, the "Son."What Paul must have in mind, then, are multiple, succeeding chapters in the one Son's biography. Paul's line of thought seems to run something like this: God has a Son, known through the Hebrew prophets prior to the appearing of Jesus. The earthly life of the Son—his life "according to the flesh,"as Paul's Greek literally reads—shows him to have descended from David. But there is another phase the Son embarks on after his death and resurrection—a new era, by virtue of God's work through the Spirit in raising him, in which he enjoys power and can impart that power to specially commissioned spokespersons like Paul. Putting

---

3.   See Daniel Falk, "Prayers and Psalms,"in *Justification and Variegated Nomism: Volume 1—The Complexities of Second Temple Judaism* (ed. D. A. Carson, P. T. O'Brien, and M. A. Seifrid; Grand Rapids: Baker, 2001), 7–56.

4.   If Paul is the author of 2 Tim 2:8, then Rom 1:3 is one of two mentions of Jesus' Davidic heritage in Paul's letters.

5.   Other NT texts that emphasize Jesus' Davidic sonship include Matt 1:1–16, 20; 9:27; 12:23; 15:22; 20:30–31; 21:9, 15; Mark 12:35–37a; Luke 1:27, 32, 69; 2:4; 3:23–31; John 7:42; Acts 2:30; Rev 5:5; 22:16.

each of these biographical chapters together in sequence, we can see that it is the *Son* whom God already has in view when he imparts prophetic insight in Israel's Scriptures; it is the same *Son* who stands in David's royal line when he lives out his earthly existence in the shadow of weakness and frailty; and it is that same *Son* who is appointed to be not only "Son" but "Son-in-power" at his resurrection through the agency of the Spirit of holiness (see figure 1.1).

Figure 1.1: The Son's Biography in Romans 1:3–4

The preexistent "Son of God"	Descended from David according to the flesh	Appointed Son of God in power according to the Holy Spirit

It was for this reason that Athanasius, the fourth-century church father, opposed the priest Arius for the latter's teaching that the Son was less than fully equal with God the Father. Athanasius recognized that texts such as Rom 1:3–4 never envision a time when the Son is not "Son," thus undermining any literal reading of this passage that might suggest how God *became* a parent at a certain point in time by fathering a Son. Rather, Athanasius taught, Jesus is indeed God's Son, but this sonship is an eternal sonship—displayed in the time of Jesus' fleshly life but not established or determined by that earthly existence.[6] It is *analogous* but not *identical* to earthly, physical parentage and childbirth.

The Messiah's Subjugation of Gentiles. Second, Paul also modifies the messianic tradition he inherits from texts like the *Psalms of Solomon* by redefining the nature of the Son of David's victory. In *Psalms of Solomon* 17, the Messiah's victory involves the exile of Gentile idolaters (17:22), their destruction and banishment (17:24), their separation from faithful Jews (17:28), their slavery and despoilment (17:30–31). True, the Messiah's judgment will be tempered by compassion (17:34), but it will be no less discriminating for all that (17:45).

In Paul, we see an ironic reversal of many of these features of the psalm. Paul, the faithful Jew, is the one who is enslaved to the Messiah (Rom 1:1) on behalf of the Gentiles (1:5–6). The Messiah, rather than immediately triumphing, is victorious only by first dying and suffering defeat (1:4). And the Gentiles, consequently, are indeed subjugated (1:5) as *Psalms of Solomon* expected—but they are subjugated to a crucified Messiah who now lives to

---

6.   For an excellent accessible summary of Athanasius's argument on this score, see Peter J. Leithart, *Athanasius* (Foundations of Theological Exegesis and Christian Spirituality; Grand Rapids: Baker, 2011).

give them grace and peace (1:7). The gospel Paul preaches, then, is dependent on Paul's ancestral Jewish traditions (cf. 1:2), but as he goes on to make clear here and later in the same chapter, it also radically reinterprets those traditions in light of God's surprising new action in Jesus Christ. Because of Jesus, the righteousness of God is no longer defined straightforwardly as what subjects the Gentiles to obedience and vindicates Israel. Now, rather, in light of the death and resurrection of the Son, that divine righteousness is manifested in God's judging and saving *"everyone* who believes,"both Jew and Gentile, on the same basis of faith (1:16–17).

In this way, we have come full circle from what we discussed in the introduction. If interpreting Paul well depends on looking at other texts that Paul and his contemporaries might have been familiar with and allowing those texts to influence our interpretation of key terms and ideas within Paul's letters, we can also conclude that the converse is true: Paul is a creative, original thinker whose vision of Jesus—preexistent with God, manifested in the flesh and in death, set apart by the Spirit for a new life of risen power—makes Paul see the key terms and ideas he inherits from Judaism in a new light. In our effort to interpret Paul's letters, we need to attend to what came before Paul, but also to the way in which Paul unleashes a new, unprecedented, ironically incongruous insight within his own Jewish textual tradition.

FOR FURTHER READING

Additional Ancient Texts

One might compare the following **Second Temple Jewish** texts for messianic ideas similar to those we saw in *Pss. Sol.* 17: 4QFlor 1:10–13; 4Q246 2:1; 4QpGen 49; 4QpIsa[a] 2:21–28; Shemoneh Esrei 14–15. Elsewhere in Paul, Gal 4:4–6 makes clear that Paul's understanding of Jesus' sonship is both at home in Jewish messianic expectation and exceeds the boundaries of that realm by placing Jesus in an *eternal* filial relationship with God, his Father. And outside of Paul's writings, the beginning of the letter to the Hebrews draws on and interprets the "sonship"language in relation to Jesus (1:1–14).

English Translations and Critical Editions

NETS

Wright, R. B. "*Psalms of Solomon*: A New Translation and Introduction."Pages 639–70 in vol. 2 of *The Old Testament Pseudepigrapha*. Edited by James H. Charlesworth. Garden City, NY: Doubleday, 1985.

———. *Psalms of Solomon: A Critical Edition of the Greek Text*. London: T&T Clark, 2007.

Secondary Literature

Collins, John J. *The Scepter and the Star: Messianism in Light of the Dead Sea Scrolls*. 2nd ed. Grand Rapids: Eerdmans, 2010.

Dunn, James D. G. "Jesus—Flesh and Spirit: An Exposition of Romans I.3–4." *JTS* 24 (1973): 40–68.

Hengel, Martin. *The Son of God: The Origin of Christology and the History of Jewish-Hellenistic Religion*. Philadelphia: Fortress, 1976.

Hill, Wesley. *Paul and the Trinity: Persons, Relations, and the Pauline Letters*. Grand Rapids: Eerdmans, 2015.

Jenson, Robert W. "Once More the *Logos Asarkos*." *IJST* 13 (2011): 130–33.

Novenson, Matthew V. *Christ among the Messiahs: Christ Language in Paul and Messiah Language in Ancient Judaism*. Oxford: Oxford University Press, 2012.

Rowe, C. Kavin. "Biblical Pressure and Trinitarian Hermeneutics." *ProEccl* 11 (2002): 295–312.

Stuckenbruck, Loren T. "Messianic Ideas in the Apocalyptic and Related Literature of Early Judaism." Pages 90–116 in *The Messiah in the Old and New Testaments*. McMaster New Testament Studies. Edited by S. Porter. Grand Rapids: Eerdmans, 2007.

Winninge, Mikael. *Sinners and the Righteous: A Comparative Study of the Psalms of Solomon and Paul's Letters*. ConBNT 26. Stockholm: Almqvist & Wiksell, 1995.

CHAPTER 2

Wisdom of Solomon and Romans 1:18–2:5: God's Wrath against *All*

JONATHAN A. LINEBAUGH

"The wrath of God is being revealed from heaven" (Rom 1:18). This is the first word of Paul's apostolic announcement. He is eager "to preach the gospel" in Rome (1:15) because this good news about God's Son, Jesus Christ (1:3–4), is the "power of God that brings salvation," and this because "in the gospel the righteousness of God is revealed" (1:16–17). Paul's proclamation, however, does not begin with a revelation of saving righteousness; the first word is a word of *wrath*. The divine wrath that is revealed in Paul's preaching (1:18) will be fully enacted at the revelation of God's "righteous judgment" (2:5)—a judgment in which the conclusion that "Jews and Gentiles alike are all under the power of sin" (3:9) can only have one consequence: "No one will be declared righteous" (3:20).

Romans 1:18–2:5 is the first step in Paul's rhetorical revelation of the common condition of all human beings: *homo est peccator* (the human is a sinner). This is a revolutionary revelation. The language Paul employs, however, in terms of vocabulary, theme, and argumentative structure, has deep parallels in the early Jewish textual tradition. This is especially true of Wisdom of Solomon 13–15, which, like Rom 1:18–2:5, considers the relationship of Jews and Gentiles before God within the human history of idolatry. The parallels between Wisdom of Solomon and Romans make them readily comparable, but, as we shall see, the differences are even more significant.

Wisdom of Solomon

"WE WILL NOT SIN"

Wisdom of Solomon (hereafter, Wisdom), sometimes referred to as the Book of Wisdom, was probably composed in Greek in Alexandria between 200 BC and AD 50. Chapters 2–5 especially, with their vivid depiction of a suffering and vindicated righteous person, have long been read by Christians for their **christological** resonances. Wisdom is included in the **Septuagint** and is considered either **apocryphal** or **deuterocanonical** by various Christian traditions.

As the title suggests, Wisdom is best classified as Wisdom literature, though several portions of the text (e.g., chs. 2–5) display affinities with the **apocalyptic tradition**. The work appears to be occasioned, at least in part, by social tensions in Alexandria (cf. 19:13–15). But whatever the exact situation, the event was serious enough to generate a series of questions about the stability of the moral order, the patterns of history, and the past, present, and future justice of God. Into this crisis—which appears to be principally defined by the present flourishing of the ungodly and the suffering of the righteous (cf. chs. 2–5)—Wisdom announces a word of hope: the God of illimitable love is immutably just.

God's Just Judgment. Wisdom, then, like Paul in Rom 1:16–17, is relating the good news of God's justice (cf. Wis 1:1). The future form of this justice will be evident when "the souls of the righteous" (3:1), those whom God has "found worthy of himself" (3:5), are "numbered among the children of God" (5:5) and God himself fights against "those who have oppressed them" (5:1, 17–23)—that is, the "ungodly" (1:16). This pattern of symmetrical justice was paradigmatically enacted at the Red Sea. This single act of divine righteousness was simultaneously *the rescue of Israel*—"[wisdom] led [the righteous] through deep waters" (10:18)—and *the destruction of the Egyptians*—"but she drowned their enemies" (10:19). Here, divine justice is exemplified in the correspondence between the *form* (deliverance or destruction) and the *object* (the righteous or the ungodly) of divine action. This correspondence underwrites the confession that God "arranged all things by measure, number, and weight" (11:20) and therefore anchors the promise that the **eschaton** will be like the exodus.

This, then, is Wisdom's sermon to sufferers: as it was in the beginning, it will be (to echo an old prayer). The injustice of the present will be overturned as the God who acted with justice in the past will again redeem the righteous and judge the ungodly. But this good news assumes an **anthropology**: there must be a "righteous." It is this assumption that Wisdom argues for in chapters 13–15.

Israel's Distinction from Sinful Humanity. Wisdom 11–19 is a retelling of portions of Exodus and Numbers that rearranges the scriptural events as a consistent contrast between the deserved judgment of the Egyptians and the just blessing of Israel. On display in this symmetry is the "fitting judgment of God" (12:26). The destruction of the Egyptians is an enactment of just judgment because the Egyptians idolize creatures (12:24); the rescue and preservation of Israel are enactments of just grace because "the evil intent of human art" did not mislead Israel into idolatry (15:4). Wisdom 13–15, which is an extended and unrelenting polemic against idolatry and the immorality that inevitably follows, functions within Wisdom's recasting of scriptural history to reinforce the distinction between Israel and non-Israel: non-Israel is idolatrous; Israel is not.

Wisdom unleashes this rhetorical attack in three stages, moving from (1) the folly of nature worship (13:1–9) to (2) the origins of idolatry and the ethical corruption it causes (13:10–15:17) and finally on to (3) the particularly foolish and debased cultic practices of the Egyptians (15:18–19). Worshiping what God has created is less deplorable than worshiping human artifacts, yet it still reflects an inexcusable intellectual error: "If they had the power to know so much as to try to understand the material world, how did they not find the Lord of these things?" (13:8–9; cf. 13:1). This religious stupidity is on full display in the mocking depiction of those who pray to human crafts. While the idols themselves are born from feelings of loss and/or attempts at honor (14:12–21), the idolater wastes words requesting safe travel from that which cannot move, strength from that which lacks functioning limbs, and, most absurdly, life from that which is dead (13:18–19). This kind of idolatry is the source of immorality: "The worship of unnamable idols is the beginning, cause, and end of every evil" (14:27). The Egyptians are paradigmatic of both this move from idolatry to immorality—they worshiped animals so ugly that even the Creator did not bless them (15:18–19)—and the theological conclusion that "the ungodly and their ungodliness are equally hateful to God" (14:9).

In the middle of this otherwise universal indictment is a celebration of Israel's innocence from idolatry and immorality.

> [1] But you our God are kind and true, patient and managing all things
>   in mercy.
> [2] For if we sin we are yours, knowing your power;
>   but we will not sin, knowing that we are reckoned as yours.
> [3] For to understand you is complete righteousness,
>   and to know your power is the root of immortality.
> [4] For neither has the evil intent of human art deceived us,
>   nor the fruitless toil of painters …
>
> WISDOM OF SOLOMON 15:1–4

Just as unintelligence is the cause of idolatry, Wisdom anchors Israel's uniqueness in her knowledge of God, which is both the sum of righteousness and the root of immortality. Echoing Exod 34, Wisdom confesses God's graciousness, which, as promised by Moses (Exod 34:9), will mean forgiveness of potential sin. Such potential sin, however, is an actual impossibility: "we will not sin" (Wis 15:2). This is a bold employment of **LXX** Exod 34. The "if we sin" of Wisdom 15:2 grounds its (unneeded) hope of future forgiveness in Moses' words spoken in the aftermath of the golden calf incident, thereby echoing language from Israel's paradigmatic act of idolatry in an argument for the nonidolatrousness of Israel. Unsurprisingly, therefore, Wisdom's scriptural retelling never mentions the disaster of Exod 32. Unlike the ungodly, whose "unsound reason" (2:1) leads to idolatry and immorality, Israel knows God and is, for that reason, innocent. This establishes a firm distinction: non-Israel, as the idolatrous and immoral, is unrighteous; Israel, as the nonidolaters and obedient, is righteous.

Romans 1:18–2:5

"YOU WHO PASS JUDGMENT DO THE SAME THINGS"

God's Just Judgment. The story of sin starts in Eden (Wis 2:23–24; Rom 5:12). If the beginning of the story was the whole story, then Wisdom and Romans would have a similar tale to tell; and the connections between Wisdom 13–15 and Rom 1:18–2:5 can give the impression that they do. Their themes and vocabulary overlap to a considerable extent, and, most significantly, the argumentative sequence of Rom 1:18–32 develops in parallel to Wisdom 13:1–14:31—a rhetorical progression that is unique to Wisdom and Romans. The arguments move from a squandered or missed knowledge of God to the idolatry and immorality that inevitably follow and the deserved judgment that awaits (see figure 2.1).

Figure 2.1: Wisdom 13–15 and Romans 1:18–2:5—Points of Theological Contact

A (possible) creation-related knowledge of God has been squandered.	
Wisdom 13:1–9	Romans 1:19–20

The wasted opportunity to know the true God manifests itself in false religion.	
Wisdom 13:10–14:11, 15–21 (and 15:7–13)	Romans 1:21–23

The turn to idols occasions a corresponding decline into immorality.	
Wisdom 14:12–14, 22–29	Romans 1:24–31

A fitting divine judgment awaits those guilty of idolatry and immorality.	
Wisdom 14:30–31	Romans 1:32

These connections ensure that Jewish readers of Romans—that is, read-ers in the tradition of Wisdom of Solomon—would find themselves sympa-thetic to Paul's announcement that those who "served created things rather than the Creator" (Rom 1:25) and were therefore given over to immorality (1:24, 26–31) "deserve death" (1:32). Romans 2:1–5 seems to suppose and exploit this sympathy.

Israel's Inclusion among Sinful Humanity. Romans 2:1 addresses a dialogue partner whom Paul characterizes as both judging the sinful people depicted in 1:19–32 and participating in the idolatry and immorality cata-loged there. Because "you who pass judgment" also "do the same things," his condemnation of the other is necessarily a condemnation of the judge *himself* (2:1, 3). The judge, however, appears to presume that he "will escape God's judgment" (2:3), and this because God is *patient* and *kind*—an echo of Exod 34 that echoes Wisdom's appeal to LXX Exod 34:9 (Rom 2:4; cf. Wis 15:1). As mentioned above, however, Wisdom decontextualizes divine mercy, borrowing words from the aftermath of the golden calf incident to insist on Israel's innocence in relation to idolatry. But Paul is quick to remind his conversation partner of an element of Wisdom's theology: God "overlooks human sin for the sake of repentance" (Wis 11:23; cf. Rom 2:4). Like Exod 34, Paul locates mercy in the matrix of idolatry and immorality. Whereas Wisdom 13–15 *excludes* Israel from the otherwise universal history of false religion and ethical decline, Paul's reminder that "you who pass judgment" also "do the same things" (Rom 2:1, 3) serves to *include* Israel within the human story of sin.

From this vantage point, Rom 1:18–32 reads rather differently. Instead of a compressed yet faithful presentation of Wisdom's irreducible distinction between Israel and non-Israel, Paul's announcement is, as he says, a revelation of God's wrath against *all* (1:18). This revelation of wrath is connected to the revelation of *righteousness* by the repeated use of the word *for* in 1:16–18 (see figure 2.2).[1]

Figure 2.2: The Logical Progression of Romans 1:16–18

| [16] For I am not ashamed of the gospel . . . | . . . for it is the power of God for salvation . . . | [17] For in the gospel the righ-teousness of God is revealed . . . | [18] For the wrath of God is revealed . . . |

---

1. The chart follows my translation.

The progression of Paul's logic suggests that the word of wrath is the first word of a two-part proclamation: wrath and righteousness, death and life. This revelation "from above" is different from Wisdom's claim that people should have reasoned "from below"—that is, "from the greatness and beauty of created things" to "their Creator" (Wis 13:5). For Wisdom, God could have been reasoned to from creation, but this potential has gone unrealized. Paul, however, says that "what may be known about God is plain … because God has made it plain" (Rom 1:19). Thus, in contrast to Wisdom, people "knew God" (1:21), and their error is not stupidity, but sin—the failure to honor God "as God" (1:21) and the corresponding idolatry of worshiping the creature (1:25; cf. 1:21–24).

Paul's narrative of this "fall" from knowledge of God to ignorance, idolatry, and immorality tells the tragic tale of human history "since the creation of the world" (1:20). This creational context indicates that the "all" of 1:18 identifies Adamic humanity as the actor in the drama of "godlessness and wickedness." But—and this is a crucial point in conversation with Wisdom—Adamic humanity includes *Israel* (cf. Rom 5:12–14). Romans 1:23 establishes this point. Paul's depiction of humanity exchanging the glory of God for "images made to look like a mortal human being" recalls the creation of Adam (cf. Gen 1:26), but it does so by alluding to Israel's golden calf idolatry as described in LXX Ps 105:20 (106:20 NIV).[2]

LXX Psalm 105:20	Romans 1:23
"And they exchanged the glory that was theirs for the likeness of a grass-eating ox."	*"And they exchanged the glory* of the immortal God *for the likeness* of the image of a mortal man and of birds and four-footed animals and creeping creatures."

Wisdom's presentation of an idolatry-free Israel deletes this episode from Israel's history in order to preserve the distinction between the unrighteous (non-Israel) and the righteous (Israel). Paul, however, faces the **canonical** facts: Israel's original sin at Sinai includes Israel in the history of idolatry and immorality announced in Rom 1:18–32.

Therefore, as Rom 1:18 says, "all"—that is, Jews and Gentiles (cf. Rom 3:9)—are "without excuse" (1:20), because all have traded worship of the Creator for worship of the creature (1:25). As in Wisdom 14:12–14, such idolatry leads inevitably to immorality, but in Romans this is because "God gave them

---

2.   The chart follows my translation.

over" to "the sinful desires of their hearts" (1:24), to "shameful lusts" (1:26), and to "a depraved mind" (1:28). Thus, in contrast to Wisdom, for whom the movement from idolatry to immorality is a *natural devolution*, Paul presents this as an enactment of *divine judgment*: idolaters are *handed over* to immorality. For Wisdom, of course, Israel is excluded from this history. Free from various forms of idolatry and the immorality that follows, Israel is the nation that "has not been misled by the evil intent of human art" (15:4) and thus "will not sin" (15:2). Paul disagrees on both counts. Rather than describing idolatry in its diverse expressions, Paul reduces false worship to a common denominator: worshiping and serving the creature rather than the Creator (Rom 1:25). Insofar as Israel is complicit in Adamic humanity's history of idolatry—and Paul's allusion to the golden calf idolatry in Rom 1:23 exposes this complicity—Israel is included in the history of "exchang[ing] the truth about God for a lie" (1:25), is among those whom "God gave ... over" (1:24), and is therefore subject to the universal verdict that "those who do such things deserve death" (1:32).

Romans 3:22–23 provides a perfect summary of Rom 1:18–2:5: "There is no difference between Jew and Gentile, for all have sinned." But for Wisdom, there is a difference. The function of Wisdom 13–15 is to reinforce this **anthropological** division by juxtaposing the idolatry and immorality of non-Jews with the innocence of Israel. Romans 1:18–2:5 makes the opposite point. By telling the story of Adamic humanity's idolatry and immorality in a way that includes Israel, Paul announces the essential oneness of all persons before God. Jew and Gentile are both "under the power of sin" (3:9), and humanity is thereby reduced to a common denominator—sinner.

FOR FURTHER READING

Additional Ancient Texts

Texts that contain anti-idolatry polemic include *Sibylline Oracles*; Josephus, *Against Apion*; Philo, *On the Decalogue* 52–81. For other Pauline texts on idolatry, see 1 Thess 1:2–10; 1 Cor 8:1–13; 10:6–22.

English Translations and Critical Editions

NETS

NRSV

Rahlfs, Alfred, and Robert Hanhart, eds. *Septuaginta*. Stuttgart: Deutsche Bibelgesellschaft, 2007.

Secondary Literature

Barclay, John M. G. "Unnerving Grace: Approaching Romans 9–11 from The Wisdom of Solomon." Pages 91–110 in *Between Gospel and Election*. WUNT 257. Edited by F. Wilk and J. R. Wagner. Tübingen: Mohr Siebeck, 2010.

Collins, John J. *Jewish Wisdom in the Hellenistic Age*. OTL. Louisville: Westminster John Knox, 1997.

Dodson, J. R. *The Powers of Personification: Rhetorical Purpose in the Book of Wisdom and the Letter to the Romans*. BZNW 161. Berlin: de Gruyter, 2008.

Linebaugh, Jonathan A. *God, Grace, and Righteousness in Wisdom of Solomon and Paul's Letter to the Romans: Texts in Conversation*. NovTSup 152. Leiden: Brill, 2013.

McGlynn, M. *Divine Judgment and Divine Benevolence in the Book of Wisdom*. WUNT 2.139. Tübingen: Mohr Siebeck, 2001.

Watson, Francis. *Paul and the Hermeneutics of Faith*. London: T&T Clark, 2004.

CHAPTER 3

Jubilees and Romans 2:6–29: Circumcision, Law Observance, and Ethnicity

SARAH WHITTLE

aul begins the letter to the Romans by insisting that the whole of humanity, both Jew and Gentile, is liable to the righteous judgment of God; in judgment as elsewhere, God is impartial: "first for the Jew, then for the Gentile" (Rom 2:9–10). In this case, being a recipient of the law will prove to be no advantage when it comes to God's justice, not least because Gentiles who do not possess the law may do "things required by the law" (2:14), since it is "written on their hearts" (2:15). In this complex passage, Paul engages in **diatribe**—a type of writing that may include rhetorical questions and fictional conversations and partners—and interpretation of some of Paul's statements here is contested.

The climax of Paul's argument for God's just judgment for Jews and Gentiles—both those with the law and those outside of the law—involves the issue of circumcision, the sign of the **covenant** relationship. Paul rejects the validity of circumcision in the flesh of the foreskin without the requisite obedience in favor of the circumcision of the heart, a legitimate covenant category into which he incorporates Gentiles in Christ who are physically uncircumcised. This internalization of circumcision in itself is not new—it is present elsewhere in the OT and **Second Temple Jewish** literature (Deut 10:16, 30:6, 10; Jer 4:4; 1QpHab 11.13; Philo, *Spec.* 1.305). But whereas circumcision previously marked ethnic identity, the innovation in Paul's heart circumcision is that it has become the mark of those made righteous in Christ, both Jew and Gentile. Real circumcision is not external and physical, but inward: "circumcision is circumcision of the heart by the Spirit" (Rom 2:29). Participation in the people of God, and in this case God's just judgment, is no longer on the basis of ethnicity.

Jubilees

"AND MY COVENANT WILL BE IN YOUR FLESH"

Another Jewish text that reflects on the value of circumcision is the book of *Jubilees*. This is a second-century BC rewriting of Genesis and the first half of Exodus (from creation to Sinai),[1] which begins with Moses receiving the law on Sinai and has a particular concern with the "division of the days," or a chronology (ordained by God) for jubilee.[2]

Fragments from fourteen Hebrew manuscripts found at **Qumran** now supplement translations into Greek, Latin, and Ethiopic. The numerous copies of the book of *Jubilees* at Qumran suggest that it had a level of authority on a par with that of Genesis or Exodus.[3] At the time of the **Maccabean Revolt**, there was real pressure toward **Hellenization** and assimilation; and resisting Greek culture and asserting the necessity of circumcision were two sides of the same coin. The author of *Jubilees* is likely to have been attempting to encourage a separate Jewish identity and to maintain distance from Gentiles and Gentile practices. Circumcision would be paramount in such a project.

Circumcision and Covenant Identity. Our focus chapter, *Jubilees* 15, follows the Lord's appearance to Abram and consequent announcement of the covenant. The sign of this covenant was to be the circumcision of the foreskin of "all your males" (15:11): "And my covenant shall be in your flesh for an eternal ordinance" (15:13). Any male, even the son of a purchased servant, not circumcised on the eighth day would be uprooted from his family, considered to have "broken my covenant." In this, *Jubilees* follows Gen 17 quite closely. The next part, however—the expanded laws of circumcision—likely reflects the historical context for the production of the literature; there are specific laws of circumcision peculiar to the book of *Jubilees*, described as eternal and written on heavenly tablets (15:25).

To be a son of the covenant, a male must be circumcised on the eighth day. If he is not, he is from the children of destruction (15:26): because he does not have the sign that he belongs to the Lord, "[he is destined] to be

---

1.   Translations of *Jubilees* are adapted from R. H. Charles, ed., *The Apocrypha and Pseudepigrapha of the Old Testament in English: With Introductions and Critical and Explanatory Notes to the Several Books* (Oxford: Clarendon, 1913). For additional introductory matters, see James C. Vander-Kam, *The Book of Jubilees* (GAP; London: T&T Clark, 2001), 21; James L. Kugel, *A Walk through Jubilees: Studies in the Book of Jubilees and the World of Its Creation* (JSJSup 156; Leiden: Brill, 2012).
2.   The text holds that the calendar was ordained at Sinai. There are seven days in a week; seven years are treated as a week of years; and seven weeks of years equals a jubilee—forty-nine years. Which calendar to follow (solar or lunar) was the source of major disagreement between parts of Judaism.
3.   VanderKam, *Book of Jubilees*, 7.

47

destroyed" (15:26). The reason given is that the angels of the Presence and the angels of sanctification were circumcised from the day of their creation; and the people of Israel were circumcised in order to be with the Lord and the holy angels (15:27). God's lordship over all people is acknowledged, but Israel alone is to be a people for the Lord, gathered and sanctified. In contrast, the Lord caused spirits to rule over the other peoples and nations to lead them astray.

Judgment for the Uncircumcised. Finally, the section contains a prediction: some of Israel, named as the sons of Beliar (i.e., wicked or worthless people), will not circumcise their sons (15:33). In this they will blaspheme and make themselves like Gentiles and consequently will be recipients of the wrath of God, to be removed and uprooted from the land. There will be no pardon, for this is an eternal error (15:34). Following these special laws, *Jubilees* returns to Genesis to pick up the narrative at chapter 18. So we have an excursus in the eternal laws of circumcision for the sons of Israel, written in heaven; and disobedience will lead to destruction.

Romans 2:6–29

"CIRCUMCISION IS A MATTER OF THE HEART"

Justification for Law Keepers. Paul, however, seeks to establish the fact that people will not be judged on the basis of their ethnicity. First he addresses the issue of whether or not persons are recipients of the law (Rom 2:12–13). He asserts that it is not the hearers, those who have been given the law, who are made righteous, but the doers. Then he introduces the category of Gentiles who are not in *possession* of the law but who keep the *requirement* of the law; and in this they show that the law is "written on their hearts" (2:15). Conversely, a Jew who might rely on possession of the law, even making it the basis of a boast, is rebuked for being overconfident: "You who boast in the law, do you dishonor God by breaking the law?" (2:23). The implication is that Paul's hypothetical subject does indeed break the law and so should keep in check any sense of superiority.

Law Keeping and Heart Circumcision. The argument about ethnicity and judgment reaches its climax in a discussion of circumcision. It remains of value for the person who is observant, but for the one who breaks the law, "you have become as though you had not been circumcised" (2:25). Correspondingly, according to Paul's rhetoric, the one who keeps the requirement of the law but is uncircumcised will be regarded as circumcised. In other words, physically uncircumcised "law keepers" will condemn circumcised law breakers. Of course, Paul's description of the uncircumcised person who keeps the requirement of the law is severely challenged by the fact that circumcision was a requirement of the law! So in order to make this move, Paul has to redefine not only "circumcision" and "Jew" but also "law keeping." And that is what he does: "For no one is a Jew who is merely one outwardly, nor is circumcision outward and physical. But a Jew is one inwardly, and circumcision is a matter of the heart, by the Spirit, not by the letter" (2:28–29 ESV).

Whereas the special laws of circumcision in *Jubilees* implored Israel to be circumcised in the flesh of the foreskin and avert the wrath of God—an imperative arising out of the necessity to maintain a separate identity from Gentiles—Paul focuses on the inward: circumcision is spiritual, not physical; it is a matter of the heart. But Paul did not initiate this hermeneutical move. Scripture has already redefined circumcision (Deut 10:16; 30:6, 10; Jer 4:4). The idea of the "inward" (things) from Rom 2:29, which may be translated "secret" or "hidden" things, is only found elsewhere in Scripture in the section of Deuteronomy concerned with Israel's covenant renewal (29:28), the much-anticipated **eschatological** event at which God will intervene to restore the covenant relationship by enabling Israel's obedience.

David Lincicum says that this term for "inward" or "hidden" had an important hermeneutical function in **sectarian** Judaism. Heart circumcision belongs to the category of "eschatologically 'hidden' mysteries" that Paul believes have come to pass in Christ.[4] And while there is no explicit citation, Paul's "heart" and "Spirit" language in 2:29 is likely to be reflecting the tradition that associates the giving of God's Spirit (Ezek 36:26–27) or writing law on the heart (Jer 31:33–34//**LXX** Jer 38:33–34).

Jubilees itself picks up on this idea of "internalizing" circumcision as an eschatological category in 1:23–24.

> And after this they will turn to me [God] in all uprightness and with all their heart and with all their soul, and I shall circumcise the foreskin of their heart and the foreskin of the heart of their seed, and I shall create in them a holy spirit, and I shall cleanse them so that they shall not turn away from me from that day unto eternity. And their souls will cleave to me and to all my commandments, and they will fulfill my commandments, and I shall be their Father and they will be my children.

---

4. David Lincicum, *Paul and the Early Jewish Encounter with Deuteronomy* (Grand Rapids: Baker, 2013), 150–51.

The key difference between the eschatological interpretation of Scripture in *Jubilees* and Paul's letter to the Romans is that for the former this remains a category for Israel only. Paul uses the theme of internalization to argue that persons may be obedient without being physically circumcised, a category into which he places the Gentiles.

It would be possible to conclude from Paul's argument so far that the result of this eschatological state of affairs is that the Spirit now enables one to observe the law in a way that Exodus and Deuteronomy anticipated. Yet Paul's rewriting of Deut 30:11–14 in Rom 10:6–8, where righteousness by faith gives the Torah a **christological** interpretation, affirms that this covenant renewal takes place on a very different basis from a commitment to "follow all the words of this law" (Deut 28:58; 29:29). The righteous requirement of the law is fulfilled in those who walk according to the Spirit. Indeed, believers are said to fulfill the law when they walk in the Spirit (Rom 8:4), which manifests in loving others: "Whoever loves others has fulfilled the law" (13:8); "love is the fulfillment of the law" (13:10; cf. Gal 5:12–13).

In conclusion, circumcision, as established with Abraham in Gen 17, was the sign of the covenant, identifying Israel as the people of God. Jews were circumcised; Gentiles were not. The "special laws" in *Jubilees* 15 reinforce the gravity of the issue, condemning to eternal destruction any Israelites who did not circumcise their sons—so critical was the need to maintain a Jewish identity in the face of pressure from **Hellenism**. In Rom 2 the very things that separate Jewish and Gentile identity become the issues by which Paul includes Christ-believing Gentiles in the people of God—namely, law and circumcision. Not a circumcision of the flesh of the foreskin, but a circumcision of the heart, spoken of in Israel's covenant renewal texts—an internal work of God, carried out by the Spirit, which meant that even those not in possession of the law might do the things that the law requires. While he maintains the order— "first to the Jew, then to the Gentile" (Rom 1:16)—Paul redefines the covenant categories along nonethnic lines to establish the fact that God's just judgment applies to Jews and Gentiles impartially.

FOR FURTHER READING

Additional Ancient Texts

A foundational text on Jewish identity and circumcision is Exod 19 and 32–34, which Paul reflects on in 2 Cor 3–4. See also Rom 4; Gal 2:4; 3:3, 13; 5:2; 6:12. See also the foundational documents for the Qumran community: CD *Damascus Document* and 1QS *Rule of the Community*.

English Translations and Critical Editions

Charles, R. H., ed. *The Apocrypha and Pseudepigrapha of the Old Testament in English: With Introductions and Critical and Explanatory Notes to the Several Books*. 2 vols. Oxford: Clarendon, 1913.

Wintermute, O. S. "Jubilees." Pages 35–142 in vol. 2 of *The Old Testament Pseudepigrapha*. Edited by James H. Charlesworth. Garden City, NY: Doubleday, 1985.

VanderKam, James C. *The Book of Jubilees: A Critical Text*. 2 vols. CSCO 510. Leuven: Peeters, 1989.

Secondary Literature

Berkley, Timothy W. *From a Broken Covenant to Circumcision of the Heart: Pauline Intertextual Exegesis in Romans 2:17–29*. SBLDS 175. Atlanta: Society of Biblical Literature, 2000.

Gathercole, Simon J. *Where Is Boasting? Early Jewish Soteriology and Paul's Response in Romans 1–5*. Grand Rapids: Eerdmans, 2002.

Kugel, James L. *A Walk through Jubilees: Studies in the Book of Jubilees and the World of Its Creation*. JSJSup 156. Leiden: Brill, 2012.

Lincicum, David. *Paul and the Early Jewish Encounter with Deuteronomy*. Grand Rapids: Baker Academic, 2013.

Stowers, Stanley K. *The Diatribe and Paul's Letter to the Romans*. SBLDS 57. Atlanta: Society of Biblical Literature, 1981.

VanderKam, James C. *The Book of Jubilees*. GAP. London: T&T Clark, 2001.

Whittle, Sarah. *Covenant Renewal and the Consecration of the Gentiles in Romans*. SNTSMS 161. Cambridge: Cambridge University Press, 2014.

Wright. N. T. "The Law in Romans 2." Pages 131–50 in *Paul and the Mosaic Law*. Edited by James G. Dunn. Grand Rapids: Eerdmans, 2001.

CHAPTER 4

4QMMT and Romans 3:1–20: Works of the Law and Justification

JASON MASTON AND AARON SHERWOOD

At a key point in his letter to the Romans, Paul declares, "Now we know that whatever the law says, it says to those who are under the law, so that every mouth may be silenced and the whole world held accountable to God. Therefore no one will be declared righteous in God's sight by the works of the law; rather, through the law we become conscious of our sin" (3:19–20). This statement is the conclusion to Paul's argument that began in 3:9 and ultimately traces back to 1:18. For three chapters Paul has been exposing the sinfulness of humanity, reminding his readers of the complete failure of *all* people—both Jew and Gentile—to live in a manner pleasing to God. The unmasking of humanity's sinfulness (in stark contrast to God's faithfulness) reaches its climax in the catena of 3:10–18, where Paul draws on statements from the "law" (3:19)[1] to provide evidence for his assertion in 3:9 that all are "under the power of sin." Now, having established humanity's sinfulness, Paul draws the conclusion that "no one will be declared righteous in God's sight by the works of the law" (3:20). Paul's claim raises many questions, one crucial question being this one: What does he mean by "works of the law"? To help answer this question, we will draw on the only other Jewish text outside the Pauline corpus that uses this phrase, namely, *Some Works of the Law* (4QMMT).[2]

---

1. He is actually quoting the Psalms and Prophets as interpreters of the law.
2. The expression "works of the law" also appears in Rom 3:28; Gal 2:16 (3x); 3:2, 5, 10.

4QMMT

"WORKS OF THE LAW ... WILL BE RECKONED
TO YOU AS RIGHTEOUSNESS"

The label 4QMMT stands for six **Dead Sea Scrolls** found in cave 4 beside Khirbet **Qumran** (4Q394–4Q399). The documents receive their title from the distinctive phrase translated in English as "some works of the law." The original may have been a letter written from one group of Jews to another. Many scholars claim it was written by the "Teacher of Righteousness" who apparently led the community at its formative stage. The reconstructed document—that which is restored when fragments from all six extant copies are pieced together to form a single text—is customarily divided into three sections: §A is a calendar; §B contains interpretative comments on some commandments in the Torah; and §C is an exhortation to obedience, drawing on the blessing and cursing language of Deut 27–28.[3]

Bringing their exhortation and letter to a conclusion, the authors announce that they have written about "some works of the law," and they have done this so the recipients will obey and righteousness will be reckoned to them. The epilogue reads:

> [26] And so we have written to you [27] *some works of the law* that we consider are beneficial for you and your people, since we have seen [28] you have aptitude and knowledge regarding law. Be perceptive in all these matters and in his presence seek for him to uphold [29] your counsel, in order to keep the wickedness and counsel of Belial far from you, [30] with the result that, at the end of time, you may rejoice, finding our words sound. [31] And it will be reckoned to you as righteousness when you do what is upright and what is good in his presence, for the good of yourselves [32] and for Israel. (§C 26–32)

To help us navigate this complex document, we will answer three questions: (1) What does the phrase "works of the law" mean? (2) What does the author mean by "reckoning as righteousness"? and (3) What is the relationship between righteousness and works of the law?

Works of the Law. On the one hand, the phrase "works of the law" could stand as a summary for the instructions found in §B. There may be a link between the phrase in §C 27 and the opening lines of §B: "These are some

---

3.   It is fairly widely agreed that §A was originally transmitted separately (cf. 4Q237) but was attached to 4Q395 at some stage. Section A has no bearing on the issues discussed here.

of our words/rulings […] which […] the works which we […]."The Hebrew wording is different between the two sections, however, and the text is highly fragmented, so it is difficult to draw a firm link between the two. Nevertheless, the connection with §B makes good conceptual sense. Section B refers to twenty-four different commandments from the Torah and includes the community's own view about how these precepts are to be applied. The uniting feature is that they all address issues of purity and impurity. The authors have written about these things because they believe the readers have the ability to understand the Torah and thus they are encouraging them to study the interpretive decisions. On the other hand, the phrase can refer to observing the Torah. Here the focus is not on the precepts of the Torah, but on the human agent obeying what the Torah commands. This meaning fits well with the overall focus of the final paragraph and indeed all of §C, which is an exhortation for the readers to practice the distinctive interpretations offered in §B.

Since both positions seem to have some supporting evidence, the best solution may be a mediating one. The phrase is probably best understood in the first sense as a reference to the works required by the law, specifically those described in §B. This, though, needs to be set firmly in the overall purpose of the letter, which is to motivate the readers to *do* certain things: the "works of the law" are to be observed.

Reckoning as Righteousness. The statement "And it will be reckoned to you as righteousness" (§C 31), as with much of §C, is derived from the Scriptures. In form, this expression is probably closest to the account of Phinehas, who intervened to bring an end to God's judgment against the Israelites who were worshiping the Baal of Peor (Num 25:6–13; Ps 106:28–31). Because of this action, righteousness was credited to him—that is, he was *justified*. The account of Phinehas also has conceptual and linguistic links to the Abraham narrative. Genesis 15:6 states, "Abram believed the LORD, and he credited it to him as righteousness." Taking note of this scriptural background is important because it helps us to see that when God credits righteousness to someone, that person is already part of the **covenant community**. Therefore, while many Christians understand "justification" as equivalent to forgiveness of sins (see below), this does not seem to be the way it was understood by many Second Temple Jews. God's justifying act does not *make* somebody a member of the covenant, but *confirms* the person's already existing status within the covenant people.

Relating Righteousness and Works of the Law. The final sentence of the epilogue states that righteousness is reckoned when one does "what is upright and what is good." Reading backward from this statement, it is probably the case that the upright and good deeds that the recipients should do are in fact the "works of the law" mentioned earlier. This conceptual link indicates that, according to 4QMMT, justification is finally based on one's observance of the Torah. This does not mean, though, that the authors held some notion of "legalism," for their aim was not to *earn* God's favor. They believed that God was already favorable to them because he had established a covenant relationship with them. Moreover, they insisted that God, in some manner, helps them to obey: "in his presence seek for him to uphold your counsel" (§C 28–29). The authors of 4QMMT do not present the human as the only or even primary agent in gaining salvation. Nevertheless, as we will see, one must not downplay the emphasis here on obeying the Torah as the means to righteousness.

Romans 3:1–20

"NO ONE WILL BE DECLARED RIGHTEOUS ... BY THE WORKS OF THE LAW"

When we turn to Paul's claim that "no one will be declared righteous in God's sight by the works of the law" in Rom 3:20 with 4QMMT in mind, we find that some light can be cast on Paul's statement. In the discussion of 4QMMT above, we noted that there is some ambiguity about whether the expression "works of the law" refers to the specific matters identified in §B or indicates the "doing" of the Torah. The same issue arises in Rom 3:20. Compare, for example, the 1984 NIV translation with the 2011 version:

Romans 3:20 (1984 NIV, italics added)	Romans 3:20 (2011 NIV, italics added)
"Therefore no one will be declared righteous in his sight by *observing the law*."	"Therefore no one will be declared righteous in God's sight by the *works of the law*."

Although the change could be explained as a move toward a more "literal" translation, it recognizes more clearly the uncertainty regarding whether the phrase refers to doing the law or to some specific commandments contained within the law.

Works of the Law. As we saw with 4QMMT, a mediating position may be best. If we trace Paul's statements about the Torah through Rom 2 and 3, we see that he covers a range of topics—stealing (2:21), adultery (2:22), idolatry

(2:23), blaspheming (2:24), and circumcision (2:25–29)—and often refers to the Torah in a broad sense (2:12–15, 18–20). In the context of Rom 3:19–20, Paul does not appear to have any particular commandments in mind, so it is probably best to view the works of the law broadly as any act of obedience to the Torah.[4] To limit ourselves to this conclusion alone, though, misses part of what Paul is doing, as we will see below.

Declaring Righteous. At this point in the argument of Romans, there is little to help us make sense of Paul's view of justification or righteousness. The previous mention in 1:17 links righteousness with faith, and the following sections (3:21–26; 4:1–25) will make the same connection.[5] In these other places, most particularly in 4:1–8, Paul seems to advocate a different understanding of justification from what we saw in 4QMMT. Paul links justification with forgiveness of sins, and he stresses that God justifies "the ungodly" (4:5). Whereas the authors of 4QMMT viewed God's declaration of righteousness as applying to those already *in* a covenant relationship with him, Paul presents God as declaring righteous those who are *outside* the covenant. Paul brings "justification" closer to conversion and the establishment of the person among the people of God.

Relating Righteousness and Works of the Law. For Paul, then, what is the relationship between justification and works of the law? Or we might put it this way: Why does Paul reject works of the law as an acceptable means to righteousness? This question brings us to the heart of our comparison of 4QMMT with Paul: however we answer the previous two questions, the primary similarity is the link between righteousness and works of the law. Both affirm that God is the one who declares a person righteous. For the authors of 4QMMT, it is on the basis of doing the works of the law that God declares one righteous. Paul, however, turns this idea upside down. According to Paul, doing the works of the law will *not* bring justification. Two observations are in order, which correspond to the key words *works* and *law*.

Works. Like 4QMMT, Paul draws on a scriptural claim, namely, Ps 143:2 (**LXX** Ps 142:2), which he modifies to fit his purposes. The psalmist uses the claim "for no one living is righteous before you" as the reason that God should not judge him for his sins. The psalmist's statement is virtually a truism: in comparison with God, no one is righteous. With the addition of "by the works

---

4. This claim is in contrast to much recent scholarship, especially the New Perspective on Paul, which has held that, even if "works of the law" refers to all the commandments, Paul has in mind particularly the Jewish covenant identity markers: circumcision, the food laws, and Sabbath regulations. These three things in particular are what distinguished Jews from their neighbors.
5. Note also Paul's use of "unrighteousness" in Rom 1:18, 29; 2:8; 3:5.

of the law," Paul shifts the focus so that the statement stresses the *means* by which one cannot become righteous before God. The point is no longer a comparison between sinful humans and the righteous God; rather, the focus is now on the way in which one attains (or cannot attain) a righteous verdict from God. In comparison to 4QMMT, Paul presents another way to think about how God and humans interact in the salvation process. Paul finds in claims like that of 4QMMT §C 27 assertions that humans are the primary acting agent for the reason that one is declared righteous. Paul highlights the human act of *doing* the Torah, and he rejects this as a means to attaining righteousness.

Law. Although not made clear at this point in his argument, Paul's following statements shift the focus away from the Torah and obedience to it as the defining characteristic of the people of God. Instead, he will stress the divine act in Christ and the faith response to it as that which characterizes God's people. Here we find a major reason that Paul contends justification is not by works of the law, namely, because God has worked through his Son to effect justification for his people. At the same time, Paul assigns the law a new role. Rather than being a dividing wall between Jew and Gentile and a source of justification for the Jew, the Torah, Paul maintains on the basis of Scripture itself, has silenced every mouth and holds the whole world—both Jew and Gentile—accountable to God (3:10–19). Such a move, radical in its day, serves to reinforce this profoundly countercultural gospel message: that God was at work in Jesus Christ to justify all who will believe in him apart from the works of the law (3:21–26).

For Further Reading

Additional Ancient Texts

For other Jewish texts that (possibly) use an expression similar to "works of the law," see 4QFlor 1:7 (disputed); 1QS 5:21; 6:18. The whole of 1QS (*Rule of the Community*) could be profitably studied for how some Jews viewed obedience to the Torah. For other Pauline texts, see Gal 2:15–21; 3:1–14.

English Translations and Critical Editions

Qimron, Elisha, and John Strugnell, eds. *Qumran Cave 4. V, Miqṣat Maʿaśe ha-Torah.* DJD 10. Oxford: Clarendon, 1994.

García Martínez, Florentino, and Eibert J. C. Tigchelaar, eds. *The Dead Sea Scrolls: Study Edition.* 2 vols. Leiden: Brill, 2007.

Secondary Literature

Abegg, Martin G. "4QMMT C 27, 31 and 'Works Righteousness.'" *DSD* 6, no. 2 (1999): 139–47.

de Roo, Jacqueline C. R. *"Works of the Law" at Qumran and in Paul.* NTM 13. Sheffield: Sheffield Phoenix, 2007.

Dunn, James D. G. "4QMMT and Galatians." *NTS* 43, no. 1 (1997): 147–53.

Hogeterp, Albert L. A. "4QMMT and Paradigms of Second Temple Jewish Nomism." *DSD* 15, no. 3 (2008): 359–79.

Kampen, John, and Moshe J. Bernstein, eds. *Reading 4QMMT: New Perspectives on Qumran Law and History.* Atlanta: Scholars Press, 1996.

Sprinkle, Preston M. *Paul & Judaism Revisited: A Study of Divine and Human Agency in Salvation.* Downers Grove, IL: InterVarsity Press, 2013.

von Weissenberg, Hanne. *4QMMT: Reevaluating the Text, the Function, and the Meaning of the Epilogue.* STDJ 82. Leiden: Brill, 2009.

Wright, N.T. "Justification and Eschatology in Paul and Qumran: Romans and 4QMMT." Pages 104–32 in *History and Exegesis: New Testament Essays in Honor of Dr. E. Earle Ellis on His Eightieth Birthday.* Edited by Sang-Won Son. New York: T&T Clark, 2006.

CHAPTER 5

The *Epistle of Enoch* and Romans 3:21–31: The Revelation of God's Righteousness

JONATHAN A. LINEBAUGH

Romans 3:21 announces something new—an unheard-of possibility. Following the despairing conclusion that "no one will be declared righteous in God's sight by the works of the law" (3:20), Paul declares that the "the righteousness of God has been made known" in an event he calls "the redemption that came by Christ Jesus" (3:21, 24). Rather than carrying out the condemnation that concluded 3:20, however, this righteousness is demonstrated in the death of Jesus (3:25), which results in the unexpected declaration that sinners (3:23) are called righteous—that is, "justified freely by his grace" (3:24).

To underline the newness of Paul's proclamation is not to suggest he was alone in thinking that the disclosure of divine righteousness would be enacted in a history-altering (or in many cases, history-ending) moment of divine judgment. Such an expectation is a common theme in early Jewish texts, especially in the literature classified as **apocalyptic**. Paul's place within this tradition, and the ways in which he points to something radically new, can be illuminated by comparing Rom 3:21–31 with another text that claims to pass on received revelation and depict the decisive climax of divine righteousness: the *Epistle of Enoch*.

The Epistle of Enoch
"THE RIGHTEOUS WILL NOT BE FOUND AS SINNERS"

The *Epistle of Enoch* (*1 En.* 92:1–5; 93:11–105:2; hereafter, the *Epistle*) is a relatively late moment in the literary history of *1 Enoch*, which is a collection of writings from different times,[1] in different genres, but all in the voice of Enoch. The oldest manuscript fragments from **Qumran** cave 4 are in Aramaic, though some scholars suspect that portions of the text were originally composed in Hebrew. *First Enoch* is a non**canonical** text for most Jewish and Christian traditions, though the Ethiopian and Eritrean Orthodox churches include it in their canon. The *Epistle*, in both frame and body, probably dates from just before the **Maccabean Revolt** (167–142 BC).

The *Epistle* speaks in the **pseudepigraphic** voice of Enoch, addressing "my sons ... and the last generation who will do uprightness and peace" (*1 En.* 92:1). Despite the present time of trouble, "the righteous ones" have no need to "be saddened ... for the Holy and Great One has appointed days for everything" (92:2). Now is the time of injustice. Those who walk in the way of "wickedness" enjoy the riches and rewards promised to the righteous (96:4; cf. 94:1–5) while the lived experience of the righteous is characterized by the **covenant** curses of Deut 28–30. "Having hoped to become the head," the righteous lament, "we have become the tail" (103:11; cf. Deut 28:13, 44).

God's Justice Will Be Revealed. The question is whether this upside-down existence, implying as it does the inversion of the **Deuteronomic pattern** of blessings and curses, reflects reality or is simply a temporary aberration of injustice. The sinners express one opinion: "The pious die according to fate, and what is gained for them by their works?" (102:6). Enoch offers an alternative: at the judgment the righteous "will not be found as sinners" (104:5). The apparent righteousness of the rich (96:4) and the assumed disobedience of the downcast (103:9–15) will both be exposed as illusions of injustice in an **eschatological** reversal of fortunes (104:5–6). In an act of total rebalancing, the judgment will both punish the wicked and reward the righteous, and to complete the compensation, what is upside down in the present will be turned right side up as the oppressed become the oppressors of the sinners.

Epistle of Enoch 95:3	*Epistle of Enoch* 96:1
"For the Lord will again deliver them into your hand so that you may carry out judgment on them as you wish."	"For sinners will quickly be destroyed before you, and you will have authority over them, as you wish."

Both the *end* (the blessing of the righteous and the destruction of the sinners) and the *instrument* (sinners judged by the righteous) of the final judgment ensure that the present injustice will be undone at the **eschaton**. The unjust

---

1. The various strands of the Enochic tradition date from the third to the first century BC.

links between sinners and blessing, on the one hand, and the righteous and curses, on the other, will be erased, and the straight lines of justice will be redrawn as, positively, the righteous are blessed, and, negatively, the wicked are cursed.

The Righteous Will Be Saved. But the sinners have a reply: "The godly die" (102:6). Open your eyes, the sinners say, for wishful thinking about some unseen reversal is just a fanciful avoidance of the obvious. The Enochic retort is, of course, that death is not the end. Within the world of the text, however, this claim is not naive speculation; the announced future is a record of revelation. Because Enoch "knows" and has "seen" (cf. 94:5, 10; 97:2; 98:8, 10, 12; 100:10; 103:2, 7–8; 104:10, 12), he can speak under oath (103:1) and make a promise: "Blessed will be those who receive the words of the wise and understand them, to do the commandments of the Most High; and they will walk in paths of his righteousness and not go astray with those who err, and they will be saved" (*1 En.* 99:10).

The *Epistle* is a revelation that the righteousness of God will be disclosed. The present is a time of trouble because, from the vantage point of righteousness, the wrong people are rewarded: the righteous suffer the covenant curses, while the sinners are blessed. But God's justice is coming; the final judgment will overcome injustice with justice as the sinners are punished and the righteous are blessed—this is the good news of the *Epistle of Enoch* (see figure 5.1).

Figure 5.1: The Epistle of Enoch's Presentation of Justice

Party	The Unjust Present	The Just Eschaton
The Righteous	Cursed	Blessed
The Unrighteous	Blessed	Cursed

Romans 3:21–31
"THE RIGHTEOUSNESS OF GOD HAS BEEN MADE KNOWN"

God's Justice Revealed Now. The Enochic apocalypse ("revelation") is future oriented. *Now* is the scene of the crime, the time of trouble when the righteous suffer and the wicked experience the covenant blessings. *Now* is the problem. This *now* is confronted with the eschatological *but then*—a promised future judgment that enacts and restores justice. *Now* the righteousness of God is hidden, *but then* the righteousness of God will be revealed.

Paul, by contrast, locates the revelation of divine righteousness in the *now*: "But *now* apart from the law the righteousness of God has been made known" (Rom 3:21). To Enochic ears, these words can only be heard as an announcement that what was promised to happen at the future judgment has occurred in the event Paul calls "the redemption that came by Christ Jesus" (3:24). Like the *Epistle*, Romans describes "the day ... when [God's] righteous judgment will be revealed," when "God will repay each person according to what they have done" (2:5–6). The time preceding this judgment is a period of "forbearance" (2:4), but the days of passing over sins (3:25) will give way to the "day of God's wrath" (2:5). Romans 3 joins Romans 2 in describing the era before the demonstration of divine righteousness as a time of "forbearance" (3:25). But rather than seeing this period as the present, Rom 3:21–26 puts it in the past. For Paul, the period of forbearance—the time when God "left the sins committed beforehand unpunished" (3:25)—ended in the enactment of divine righteousness that is the death of Jesus Christ. What the *Epistle* promises as an end-time judgment, Paul proclaims as apocalypse now: God's act of "present[ing] Christ as a sacrifice of atonement" (3:25) is the revelation of God's "righteous judgment" (2:5)—the judgment of God against sin.

All Are Unrighteous. It is not just the timing of this revelation of righteousness that would shock Enoch, however. The *Epistle* is predicated on a distinction between the righteous and the sinners. The existence of the righteous and the sinners is presupposed by the problem (the righteous experience the covenant curses, while the sinners are blessed), and it shapes the solution (at the judgment the righteous will be blessed and the sinners will be cursed). But Paul, summarizing his conclusion from Rom 1:18–3:20, says "there is no difference ... for all have sinned" (3:22–23; cf. 3:9). For the *Epistle*, such a claim can lead to only one conclusion: condemnation. And this is exactly what Paul concludes within the closed circle of the law in Rom 3:20: "No one will be declared righteous in God's sight by the works of the law."

Justification of the Ungodly. "But," 3:21 opens in antithesis to 3:20, God's righteousness has been revealed in what Karl Barth called the "impossible possibility ... of acquittal in condemnation."[2] This impossible possibility, however, this righteousness "apart from law" (3:21), does not go around the law's verdict of guilt and sentence of death; it goes through it. According to the righteous decree of the righteous judge (2:5; 3:5–6), sinners deserve to die (1:32; cf. 6:23). The cross, as the enactment of God's final judgment in the death of Jesus, is

2. Karl Barth, *The Epistle to the Romans* (trans. E. Hoskyns; London: Oxford University Press, 1993), 92.

the revelation of righteousness because it is the carrying out of this decree: the death of Christ for sinners is the death of the sinner (cf. Gal 2:20). But—and this is the unheard-of possibility—the God who judges ungodliness at the cross also, by that same event, justifies the ungodly (Rom 4:5). In the eschatological judgment scene that is the cross, sinners are put to death, so that they exist in a state of *nonbeing* ("things that were not," 4:17); but out of their postjudgment *nothingness* the resurrecting God re-creates (cf. 4:5, 17).

A Different Kind of Justice. Here we come to the line in the sand separating the *Epistle* and Romans. For the *Epistle*, the problem of the present is the injustice evident in the link between sinners and blessings. Paul is confronted by a different problem and, accordingly, a different solution—a solution, moreover, that would look to our Enochic author unnervingly like his problem. If "all have sinned" (3:23), and thus "there is no one righteous" (3:10), then "no one will be *declared* righteous"—that is, justified (3:20). Thus spoke the law. But now the righteousness apart from law speaks. It affirms the law's verdict ("all have sinned," 3:23) and enacts the law's sentence (judgment against sin in the form of death, 3:25–26). But this judgment is justifying: it declares the unrighteous righteous. It is precisely those who sinned (3:23) who are the objects of justification in Rom 3:24. From the perspective of the *Epistle*, a righteousness that calls the unrighteous righteous is a theological oxymoron. Paul seems to be proclaiming an instance of forensic "doublethink,"[3] as the judge identifies sinners as sinners (3:23) but then overturns his verdict with the seemingly unjust word of justification (3:24).

For Paul, of course, the rightness of this apparently unjust justice is grounded in the death of Jesus (3:25–26). But to Enochic ears, this is to go from bad to worse. In the *Epistle*, the injustice of the present is felt most acutely in the death of the righteous (e.g., *1 En.* 99:15; 102:4–11; 103:3, 9–10, 15). From this vantage point, Paul's explanation looks like an attempt to justify an act of injustice (calling sinners righteous) by anchoring it in a prior instance of injustice (the death of a righteous person). Rarely do two wrongs make a right, and it is wholly unlikely that Enoch would concede what he would hear as the Pauline claim that two wrongs make God righteous. But, and this is the point these differences have been uncovering, Paul is announcing a different kind of justice. This is a righteousness apart from law (3:21), a righteousness Paul calls "the righteousness of God through faith in Jesus Christ" (3:22, my translation).

That "the righteousness of God" is revealed "apart from law" disqualifies any grounds for human boasting (3:27) because it means that a person "is

---

3.   George Orwell, *1984* (New York: Penguin, 1949), 213–14.

justified by faith apart from the works of the law" (3:28). This elimination of works provides a negative definition of faith: faith says "no" to the human as the subject of justification. This faith, however, which is an **anthropological** "no," is also a **christological** "yes"—it confesses Jesus Christ, the one who is "present in faith,"[4] as the one by, in, and on the basis of whom God justifies the ungodly. Thus Paul's compact summary of this saving revelation of righteousness (cf. 1:16–17): this is "justification as a gift, by God's grace" (3:24, my translation). Paul calls this gift "the redemption that came by Christ Jesus" (3:24), suggesting it is the crucified Christ who graciously suffers God's judgment against sin (3:25–26) and who is graciously given to sinners as their righteousness (5:6–10, 17; cf. 1 Cor 1:30; 2 Cor 5:21).

This gift is given to sinners (3:23–24), a category that includes "all"—that is, Jew and Gentile (3:9)—and therefore the one God is the God of all, Jew and Gentile (3:29), justifying both the circumcised and the uncircumcised through faith (3:30). It is this unconditioned gift, the gift of Jesus for the justification of the ungodly, that mobilizes Paul's revolutionary mission to the Gentiles. An apostolic announcement to all is an effect—better, an aftershock—of the earthquake that is the enactment of God's justifying judgment against and for all. In Jesus, the law is upheld (3:31), not least because the death of Jesus is God's judgment against sin. But there is a deeper mystery in this judgment: the demonstration of God's righteousness reveals that God's judgment of sin, because it is placed on the one "who loved me and gave himself for me" (Gal 2:20), ultimately aims at and effects the justification of sinners.

For Further Reading

Additional Ancient Texts

The apocalyptic and testament literature is extensive. A sample of the apocalyptic texts includes *Apocalypse of Zephaniah*, *4 Ezra*, and *2 Baruch*. For examples of testaments, see *Testament of Moses*, *Testaments of the Twelve Patriarchs*, and *Testament of Job*. For a text that is influenced by and reflective of the *Epistle of Enoch*, see Wisdom of Solomon 2–5. For other Pauline texts, see 2 Cor 5:17–21; Gal 2–3; Phil 3:2–11.

---

4.   Martin Luther, *Lectures on Galatians* (1531/35) = LW 26:129. In other words, Christ himself is given in the word, which creates the faith that clings to him. Christ, then, as Luther insists (following 1 Cor 1:30), is "our righteousness."

English Translations and Critical Editions

Olson, D. *Enoch: A New Translation*. North Richland Hills, TX: BIBAL Press, 2004.

VanderKam, James C. *1 Enoch: A New Translation*. Minneapolis: Fortress, 2004.

The Aramaic fragments from Qumran cave 4 are included in:
García Martínez, Florentino, and Eibert J. C. Tigchelaar, eds. *The Dead Sea Scrolls: Study Edition*. 2 vols. Leiden: Brill, 2007.

For the Ethiopic texts:
Knibb, M. A. *The Ethiopic Book of Enoch*. 2 vols. Oxford: Clarendon, 1978.

For the Greek fragments:
Black, M. *Apocalypsis Henochi Graece*. PVTG 4. Leiden: Brill, 1970.

Secondary Literature

Linebaugh, Jonathan A. "Debating Diagonal Δικαιοσύνη: The *Epistle of Enoch* and Paul in Theological Conversation." *Early Christianity* 1 (2010): 107–28.

———. *God, Grace, and Righteousness in Wisdom of Solomon and Paul's Letter to the Romans in Conversation: Texts in Conversation*. NovTSup 152. Leiden: Brill, 2013.

Seifrid, Mark, A. *Christ, Our Righteousness: Paul's Theology of Justification*. NSBT 9. Leicester: Apollos, 2000.

Stuckenbruck, Loren T. *1 Enoch 91–108*. CEJL. Berlin: de Gruyter, 2007.

Westerholm, Stephen. *Perspectives Old and New: The 'Lutheran' Paul and His Critics*. Grand Rapids: Eerdmans, 2004.

CHAPTER 6

Sirach and Romans 4:1–25:
The Faith of Abraham

───────◇◇◇───────

MARIAM J. KAMELL

braham stands at the pinnacle of both Jewish and Christian traditions as the patriarch who, on the basis of his faith in God's promises, fathered the people of God. He was a towering figure in Jewish literature, who modeled faith for everyone to follow, a faith so vital that God spoke to and even covenanted with him. Throughout the OT, the Israelites are said to worship the God of Abraham, for Abraham had left his pagan culture at this God's word and covenanted that his descendants would worship this God alone.

For Paul, therefore, seeking to ground his argument of God's faithfulness to both Jews *and* Gentiles, Abraham stands as a fundamental character to draw on, anchoring his argument for the unity of God's purposes. In Rom 1–3, Paul contrasts human unfaithfulness with God's faithfulness, concluding with a triumphant set of rhetorical questions: "Or is God the God of Jews only? Is he not the God of Gentiles too? Yes, of Gentiles too, since there is only one God, who will justify the circumcised by faith and the uncircumcised through that same faith" (3:29–30). Paul confidently argues that faith in Christ is the basis of righteousness for everyone—whether Jew or Gentile. But because of his affirmation that the oneness of God ensures the oneness of his people via faith in Christ, Paul has to deal with the accusation that he nullifies the law since he undermines it drastically in his relegation of circumcision (3:31). And he does so in Rom 4, where he points to the story of Abraham for his defense, particularly drawing on the praise of Abraham in Gen 15:6. But while Paul's appeal to Gen 15:6 may seem for modern readers an obvious way to demonstrate how the law "testifies" to justification by faith (cf. 3:21), it is instructive to observe how some Second Temple Jews looked to

Abraham to legitimate quite different theological claims. To show how Paul read and used the Abraham narratives for his argumentative purposes, we shall in this chapter compare Rom 4 with another Jewish text that draws on the life and experience of Abraham—the book of Sirach.

Sirach

"IN THE TEST HE WAS FOUND FAITHFUL"

The book of Sirach, also known as Ecclesiasticus, is a lengthy piece of Wisdom literature written by Jesus Ben Sira, a resident of Jerusalem, who composed the work shortly before the outbreak of the **Maccabean Revolt** (167–142 BC).[1] The book was originally written in Hebrew and subsequently translated into Greek by Ben Sira's grandson, who also appended a prologue. Although Sirach was never canonized in Judaism, it was included in the **Septuagint** and is considered **deuterocanonical** in some branches of Christianity, including the Roman Catholic, Eastern Orthodox, and Anglican Churches.

Because of his importance, standing at the head of the Israelite tradition in faith and lineage, Abraham shows up in an assortment of hero lists (e.g., Heb 11), including the one found in Sirach 44–49. While much of the book stands in the tradition of Proverbs, in Sirach 42:15 Ben Sira switches to an *encomium* (a series of praises). He begins by praising the "works of God" (42:15), and in 44:1, he starts to "extol faithful/glorious men." Ben Sira's focus on "faithful men" (44:10) begins in 44:16 with Enoch and in 44:17–18 moves to Noah. Third in Israel's heritage comes Abraham, described in 44:19–21. The text reads thus:

> [19] Abraham, father of a multitude of nations,
>> did not tarnish his glory (with a blemish),
> [20] Who kept the commandments of the Most High,
>> and entered into a covenant with him;
> in his flesh he carved his decree,
>> and in the test he was found faithful.
> [21] Therefore, with an oath he [the Lord] raised him up
>> to bless the nations by his seed;[2]
> to give them an inheritance from sea to sea,
>> and from the river to the end of the earth.

---

1. *Ben* is Hebrew for "son of." The author's full name was "Jesus ben Eleazar ben Sira" (Sir 50:27); Eleazar was his father, and Sira his grandfather.
2. This translation is based on the Hebrew text. The Greek adds an extra two lines following this first blessing, based on the promises in Genesis: "to multiply him as the dust of the earth, / to raise his offspring/seed as stars."

Abraham as Law Keeper. One of the first things about Abraham we see in this text is an important development: before Moses ever ascended to Sinai, Abraham is said to have "kept the commandments of the Most High." This echoes God's affirmation of Abraham in Gen 26:5, "Abraham obeyed me and did everything I required of him, keeping my commands, my decrees and my instructions." Sirach goes beyond the praise of Gen 26, however, because in Genesis the Torah—as given to Moses—has not yet come! In Sirach, however, the law refers to Torah, the commandments given to Moses (cf. Sir 24:23). Sirach, then, expands on the assessment of Gen 26:5 by exemplifying what becomes common in later Jewish tradition, that Abraham did indeed keep Torah even before it was given.[3]

Figure 6.1: Abraham's Life according to Genesis

Call of Abram to leave Harran	(Gen 12)
Promise to make his descendants like the dust	(Gen 13:14–17)
Promise that the Lord is his shield and inheritance	(Gen 15:1–5)
"Abram believed the LORD, and he credited it to him as righteousness"	(Gen 15:6)
Covenant of a nation	(Gen 15:7–20)
Name change to Abraham and covenant of circumcision	(Gen 17)
Promise of Isaac	(Gen 18)
Birth of Isaac	(Gen 21)
Binding of Isaac	(Gen 22)

Narrative Sequence of Abraham's Life. Beyond the bigger chronological question, however, the subtle difference in the ordering of events in Abraham's life is important (see figure 6.1). In the original story, Gen 15 stands as a high point of the Abraham narrative. God engages Abram, who has left everything in trust of God's promise, in conversation. God reminds him that his reward will be great, but Abram pushes back: What good is a reward if he has no one to inherit it? God, in 15:4–5, reaffirms his promise of true descendants that would be countless, like the stars. Then, dramatically, Gen 15:6 summarizes: "Abram believed the LORD, and he credited it to him as righteousness." Then ensues another conversation following the same pattern of promise, question, and affirmation (15:7–21). As such, Gen 15:6 stands as a hinge for the chapter and a summary of Abraham's story as a whole. Two chapters later, God again promises a multitude of descendants, and it is at

---

3. Cf. *m. Qidd.* 14; *Jub.* 6:18–19; *2 Bar.* 57:1–2; *Gen. Rab.* 61:1; 1QapGen 19:24b–26.

this point in the story that God also changes Abram's name to Abraham and institutes circumcision as the sign of God's **covenant**. Finally, the culmination of the narrative comes in Gen 22 (the so-called *Aqedah*, or "binding") when Abraham is willing to sacrifice his son, Isaac, in obedience to God's command. Here the ultimate test of Abraham's faithfulness is enacted.

When we look at the story in Sirach, however, the ordering of the narrative shows some theologically significant shifts (see figure 6.2). In 44:20, there are four descriptions: (1) Abraham "kept" the Torah, (2) entered into covenant with God, (3) underwent circumcision, and (4) proved faithful when tested (Gen 26:5; 15:18; 17:23; and 22:1–19, respectively). The emphasis is on Abraham's *actions*: Abraham was faithful in all ways. "*Therefore,*" Ben Sira concludes, God promised that Abraham's descendants would be numberless (44:21)—a promise that first involved becoming a "great nation" (Gen 12:2), but subsequently meant that his children would number "like the dust of the earth" (13:16).

Figure 6.2: Abraham's Life according to Sirach

Abraham "kept" the Torah	(Gen 26:5)
Entered into covenant with God	(Gen 12:1–3; 15:7–20)
Underwent circumcision	(Gen 17)
Proved faithful in testing	(Gen 22)
Therefore, God promised Abraham numberless descendants	(Gen 12:2; 13:14–17)

Faithfulness and the Promise. Sirach provides us with an interesting though different way of reading the Abraham narrative from the one that Paul presents in Rom 4. In Sirach, Abraham's faithfulness is at the center: he was faithful to the law in all ways—most particularly through his circumcision and his willingness to sacrifice his son—and, as a result, God blessed him. Included amongst the heroes, Abraham illustrates the point with which the entire book of Sirach concludes: "Do your *work* with integrity and he will give you your *wages* in his time" (Sir 51:30, italics added). Ben Sira's reading is not unique: "Judaism insisted that Abraham's faith as referred to in Gen 15:6 must always be coupled with Abraham's acceptance of circumcision in the covenant of Gen 17:4–14, so that the two matters of believing and keeping the covenant must be constantly brought together when one speaks of the righteousness of Abraham."[4]

---

4.   Richard N. Longenecker, "The 'Faith of Abraham' Theme in Paul, James and Hebrews: A Study in the Circumstantial Nature of New Testament Teaching," *JETS* 20 (1977): 205.

Romans 4:1–25

"ABRAHAM IN HOPE BELIEVED"

In Rom 4 Paul presents a quite different picture of Abraham from the one found in Sirach 44:19–21. For our purposes, we will expose two major differences between the two passages: (1) the *chronological sequence* of Abraham's life, and (2) the related issue about the *basis* of Abraham's justification. We will see that, in stark contrast to Ben Sira, Paul points to Abraham to demonstrate that God blessed the patriarch on account of his faith (Gen 15:6).

Narrative Sequence of Abraham's Life. For Paul, unlike Ben Sira, the ordering of the events in Genesis is crucial for his argument, and his argument follows closely the sequence of the Genesis narrative presented in figure 6.1. Importantly, Paul highlights that Abraham's righteous status is declared in Gen 15:6 *before* the covenant of circumcision is established between God and Abraham in Gen 17. Indeed, since Abraham was seventy-five years old when God established a covenant with him (Gen 12:4), eighty-six years old at Ishmael's birth (16:16), and ninety-nine years old when circumcised (17:24), Abraham must have been declared righteous (Gen 15:6) between thirteen and twenty-four years *prior* to his circumcision (see figure 6.3).

Figure 6.3: Abraham's Age at Key Moments in Genesis

Abraham's covenant with God	75 years old	(Gen 12:4)
Abraham declared righteous	?? years old	(Gen 15:6)
Ishmael's birth	86 years old	(Gen 16:16)
Abraham's circumcision	99 years old	(Gen 17:24)

Paul even quotes Gen 15:6 in Rom 4:9—"Abraham's faith was credited to him as righteousness,"a phrase he uses to refer to the forgiveness of sins and justification before God (4:6–8, 24–25)—so that he can point to the temporal inconsistency of ascribing too essential a role to circumcision. Faith, Paul insists, was credited as righteousness "not after, but before"Abraham was circumcised (4:10), and it was only *after* God promised Abraham innumerable descendants that God instituted the covenant of circumcision. Thus, according to Paul, God's covenant with Abraham reveals that it is *faith* in God's word and *trust* in God's faithfulness, not *circumcision*, that is the mark of Abraham's descendants, a shocking argument that thereby includes believing Gentiles in God's family (4:11–12).

Faith and the Promise. This leads Paul to a second contrast with the traditional interpretation of Abraham as depicted in Sirach 44:20: While Ben

Sira celebrates Abraham's *obedience to the law*, Paul asserts that the promise to Abraham came on the basis of his *faith*: "It was not *through the law* that Abraham and his offspring received the promise that he would be heir of the world, but through *the righteousness that comes by faith*" (Rom 4:13, italics added). Although the two authors agree on the *breadth* of the inheritance— since Jewish interpretation came to the consensus that it was not simply the land of Israel but the entire "world" that would be the fulfillment of God's promise—Paul's understanding regarding the basis of Abraham's receipt of the inheritance in Rom 4:13 goes against the inference made by Sirach in 44:21 ("Therefore …"). For Paul, it was in no way Abraham's *obedience* that led to God's oath. Instead, Paul equates Abraham with the "ungodly" (Rom 4:5) and insists that it was the patriarch's trust in God to fulfill his word that led to God praising him.

Paul's discussion about the place of the law concludes with "therefore … by faith," transforming the grounds of Sirach's "therefore" from *obedience* to *faith*. Thus, in 4:16 Abraham is not the father merely of those who by blood and circumcision are his offspring, but rather, of those who share his *faith*. Just as Abraham believed that God could grant children to him, raising his own body, which was already "as good as dead" (4:19), so we who believe that God raised Jesus from the dead exercise the same faith (4:24). Abraham's trust that God could provide him an heir—despite every physical reason that God could not—shows he truly believed that God is the one "who gives life to the dead and calls into being things that were not" (4:17): Abraham trusted that God could bring back to fruitfulness his and Sarah's deadened fertility ("gives life to the dead") and thus create an heir *ex nihilo* ("calls into being things that were not"). As Christians, who believe Christ is raised from the dead (cf. Eph 1:18–20), we also hold in faith God's ability to give life to his created works, even when there seems to be no hope, and we affirm that he does this in response to *his promise*, not as a result of *our obedience* (Rom 6:8–11). God's faithfulness may call obedience out of us (6:12–15), but it is because God brings us to life that this obedience occurs, not the other way around.

And so in Rom 4:22, having explored the extent of Abraham's faith, Paul returns to the praise of Gen 15:6. Abraham was convinced "that God had power to do what he had promised. This is why 'it was credited to him as righteousness.' The words 'it was credited to him' were written not for him alone, but also for us, to whom God will credit righteousness—for us who believe in him who raised Jesus our Lord from the dead" (Rom 4:21–24). Faith in God's faithfulness and power is primary for Paul, and Abraham perfectly illustrates its importance (4:18–21). Elsewhere, Paul will urge the followers of

Jesus to continue in faithfulness (cf. 6:1–23), but here in Rom 4 he deliberately shifts the focus from Abraham's acts of faithful obedience so prominent in the Sirach account (obeying the law, being circumcised, and sacrificing Isaac) to Abraham's continued trust that God would be able to accomplish his promise, no matter the difficulties. It is a profoundly different account.

FOR FURTHER READING

Additional Ancient Texts

Jewish literature that retells Abraham's story includes Neh 9:6–8; Isa 51:1–2; 1 Maccabees 2:51–52; 2 Esdras 3:12–15; *Testament of Abraham* 1:1–5; *Jubilees* 6:18–19; chs. 12–17; Josephus, *Jewish Antiquities* 1. Philo celebrates Abraham in several texts, such as *On the Life of Abraham; On the Virtues* 212–219; *Allegorical Interpretation* 3.83–84, 203, 228. For Abraham as the model of faithfulness in testing as a parent, see 4 Maccabees 14–15; 16:20. In the NT, see Gal 3:6–29; Heb 11:8–19; Jas 2:20–24.

English Translations and Critical Editions

NETS

NRSV

Beentjes, Pancratius C. *The Book of Ben Sira in Hebrew: A Text Edition of All Extant Hebrew Manuscripts and a Synopsis of All Parallel Hebrew Ben Sira Texts.* Leiden: Brill, 1997.

Ziegler, Joseph. *Sapientia Iesu Filii Sirach.* 2nd ed. Septuaginta 12.2. Göttingen: Vandenhoeck & Ruprecht, 1980.

Secondary Literature

Gregory, Bradley C. "Abraham as the Jewish Ideal: Exegetical Traditions in Sirach 44:19–21." *CBQ* 70 (2008): 66–81.

Lambrecht, Jan. "Romans 4: A Critique of N. T. Wright." *JSNT* 36 (2013): 189–94.

McFarland, Orrey. "Whose Abraham, Which Promise? Genesis 15.6 in Philo's *De Virtutibus* and Romans 4." *JSNT* 35 (2012): 107–29.

Schliesser, Benjamin. *Abraham's Faith in Romans 4: Paul's Concept of Faith in Light of the History of Reception of Genesis 15:6.* WUNT 2.224. Tübingen: Mohr Siebeck, 2007.

Wright, N. T. "Paul and the Patriarch: The Role of Abraham in Romans 4." *JSNT* 35 (2013): 207–41.

CHAPTER 7

Community Rule and Romans 5:1–11: The Relationship between Justification and Suffering

MARK D. MATHEWS

One can scarcely dip their toe into the waters of Pauline studies without quickly feeling the swift and often tumultuous undertow of conversations concerning justification. In Rom 3:19–4:25, Paul establishes his argument on *how* people are justified by faith. But in Rom 5:1–11, he develops the results or benefits of being counted among the people of God. That is the focus of this chapter.

In Rom 5:1–2, Paul begins by indicating that those who have been justified enjoy peace with God on account of having access into the justifying grace provided in Christ and thus take joy in the hope of future glory. This establishes an **already/not yet** understanding of the believer's salvation. Paul follows in 5:3–5 with "Not only so, but we also *glory in our sufferings*, because we know that suffering produces perseverance; perseverance, character; and character, hope. And hope does not put us to shame, because God's love has been poured out into our hearts through the Holy Spirit, who has been given to us"(italics added).

In essence, Paul is saying that the hope of future glory that believers take joy in is grounded in *suffering*. This perspective on the life of God's people, of course, poses significant problems in light of the blessings and curses of Deut 28–30. This text is the basis for a **Deuteronomic theology** in which God promises material blessing and protection for his people for **covenant** obedience, and poverty and suffering for disobedience.[1]

---

1. For a discussion of the doctrine of reward for faithfulness in relation to the Deuteronomic scheme, see Moshe Weinfeld, *Deuteronomy and the Deuteronomic School* (Oxford: Clarendon, 1972), 307–19.

Thus the question arises: If Christ has become a curse for his people under the law and removed the enmity between them and God (Rom 5:10–11; Gal 3:10–14), why do those who have been counted righteous suffer? Stated differently, if all of the promises of God find their "yes" in Jesus (2 Cor 1:20), why then would those in covenant faithfulness with God in Christ be experiencing what appear to be the covenant curses under the law (Deut 28–30)?

Paul's worldview is best understood by examining **apocalyptic traditions** from the **Second Temple Period**, for these traditions may have shaped Paul's understanding of what life looks like "on the ground" for the people of God in the present age. These apocalyptic texts reflect a theology that suggests a postponement of the Deuteronomic blessings and curses until a future age, while in the present age the wicked prosper and the righteous suffer. This is an apocalyptic answer, if you will, to the question of **theodicy**. One such tradition that helps to illuminate this ideal is the *Community Rule*.

Community Rule
"PRACTICING JUSTICE AND SUFFERING AFFLICTION"

Community Rule is a document that is attested in the **Dead Sea Scrolls** manuscript 1QS, one of the original finds of the **Qumran** caves.[2] 1QS represents the latest stage in the development of the *Community Rule*, dating to around the beginning of the first century BC. It is a **sectarian** document that represents the construction of the identity of either one or several communities related to the Qumran site. That is to say, whether it reflects the actual practices of any given community is debatable. Nonetheless, the traditions contained therein demonstrate the identity that the community/communities created as the ideal for the people of God.[3] It is possible that this document in its various stages was used as either a manual for the teacher of the community or a guide for initiates. In either case it expresses the apocalyptic mind-set of the group.

Suffering of the Faithful. The following passage reflects the community's commitment to covenant faithfulness, which includes the idea of suffering, while they await a future time when there will be a reversal of fortunes:

> [1] In the Society of the Yahad there will be twelve laypersons and three priests all of whom are blameless with regard to all that has been revealed from the entirety of the [2] Law, in order to work truth, righteousness, justice, love and humility, with one another. [3] These

---

2. *Community Rule* is also attested in 4Q255–264, 5Q11, and 5Q13.
3. Carol A. Newsom, *The Self as Symbolic Space: Constructing Identity and Community at Qumran* (STDJ 52; Leiden: Brill, 2004), 186–90.

are to keep faith in the land through self-control and a broken spirit, and making atonement for sin by practicing justice and [4] *suffering affliction.* They are to live with everyone according to the way of truth and the precepts of this age. When these men are in Israel, [5] then the Society of the Yahad will be truly established, it will be an "eternal planting," a temple for Israel, and—a mystery—a Holy [6] of Holies for Aaron; true witnesses to justice, chosen according to God's will to make atonement for and restore the land, and to [7] repay the wicked.

1QS 8:1–7, italics added

The "Society of the Yahad" refers to the whole community. There is no mention of the community structure referred to here in the entirety of the other documents found among the Dead Sea Scrolls. This lack suggests that this passage most likely represents the rule or expectation for all who would become members of the community.[4] Thus, one can see how 8:3–4 demonstrates a decided expectation for suffering among the faithful.

The correlation that these apocalyptic communities envision between practicing justice and experiencing affliction becomes clear when one considers the degree to which they align themselves more with the prophetic tradition than with the Deuteronomic school. For the biblical prophets, the righteous are those who are oppressed by the wicked leaders of the Jerusalem temple, who gain wealth by unjust means. These same leaders use the Deuteronomic tradition to support their righteousness in view of their wealth and prosperity, leaving the poor to question their own piety. By aligning themselves with the prophetic tradition, the Yahad associates their wicked opponents with those who have the appearance of righteousness due to their prosperity but are actually in breach of covenant faithfulness (cf. *1 En.* 96:4). For this reason, the Qumran community presents itself as the true temple of God (1QS 8:5), in contrast to the wicked leaders of the Jerusalem cult. Thus, like the righteous in the prophetic tradition, the Yahad expects to be persecuted by the wicked, rich leaders and thus demonstrate tangibly their own faithfulness and through their suffering make atonement for the land.

Suffering and Angelic Influence. Also included within the *Community Rule* is a text known as the *Two Spirits Treatise* (1QS 3:13–4:26), which again refers to the suffering of the righteous:

---

4. Michael A. Knibb, *The Qumran Community* (Cambridge: Cambridge University Press, 1987), 129. Cf. 1QS 3:2.

[21b] The rule of the Angel of Darkness also includes the corruption
[22] of all the righteous ones. All their sins and iniquities, their disgrace-
ful and rebellious acts are by his prompting, [23] a situation that in the
mystery of God he allows to take place until the end of the age. In
addition, all the *sufferings* of the righteous, and every *trial* that comes,
occur because of this angel's diabolic rule.

1QS 3:21B−23, italics added

This passage demonstrates an idea concerning the cause of suffering for the
righteous that is similar to ideas we see in other sectarian documents (CD
4:12−19; 1QM 14:9−10). That is, an external, diabolical force in the world is
set against the people of God and seeks to deceive them and impose suffering
on them.

Suffering and Salvation. Another passage also reflects the idea that the
righteous will suffer but includes the idea of praise:

[16] Him shall I praise. I will meditate upon His miracles and deeds of
power and upon His unfailing love will I rely all day long. Then I will
know that the judgment of [17] every living thing is in His hand and
that all His works are true. When *affliction* comes forth I will praise
Him, and in His salvation I will rejoice.

1QS 10:16−17, italics added

It is important to see here that "affliction" is held in synonymous parallelism
with "salvation," suggesting their close relationship. Interestingly, this is the only
occurrence of "salvation" in the entire document. Yet its placement within the context of the "Day of Vengeance" (10:19) indicates that its use here is **eschatological**.
Thus, the *suffering* and subsequent *salvation* that are in mind are closely associated with the idea of future *vindication*. That is, the people of God, though they
suffer in this life, will be vindicated in the last day when the wicked, who currently
prosper, will be destroyed. This understanding of the expectation of suffering was
likely shaped by other, likewise apocalyptic, traditions that were collected and
copied at Qumran but are not sectarian documents (*1 En.* 93:9−10; 91:11).

These apocalyptic texts reveal a worldview that assumes a life of suffering
for the faithful people of God in the present age with a view toward future
reversal and reward. Certain Qumran texts (e.g., the earliest Enochic traditions)
lack any mention of praise or rejoicing during, or on account of, this affliction
since they deal primarily with the question of theodicy. They seek to answer the
question of *why* the righteous suffer unjustly at the hands of the wicked and
to provide assurance for those who appear to be experiencing the curses of the

covenant. The sectarian text of the *Community Rule* reshapes the issue of suffering to the degree that it is no longer forced and unjust but is a voluntary period of testing by God, one that serves to identify and mark out God's people.

Romans 5:1–11

"WE ALSO GLORY IN OUR SUFFERINGS"

Suffering of the Faithful. Paul agrees with his apocalyptic predecessors that suffering is indeed an identifying mark of the faithful people of God. But in Romans, suffering is not merely for the sake of suffering, nor is it necessarily a form of testing. Rather, it is the process by which the believer's assurance in the hope of future glory is procured (8:17). Still, it is not a hope in something that may or may not happen. Rather, the gift of the Holy Spirit and the love God has already demonstrated in giving his own Son testify to the reality of this hope (5:5). Therefore, the people of God have an eager expectation of a hope that is sure and not simply a desire. This, too, follows the apocalyptic tradition that frequently alludes to the surety of the vindication of the righteous and the judgment of the wicked, based not on opinion but on heavenly revelation and knowledge (8:16; cf. *1 En.* 103:1–4).

Suffering with Christ and Salvation. If God did these things to provide reconciliation for his enemies, certainly now being reconciled, those who have been justified can know that God will finish what he has begun (Rom 5:10), though the surety of that hope comes through suffering. This corresponds to Paul's expectation for believers that they be conformed to the image of Christ (8:28–29), which suggests that those who follow him will follow the same road to glory that he himself traveled.

This is attested in another, similar theme that runs through the passage that suggests suffering is to be viewed in relation to identity "with" Christ. While the details of Christ's passion are not elucidated, there are several verses that refer to it: "Christ *died* for the ungodly" (Rom 5:6); "Christ *died* for us" (5:8); "we have now been justified *by his blood*" (5:9); "reconciled to him *through the death* of his Son" (5:10, italics added in all instances in this paragraph). Here one can see that Paul differs from the *Community Rule*, since it is Christ and his suffering that have atoned for the sins of the people (cf. 1QS 8:3–4). Although *Community Rule* understands the idea of doing justice and suffering as a means of atonement, Paul has argued in Rom 1–4 that humans are unable to do this on their own.

So for Paul, it is the believer's union with Christ that now identifies them with him. But that identification does not stop with justification. The justified are now aligned with Christ, who suffered on their behalf, and are now expected to follow the same road to glory that Jesus himself walked: suffering in a world that is hostile to God and his people (cf. Col 1:24). Thus, suffering on the part of the justified is intrinsically linked to future glory. If Rom 5:1–5 and 8:16–39 serve as an **inclusio** for chs. 5–8, then the following verses from chapter 8, along with Rom 5:1–11, could serve to establish a climax/conclusion for what is being stated here:

> [16] The Spirit himself testifies with our spirit that we are God's children. [17] Now if we are children, then we are heirs—heirs of God and co-heirs with Christ, *if indeed we share in his sufferings* in order that we may also share in his glory.
> [18] I consider that *our present sufferings* are not worth comparing with the glory that will be revealed in us.
>
> ROMANS 8:16–18, italics added

Romans 8:17 does not present a cause/effect conditional sentence but is better viewed as evidence/inference. In other words, if we are children, then we are heirs, and the evidence that we are heirs is that we share in his sufferings. At the same time, the final clause demonstrates God's intention for his people and its sure accomplishment. That is, our sharing in Christ's sufferings is for both the purpose and result of sharing in his glory. For this reason, believers can have joy in their sufferings. Christ was vindicated in his resurrection, and therefore believers in turn will be saved by his life (5:10). This transfer from the realm of death, on the one hand, into the realm of life as a result of God's grace and righteousness, on the other, comes with an expectation of suffering in the present age. This suffering, then, is an identifying mark of the righteous and is thus a cause for rejoicing. And not simply as some masochistic joy in difficulties, but because our present sufferings validate the reality of our hope in sharing in the future glory of God. What emerges from this comparison of Paul and the *Community Rule* is two perspectives on how to explain present suffering and its relationship to the future. Figure 7.1 captures these perspectives.

Figure 7.1: The Suffering of the Righteous

Deuteronomic Tradition (Deut 28–30)	Suffering in the present age is a sign of covenant disobedience.
Second Temple Apocalyptic Traditions	Suffering in the present age is a sign of covenant faithfulness. Suffering looks forward to future reversal.
Romans	Suffering in the present age identifies the faithful. Suffering looks forward to future glory.

For Further Reading

Additional Ancient Texts

One might consider other sectarian documents from Qumran to find similar motifs of the righteous suffering (*Damascus Document, War Scroll, Pesher Habakkuk, Hodayot*), as well as more widely circulated works (*1 Enoch*, Wisdom of Solomon 1:16–3:10). For other Pauline texts, see 2 Cor 1:3–11; 4:7–18; 11:16–12:10; Phil 3:2–11; 2 Thess 1:2–10.

English Translations and Critical Editions

Charlesworth, James, ed. *The Dead Sea Scrolls: Rule of the Community and Related Documents (Hebrew, Aramaic, and Greek Texts with English Translations).* Tübingen: Mohr Siebeck, 1995.

Parry, Donald W., and Emanuel Tov. *The Dead Sea Scrolls Reader.* 6 vols. Leiden: Brill, 2004.

Secondary Literature

Collins, John J. *The Apocalyptic Imagination.* 2nd ed. Grand Rapids: Eerdmans, 1998.

Gorman, Michael. *Cruciformity: Paul's Narrative Spirituality of the Cross.* Grand Rapids: Eerdmans, 2001.

Jervis, L. Ann. *At the Heart of the Gospel: Suffering in the Earliest Christian Message.* Grand Rapids: Eerdmans, 2007.

Knibb, Michael A. *The Qumran Community.* Cambridge: Cambridge University Press, 1987.

Newsom, Carol A. *The Self as Symbolic Space: Constructing Identity and Community at Qumran.* STDJ 52. Leiden: Brill, 2004.

CHAPTER 8

Philo of Alexandria and Romans 5:12–21: Adam, Death, and Grace

JONATHAN WORTHINGTON

Romans 5:12–21 is striking. Paul suddenly introduces Adam, and his claims are extreme: we are condemned, enslaved, and dead because of Adam; we are justified, enthroned, and alive because of Jesus. In Romans, Paul has already demonstrated humanity's sinfulness and need of God's gracious justification. Moving steadily backward through history, he described contemporary Gentiles and Jews (Rom 1–3), briefly evoked the exodus ("redemption," 3:24) and God's patience throughout the Mosaic era (3:25–26), then focused on Abraham's life (Rom 4). Romans 5:12–21 is the lethal climax of Paul's reverse trajectory: Adam is the root-source of our predicament.

The content of Rom 5:12–21 is not its only striking feature. Paul's train of thought is equally surprising, for just as he introduces the discourse, he interrupts himself. He begins a comparison but omits the actual comparison: "*Just as* sin entered the world through one man, and death through sin, and in this way death came to all people, because all sinned" (5:12, italics added). Stopping midsentence, he withholds the "so also"—until 5:18! When introducing Adam and Gen 3, why does Paul interrupt himself?

Paul seems to realize that others may disagree with his account of Adam. Is Adam's "death" really for "all," if others did not transgress like him? Everyone dies, but is that *because* of Adam's choice? Did Adam himself even die for his disobedience? We need not speculate about such views "out there." Paul is right; there would be disagreement. This becomes more clear and concrete (and, consequently, so too does Paul's own view) when we listen carefully to another Jewish interpreter of Adam—**Philo** of Alexandria.

Philo is uniquely situated as a comparison-partner with Paul at this point. Paul's *interpretation* of Adam in Gen 3 is integral to his whole point within Rom 5:12–21, and out of all others who were writing in Paul's day, Philo provides the most deliberately detailed and exegetical interpretation of Gen 3. Thus, amidst many arresting ideas and intriguing ambiguities within Rom 5:12–21, our question is particular: How do Philo and Paul interpret Adam's sin and death and the effect on his progeny?

Philo of Alexandria
"THEIR DEEDS WERE WORTHY OF WRATH"

Philo lived in Alexandria, Egypt, from around 20 BC to AD 50. A Jewish commentator on the Pentateuch, Philo sought to provide a scripturally focused and philosophically respectable picture of how people could please God. Though we have twenty of his commentaries on passages in Genesis, we will focus on the one titled *On the Creation of the World* (*De opificio mundi*).

Adam's Sin and the Nature of Death. For Philo, Adam (in Gen 2) provides the model according to which humanity takes shape (*Opif.* 145–146). Adamic likeness can be beautiful, not least in bodily structure and mental capacity. But Adam (in Gen 3) committed a grievous wrong: he (and Eve) disobeyed God. Eating the forbidden fruit "instantly changed" them "out of a state of simplicity and innocence into one of treachery" (*Opif.* 156). And so the Father was "sorely angry." Philo writes that "[their] deeds were worthy of wrath, since passing by the tree of immortal life (which is the consummation of virtue) … they chose instead the daily and mortal time—I cannot even say 'life,' but rather merely 'time'—full of unhappiness. God appointed for them the punishments that were fitting" (*Opif.* 156).

Adam and Eve were "the first to become slaves of a hard and incurable passion" (*Opif.* 167–168). They "immediately found the wages paid by pleasure": for Eve, violent birth pangs and the deprivation of liberty; for Adam, labors, distress, and unceasing sweat merely to gain life's bare necessities. Cosmically, the moment God saw that "evil began to get the better of the virtues," he shut his "ever-flowing springs of graces" so as not to "bring supplies to those felt to be unworthy of them" (*Opif.* 167–168). Total destruction would be God's "fitting justice" due to Adam and Eve's "thanklessness toward God, who is the benefactor and savior" (*Opif.* 169a). This was a very dark day.

But God, who is "merciful by nature, took pity and moderated their punishment": he "permitted the race to continue" (*Opif.* 169). Philo notes the apparent tension in Gen 2–3: God promised Adam that "when you eat from [the forbidden tree] you will certainly die" (Gen 2:17). But when the fatal moment arrived, God allowed Adam to remain alive, pronouncing only a difficult life (Gen 3). God's *threat* of death showed his "fitting justice," for the crime was horrible. God's *alleviation* of the death penalty showed his "mercy." Adam did not actually die that day.

Humanity was affected by Adam's thankless treachery, though. God "no longer gave them food as he had done before from ready prepared stores" (*Opif.* 169). Also, Philo reuses his language of "slavery" from Adam and Eve (*Opif.* 167–168; see above) to explain what happens within *every* person who acts like Adam. If we succumb to temptation (like Adam), our "reason is immediately ensnared and becomes subject instead of ruler, *slave* instead of master … a mortal instead of an immortal" (*Opif.* 165, italics added).

Why is "reason" enslaved and mortalized, and how is that related to Adam and Gen 3? Underlying Philo's interpretation are philosophical assumptions and ethical aims highly influenced by **Platonism**. An example of Philo's Platonic dualism is the belief that the soul is better than the body. Within the soul, reason is chief, for it is what makes us like God. Reason *should* be like a charioteer, controlling and driving horses toward his destination. But pleasure—a bodily thing—wars against our souls, against our reason. Pleasure enters our bodily senses (touch, sight, etc.) and, through our bodies, pressures our souls to do what is *un*-reasonable (contrary to God).

Philo's Purpose for Examining Adam. With such philosophical and ethical underpinnings, Philo explores Adam's sin and its effects so as to reveal a universal psychology of temptation—*so that* his readers can resist. He reads the characters of Gen 3 in an **allegorical** manner, where each represents some deeper idea. The serpent is Philo's perfect image of pleasurable temptation: the serpent, making its appeal through Eve's physical senses (e.g., sight and taste), pressures Adam to submit to desire instead of to God—which is completely unreasonable. "What the serpent does to man, pleasure does to the soul" (*Leg.* 3.76). "Pleasures" (represented by the serpent) intrigue our physical "senses" (Eve) and put pressure on our "reason" (Adam), convincing our minds to yield. If we submit (as Adam did), then a type of *slavery* of soul and reason, even a type of *mortality*, is our lot (*Opif.* 165).

Philo uses strong language, but we should not think he is arguing for some universal state of affairs *because* of what Adam did. That is not what he writes here, and his treatment of Adam elsewhere disallows that conclusion (cf. *Leg.* 1.106–108; *QG* 1.81). Adam's sin was no less than wretched treachery. It was despicable and worthy of God's wrath, and it earned him a type of slavery and death. There even remains tough toil for us all because of Adam. There is not, however, an inescapable wrath, slavery, or death that began when and because Adam transgressed. Just do not act like he did when tempted!

Regarding our current project, we now have a more concrete vision of an available—and respected—Jewish interpretation of Adam in Gen 3. We can understand better why in Rom 5:12–21 Paul interrupts himself when introducing Adam, his sin, and his fatal influence on his progeny. And now we can be much more attentive to just how radical Paul's understanding is concerning Adam's act and influence—and therefore Jesus'.

Romans 5:12–21
"ONE TRESPASS RESULTED IN CONDEMNATION FOR ALL"

"In Adam all die,"Paul wrote to the Corinthians (1 Cor 15:22). For the Romans he elaborates. Death entered history—definitely, as a foreign invader—through the sin of one man, Adam (Rom 5:12). What was Paul envisioning? Did Adam experience "death"the moment he sinned? For Philo, God's mercy meant Adam did *not* die; he lived, even having children. The latter point is indisputable, but Paul has a different construal of what happened *to* and *because of* Adam.

Adam's Sin and the Nature of Death. "Death reigned"over everyone, from Adam to Moses (Rom 5:12–14) and ever since (5:17). This "death"is not potential, as it was for Philo, experienced only by those who act like Adam. Indeed, Paul explicitly writes, "Death reigned … even over those who did *not* sin by breaking a command, as did Adam" (5:14, italics added)! Objective and unavoidable, death is the inescapable master. But is Philo wrong that Adam continued to live? What does Paul mean that death entered through Adam's sin, that death ruled everyone, that "the many died by the trespass of the one man" (5:15)?

In Gen 1–5, the word *death* takes a prominent narratival role after Adam and Eve sin.[1] After Gen 3–4 narrates the beginnings, Gen 5 records Adam's genealogy. From this genealogy Philo had explained that Cain lost the honor of being Adam's heir because he was evil—thus *unlike* Adam—so Seth became the firstborn (*QG* 1.81). Yet another feature of this genealogy is its unique, unrelenting repetition of one phrase after each Adamic descendent (save Enoch, 5:24): "and then he died."[2] Even Noah, whom Genesis portrays as something of a new Adam, has this finale: "and then he died" (9:29).[3] For

---

1. In Gen 1–3, "death"occurs in 2:17 and 3:3–4. After Adam's sin, "death"occurs in 4:8, 14–15, 23, 25; 5:5, 8, 11, 14, 17, 20, 27, and 31.
2. Cf. the genealogies in Gen 11 (though cf. Septuagint and Hebrew); 25; 36; 1 Chr 1–9.
3. Noah's part in Adam's genealogy was begun in Gen 5:32, suspended until 9:28, and finally closed with the same Adamic epitaph (9:29).

Adam's family, death was the common experience, beginning with him. One might even say death reigned.

But in Rom 5, Paul does not merely say that "death reigned." That hardly would have been controversial enough to make Paul interrupt himself in anticipation of an objection. Philo could have agreed that everyone physically dies (though not connecting it with Adam's sin so directly, and not thinking it necessarily a bad thing, because he viewed the soul as more important than the body because of his Platonism). Paul's claim is that death dominated all people specifically *because of* "sin" and *through* "the one man." Paul reiterates: "sin entered the world *through one man,* and death *through sin*" (5:12a); "many died *by the trespass of the one man*" (5:15); "condemnation" came to all (5:16, 18), "death reigned" over all (5:17), and "the many were made sinners"—neither *naturally* nor even due to personal sin, but all *because of* "the one man," Adam, and *his* "disobedience" (5:19).[4]

Paul's Purpose for Examining Adam. Philo's primary concern while interpreting Gen 3 was for his readers' morality, that they not sin like Adam. If they did, they would experience the soulish slavery and mortality that Adam (at least temporarily) had. But in Rom 5:12–21, excluding the one ambiguous phrase in 5:12 ("because all sinned"), Paul does not show concern for whether people sin like Adam. (Of course, elsewhere in Romans Paul is very concerned with personal ethics. He has already established forcefully in Rom 1–3 that all *have* sinned—cf. 4:5–8, 25; 5:6–10—and his readers' morals take a prominent position in Rom 6, 8, and 12–14.) In 5:12–21, everyone is simply affected by *Adam's* decision/act: "made sinners" (5:19), brought "condemnation" (5:16, 18), having "died" (5:15). As mentioned above, this is so, even for those *not* exactly like Adam (5:14). Philo's interpretation was dark; Paul's is extreme.

Yet humanity's grim inheritance of Adam's fatal plight is not actually Paul's primary point either. In 5:12, Paul introduced his assumption about Adam's tragic mark mainly because he wanted to draw attention to the alternative, namely, *Jesus'* triumphal mark. Realizing that some in his audience would not agree with his assumptions about Adam, sin, and death, he delayed setting Jesus forward. As our analysis of a contemporary and prominent Jewish commentator (Philo) suggests, some would *not* have agreed with the severity of Paul's interpretation. So Paul clarified, for it was on the interpretation of Adam in Gen 3–5 that he was about to build his actual, primary, and climactic

---

4.   This fits well with the text's use of "him" in Gen 3. Adam was impassibly barred from the "tree of life," the possibility of "living forever" (3:22–24). His death was sealed that day (as was Eve's, assumed within "him" in 3:22–24). All descendants are thereby born into a realm cut off from eternal life—i.e., death—because of the action/exile of the singular "him."

edifice. Only by *Jesus'* decision and action—and not by anyone's possession or observance of the law—can Adam's dead and condemned progeny receive justification and eternal life. And this is no mere reversal. Rather, Jesus' power and influence are so "much more" than Adam's!

Paul's interpretation of Adam's sin, death, and thus condemnation for others has been brought into sharper focus by comparing it with Philo's very dark but still less tragic view. Because the hyper-severe nature of Paul's understanding of Adam's disobedience has been clarified in context, better justice can be done to Paul's primary (and much more extreme) point: God's gracious gift in Jesus. Triumphant and hyper-excessive grace—which extends to condemned, enslaved, and dead people for righteousness, enthronement, and life—is due only to *Jesus'* obedience. Death in Adam, in its extreme version given by Paul in context, is Paul's necessary foil for understanding the primary **christological** point about grace and life. And it is such gracious *life*-in-Christ that serves as a foundation and launchpad—even thesis statement in Rom 5:20–21—for what Paul writes in Rom 6–8.

For Further Reading

Additional Ancient Texts

For Philo on Gen 1–3, see *Allegorical Interpretation*, vols. 1–2; *On the Cherubim; Questions and Answers on Genesis*, vol. 1. For other Jewish references to Adam, Gen 3, and the beginning of sin and death, see Sirach 25:24; Wisdom of Solomon 2:23–24; 10:1–4; *4 Ezra* 3:6–7, 21–22; 4:30–32; *2 Baruch* 17:2–3; 23:4–5; 48:42–43; Josephus's *Jewish Antiquities* 1.40–51. For Paul, see 1 Cor 15:21–22, 45–49; 2 Cor 11:3; 1 Tim 2:13–14.

English Translations and Critical Editions

Philo. Translated by F. H. Colson et al. 12 vols. LCL. Cambridge, MA: Harvard University Press. 1929–1962.

Secondary Literature

Levison, John R. *Portraits of Adam in Early Judaism: From Sirach to 2 Baruch.* JSPSup 1. Sheffield: Sheffield Academic, 1988.
———. "Adam and Eve, Literature Concerning." Pages 1–6 in *Dictionary of New Testament Background.* Edited by C. A. Evans and S. E. Porter. Downers Grove, IL: InterVarsity Press, 2000.

Runia, David. "How to Read Philo." Pages II.185–98 in *Exegesis and Philosophy: Studies on Philo of Alexandria*. Collected Studies 332. London: Variorum, 1990.

_____. *Philo of Alexandria: On the Creation of the Cosmos according to Moses: Introduction, Translation and Commentary*. PACS 1. Leiden: Brill, 2001.

Sterling, Gregory. "Philo." Pages 789–93 in *Dictionary of New Testament Background*. Edited by C. A. Evans and S. E. Porter. Downers Grove, IL: InterVarsity Press, 2000.

Worthington, Jonathan. *Creation in Paul and Philo: The Beginning and Before*. WUNT 2.317. Tübingen: Mohr Siebeck, 2011.

CHAPTER 9

Wisdom of Solomon and Romans 6:1–23: Slavery to Personified Powers

JOSEPH R. DODSON

Romans is replete with marvelous propositions, shrewd arguments, and devotional gems. But its doctrinal richness could easily cause one to miss the epistle's literary sophistication, employing as it does an array of genres and rhetorical devices. For while it is true that Romans is **didactic** in nature, a *narrative* serves as the bedrock for the book's theological formulations. God, of course, is the story's main actor, but Paul often uses **personification** to fill in the remainder of the cast.[1]

For instance, the personification of Grace, Sin, and Death in Rom 5 creates an epic framework that brings Paul's argument to life. There, Paul recounts the story of the fall—where, through Adam's disobedience, Sin and Death are shown to have invaded the world. As spurious rulers, they sullied God's creation and conquered its inhabitants (5:12, 14). But God struck back. Paul explains how the Lord offered a bountiful gift through the Second Adam (Jesus Christ) that served a severe blow to these fraudulent monarchs (5:15–17). Now wherever Sin abounds, Grace abounds all the more. Although Sin once reigned in Death, Grace now rules in righteousness (5:21).

Paul's use of personification continues into Rom 6, where the cosmic supplanting of these personified powers leads to the question: Shall the church continue in Sin so that Grace may increase? Paul underlines the answer: "By no means!" Believers have been baptized into Christ. Therefore, for them, Sin no longer reigns and Death no longer rules. With this in mind, Paul implores his audience to offer themselves to God and not again to Sin. They are to

---

1. I have capitalized the personifications to make them more conspicuous.

live as servants of Grace, not as slaves of Sin. While the former rewards her followers with notes of holiness, righteousness, and life, Sin pays her disciples in denominations of Death.

Paul is not the only author who uses personification to persuade an audience. In fact, his personification of Grace, Sin, and Death in Rom 6 has striking similarities to and informative differences with the personifications of Wisdom and Death in the Wisdom of Solomon (henceforth Wisdom). In this essay, we will look at (1) the use of personification in Wisdom 1–2 as well as at (2) Paul's use of it in Rom 6. We will then see (3) how the points of convergence and divergence between the two works underscore all the more the message in Rom 6—especially with respect to how utterly absurd it is for believers to live as subjects of Death and Sin.

Wisdom of Solomon

"THROUGH THE ENVY OF THE DEVIL, DEATH ENTERED INTO THE WORLD"

Personified Wisdom. One of the ways the author of Wisdom seeks to persuade his readers to live rightly is through the personification of Wisdom and Death. The book opens with an appeal for the "rulers of the earth" to "love righteousness," to "study" and "seek" the Lord.[2] They should do this because God makes himself known to those who trust him, but he leaves the impious alone (1:2–3). The author then begins to speak of the concept of God's Wisdom as a *personal being*, explaining that God's Wisdom will not "enter into a soul tainted with deceit or dwell in a body enslaved to Sin" (1:4). Rather, as a "holy spirit," Wisdom "flees from fools" (1:5). "Embarrassed by their unrighteousness," she "flies from their folly" (1:5). Although she loves humanity, she will not stoop so far as to "liberate blasphemers from their guilt" (1:6).

Personified Death. The author goes on to adjure his audience to embrace Wisdom rather than to fondle Death (1:12). They must not beckon Death or escort Destruction—for God "does not delight in the desolation of his creation" (1:13). The Lord "created all things for life ... His justice is everlasting." And "the dominion of Hades was not in his holy design" (1:12–15). How then did Death enter the world? According to the author, the ungodly summoned him. "With their hands and by their words," they invited him in. As part of an illicit affair, the fools fell in love with Death. Yearning for him, they smuggled Death into God's creation. Rather than cling to God's righteousness, in an incredible turn

---

2. For more background on Wisdom, see chapter 2 (Linebaugh).

they consecrated themselves to Death. They even made a **covenant** with Death, thereby establishing themselves as subjects suited for his infernal reign (1:16).

Their pact with Death led the wicked to scheme about how to insult and torture "the righteous one" who "claimed to be the son of God." To test his goodness, they condemned "the holy one" to a "shameful death." Then they sat back to see if the Lord would descend to deliver the upright stranger (2:1, 12–20). (At least as early as the second century AD, Christians considered this passage to be a **messianic** prophecy foretelling the passion of Jesus.) The plan to execute the righteous one further instantiates the depth of the fools' wickedness and the certainty of their doom. They were "blinded by evil." Therefore, they failed to grasp "the plan of God," "to hope for the wages of piety," or "to understand the prize for purity"—namely, incorruption and life. Although God created Adam for life and "formed humanity in his own immortal image," the impious now belong to "Death, who entered into the world through the envy of the Devil" (2:21–24).

As we have seen in Wisdom 1–2, the author personifies Wisdom, Death, and other abstract concepts to show the means by which God and the devil seek to bring about their respective plans for the world. For the author, such use of personification is rhetorically and theologically strategic because it substantiates the audience's choice either to embrace God's Wisdom—leading to everlasting life—or to accept Death's fated rule.

Romans 6:1–23

"YOU HAVE BEEN SET FREE FROM SIN AND HAVE BECOME SLAVES TO RIGHTEOUSNESS"

Personified Sin, Death, and Grace. Romans 6 continues Paul's depiction of Sin and Death in 5:12–21 as illegitimate leaders in the face of regal Grace. Since Grace abounds over Sin (5:20; 6:1), the believer should live a righteous life. Paul links the reign of Grace to the person of Jesus Christ. As Paul writes, "We were therefore buried *with him* through baptism into death in order that, just as Christ was raised from the dead through the glory of the Father, *we too* may live a new life… For we know that our old self was crucified *with him* so that the body ruled by sin might be done away with, that we should no longer be slaves to sin—because anyone who has died has been set free from sin" (6:4, 6–7, italics added). The apostle reasons: (1) Jesus conquered Sin and Death by dying and rising again; (2) those who have been baptized with Christ share in his crucifixion and resurrection; consequently, (3) believers have been liberated from Sin and should no longer allow Sin to rule over them. Their allegiance belongs to a new Lord, the amazing Grace of God: "For sin shall no longer be your master, because you are not under the law, but under grace" (6:14).

Personified Sin and Righteousness. Paul goes on to delineate the rules of servitude: "Don't you know that when you offer yourselves to someone as obedient slaves, you are slaves of the one you obey?" According to Paul, people are either "slaves to sin, which leads to death, or to obedience, which leads to righteousness" (6:16). But with an interjection, he celebrates that believers "have been set free from sin and have become slaves to righteousness" (6:18). Consequently, Paul commands the church to resist the powers of Sin, Impurity, and Wickedness that once ruled their bodies: "Therefore do not let sin reign in your mortal body … Do not offer any part of yourself to sin as an instrument of wickedness, but rather offer yourselves to God as those who have been brought from death to life … Just as you used to offer yourselves as slaves to impurity and to ever-increasing wickedness, so now offer yourselves as slaves to righteousness leading to holiness" (6:12–13, 19). This cease-and-desist order leads to a serious notification for the members of the church. The currency of Sin is death (6:23), and he pays out the same wages to all people. In stark contrast, however, Paul proclaims that God offers to everyone the gift of "eternal life in Christ Jesus our Lord."

We are now in a place to see how comparing the use of personification in Wisdom and Rom 6 helps one to understand the theological claims that Paul is making at this point in his argument.

Grounds for Holiness. Paul's admonition for believers to serve Righteousness rather than Sin as their lord is similar to the challenge in Wisdom for the audience to embrace Wisdom as a "holy spirit" rather than to pine for Death as a forbidden lover. Whereas the author of Wisdom bases his argument on the character of God and his plan for creation, Paul grounds his argument on the gospel of Christ and the baptism of believers. If Paul and the author of Wisdom were to compare notes, the apostle would also shake his head at the folly of people partnering with Death rather than seeking God's Wisdom, righteousness, and life. Paul too would be nauseated at the thought of the wicked invitation to Death in the face of God's glory and creation.[3] Nevertheless, the apostle goes further than using *God's work in creation* as a foil for immorality and Death (cf. Rom 1:19–32). He goes on to stress *God's work in Christ* over against Sin and Death.

Therefore, placing Wisdom and Romans side by side reminds us of the significant reasons the gospel adds for walking in holiness. That is to say, even though God's righteousness and his cosmic plan should be incentive enough,

---

3. There would, however, likely be a disagreement between the two authors regarding the scope of fallen humanity ("some" for Wisdom versus "all" for Paul).

believers have the good news of Jesus Christ and their baptism into the new-ness of his life to motivate them to be slaves to obedience. The comparison makes the absurdity of believers living shackled to Sin especially poignant.

The Death of the Righteous One. Another benefit of reading Romans in light of Wisdom can be seen in their respective treatments of the death of the righteous one. Paul refers to Christ's crucifixion as the means of liberation for those formerly enslaved to Sin and Death. This stands in contrast to what we saw in Wisdom, where the execution of the holy one serves to illustrate the sin of the fools and to accentuate their fate. In other words, in Wisdom the partners of Death who participated in the heinous execution of God's Son are doomed forever, but according to Romans, those who participate in Jesus' death and burial are set free from Sin and Death. Through Christ's crucifixion and resurrec-tion, the ungodly receive the gift of life. Therefore, by examining Rom 6 against the backdrop of Wisdom—where the wicked await the crack of doom—Paul's incredible message of redemption and hope *for sinners* shines all the brighter.

Serving Sin. A final example of how comparing Wisdom and Romans accentuates Paul's argument concerns the critical choice he asks the church to make. In Romans, Paul implores the believers to resist offering the parts of their bodies to sin as instruments of wickedness. This is similar to the admonition from the author of Wisdom for his readers to refuse to bring on Death and Destruction by their hands. Noticing that the author of Wisdom commands his audience *never to start* serving Death helps us to realize that, in contrast, Paul calls his audience to do so *no longer.* The apostle implies that those who are redeemed may still live as servants of Sin. But he considers it a hard pill to swallow. Wisdom's tacit question regarding why anyone at the outset would choose to be enslaved to personified powers is overshadowed by the question raised in Romans: Why would those who have been set free and granted the gift of life choose to tether themselves to Sin and Death again? As Paul puts it, "What benefit did you reap at that time from the things you are now ashamed of? Those things result in death!" (Rom 6:21).

From what we've seen above, Paul's message in Rom 6 could serve as an argument *qal wahomer* (lesser to greater) to his Jewish contemporary: (1) If, as the author of Wisdom argues, people should seek God because of the purity of his cosmos and his immortal plan for Adam, *how much more* should believers do so in light of God's Grace revealed in the obedience of Christ (the Second Adam), in whose death and resurrection they live as participants? (2) Likewise, if the author's construal of the hypothetical execution of God's Son serves as a reason to reject Death, *how much more* should believers reject Sin and Death in light of the redemption offered in the actual crucifixion of the Christ? (3) Finally, while the author personifies Wisdom and Death in the appeal for his audience to take hold of salvation, Paul casts Grace, Sin, and Death to explain to the believers the significance of the salvation they already possess. *How much more* ridiculous, then, is it for believers to live under the bondage of Sin and Death now that God's Grace has set them free? Reading Rom 6 in the context of Wisdom 1–2, therefore, can not only lead to a renewed appreciation for the gospel but also stir within the reader a fresh conviction to live a life worthy of it (Phil 1:27).

FOR FURTHER READING

Additional Ancient Texts

For other uses of personification in Judaism and the NT, see Philo, *Allegorical Interpretation* 3.246; *1 Enoch* 69:8–11; Gal 3:22–29; 1 Cor 15:54–57; Jas 1:13–15.

English Translations and Critical Editions

NETS

NRSV

Ziegler, Joseph. *Sapientia Salomonis*. 2nd ed. Septuaginta 13. Göttingen: Vandenhoeck & Ruprecht, 1980.

Secondary Literature

Barclay, John M. G. "Under Grace: The Christ-Gift and the Construction of a Christian *Habitus*." Pages 59–76 in *Apocalyptic Paul: Cosmos and Anthropos in Romans 5–8*. Edited by Beverly Roberts Gaventa. Waco, TX: Baylor University Press, 2013.

Dodson, Joseph R. *The 'Powers' of Personification: Rhetorical Purpose in the Book of Wisdom and the Letter to the Romans*. BZNW 161. Berlin: de Gruyter, 2008.

Gaventa, Beverly R. "The Rhetoric of Death in the Wisdom of Solomon and the Letters of Paul." Pages 127–41 in *The Listening Heart*. Edited by Kenneth G. Hoglund. Sheffield: Sheffield Academic, 1987.

Longenecker, Bruce W., ed. *Narrative Dynamics in Paul*. Louisville: Westminster John Knox, 2002.

Southall, David J. *Rediscovering Righteousness in Romans: Personified Dikaiosyne within Metaphoric and Narratorial Settings*. WUNT 2.240. Tübingen: Mohr Siebeck, 2008.

Stafford, Emma. *Worshipping Virtues: Personification and the Divine in Ancient Greece*. London: Duckworth, 2000.

CHAPTER 10

Sirach and Romans 7:1–25:
The Human, the Law, and Sin

JASON MASTON

R omans 7:1–25 is one of the most intriguing and emotionally charged passages of the letter. It is also notoriously difficult. What Paul says in Rom 7 about the human, the law, and sin has incited debate among many of church history's most important theologians.[1] In this chapter, I hope to bring clarity to some of these matters by reading Rom 7 within its Jewish context.

The chapter begins with an analogy from marriage law. Paul illustrates how believers are freed from the Torah through union with Christ in the same way that a woman is released from a marital **covenant** when her husband dies (7:1–4). In 7:5–6, Paul explains the significance of the believer's death to the law and union with Christ. The law, Paul claims in 7:5, is incapable of producing moral transformation; it only serves to arouse sinful passions resulting in death. The believer's sanctification, which Paul in Rom 6 has just argued is an indispensable corollary of belief in and union with Christ, cannot be apprehended through Torah observance. But, Paul explains, what was formerly impossible through "the old way of the written code" is now made possible by means of "the new way of the Spirit" (7:6; cf. 2:29).

---

1. Especially difficult are the identification of the speaker ("I") in 7:7–25 and the temporal relationship between the events narrated in 7:14–25 and those in surrounding verses. See, e.g., Terry L. Wilder, ed., *Perspectives on Our Struggle with Sin: Three Views of Romans 7* (Nashville: Broadman and Holman, 2011). For the identity of the speaker, see particularly Jan Lambrecht, *The Wretched 'I' and Its Liberation: Paul in Romans 7 and 8* (Leuven: Peeters, 1992), 59–91; Michael Paul Middendorf, *The 'I' in the Storm: A Study of Romans 7* (St. Louis: Concordia, 1997), 15–51, 133–225. My argument favors the nonbeliever view, but the basic points could still work if one understood the speaker as a Christian.

Paul proceeds to elucidate the claims of 7:5–6 in greater detail throughout 7:7–8:13 (see figure 10.1). His argument here must be understood as a unity, but it is developed in two separate parts (7:7–25 and 8:1–13), each describing distinct **anthropological** conditions with corresponding **eschatological** results. In 7:7–25, Paul (elaborating on 7:5) presents a striking narrative of humanity's failure to obey God's commands revealed in the Torah. This failure and the eschatological threat it poses ("death"), Paul argues, is due not to the sinfulness of the Torah, but rather to the impotency of the fleshly human agent. The solution to this problem, however, as indicated in 7:6 and anticipated partly in 7:25, finds full expression in 8:1–13—the focus of the next chapter. For now, we shall concentrate on 7:7–25 and how Paul's **anthropology** is helpfully illuminated when read in contrast with an important and influential contemporary text—the book of Sirach.

Figure 10.1: The Logical Progression from Romans 7:5–6 to 7:7–8:13

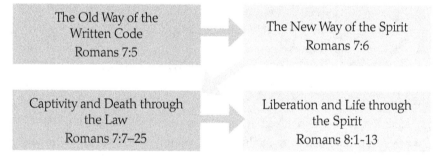

The Old Way of the Written Code Romans 7:5	The New Way of the Spirit Romans 7:6
Captivity and Death through the Law Romans 7:7–25	Liberation and Life through the Spirit Romans 8:1-13

Sirach

"IF YOU CHOOSE, YOU MAY KEEP THE COMMANDMENT"

In addition to being influenced by wisdom traditions, Sirach draws heavily on the Torah.[2] As this work demonstrates, Ben Sira was conversant with a range of contemporary issues, both theological and practical, but he was not concerned simply to enter into an academic debate. As a sage, his main goal was to train others how to live a life honoring to God. Thus, his teachings focus on the importance of fearing God and obeying his commandments. These emphases are especially apparent in Sirach 15:11–20.[3]

> [11]Do not say, "From God (comes) my sin."
> For that which he hates, he does not do.

---

2. For more on Sirach, see chapter 6 (Kamell).
3. My translation, based primarily on the Hebrew text.

¹²Do not say, "He caused me to stumble."
>For he has no need of violent men.
¹³The Lord hates abominable wickedness,
>and he does not cause it to happen to those who fear him.
¹⁴God created (the) man from the beginning,
>and he gave him into the hand of his inclination.
¹⁵If you choose, you may keep the commandment,
>and you will understand how to do his will.
¹⁶Poured out before you are fire and water:
>for whichever you choose, stretch out your hand.
¹⁷Before a man are life and death,
>and whichever he chooses will be given to him.
¹⁸The wisdom of the Lord is in abundance.
>He is strong in power and sees all.
¹⁹The eyes of God see his works
>and he observes all of man's actions.
²⁰He does not command a man to sin
>nor cause men of falsehood to dream.

Throughout this passage, Ben Sira responds to a deterministic view, which claims that the Creator, not the creature, is responsible for human sin. This erroneous teaching is introduced in 15:11–13 through an ancient debate formula ("Do not say … For …"). Then, in 15:14–20, Ben Sira argues for the autonomy of the human agent. People, he claims, are free to decide their own fate, since they possess innately the ability to obey God's commands. Presented here is a characteristic exposition of free-will theology.

In order to make his case, Ben Sira adopts the **two-ways paradigm** (see figure 10.2). This scheme portrays humans as having the option of proceeding down one of two competing paths: the first, marked by obedience, leads to life and blessing; the second, marked by disobedience, leads to death and cursing. The Jewish two-ways paradigm originated in the Pentateuch. In Deut 30:15–20, Moses sets before the Israelites the option of life or death, blessings or curses, before exhorting them to choose life by observing the commandments. Moses exhorts the Israelite community "to love the LORD your God, to walk in obedience to him, and to keep his commands, decrees and laws" (Deut 30:16). These unqualified instructions demonstrate the undivided loyalty that covenant participants must show to God. As Moses then explains, if the Israelites do in fact obey the commands, then God will grant them all the covenant blessings (30:19–20; cf. 28:1–14). If, however, they refuse to obey him and instead worship other gods, then the Lord will bring down on them all the covenant curses (30:18; cf. 28:15–68).

Figure 10.2: Two-Ways Paradigm

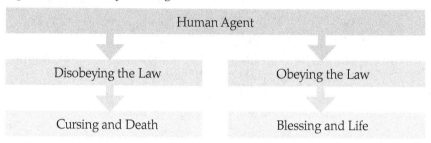

Three points should be noted about Ben Sira's use of the two-ways paradigm.

Choosing Life or Death. As with Moses, Ben Sira portrays God as having given the Torah to humans under the condition that if they keep it, then they will receive life (Sir 15:17).[4] For Ben Sira, then, as with Moses before him, life and death represent opposing human destinies, and one obtains life by keeping the Torah's commands.

The Autonomy of the Human. For Ben Sira, humans possess within themselves the ability to obey the Torah. This point is stressed repeatedly in Sirach 15:15–17. The noun "inclination" (15:14) implies that the individual possesses moral consciousness, while the verb "choose" (15:15–17)—occurring three times in as many verses—indicates that the person has functioning volitional faculties. Together these terms underscore the ability and opportunity of the individual to determine his or her own destiny, which is the very point of Ben Sira's argument in 15:14–20.

The Absence of God. When "God created (the) man from the beginning" (15:14a) and entrusted him with "the commandment" (15:15), God also gave "(the) man into the hand of his [i.e., the man's own] inclination" (15:14b). Moreover, while "[t]he eyes of God see his works and he observes all of man's actions" (15:19), God himself neither "commands a man to sin" (15:20) nor coerces him to obey. By placing the human into his own inclination, God removes himself from the scene and the decision-making process. Thus, the human is an empowered and truly autonomous being, one fully capable of determining his own destiny.

---

4. Another important text for understanding Ben Sira's view is 17:1–14, in which he describes the creation of humanity. God creates humans with knowledge and gives to them "the law of life," the "eternal covenant," in order that through their obedience to it they might obtain the life it offers.

Romans 7:1–25

"WHAT I HATE I DO"

As noted above, Rom 7 begins with an analogy based on marriage law that aims to demonstrate the believer's freedom from the law. Expanding on 7:5, 7:7–25 provides a striking contrast to Sirach's theology of free will and human ability. To be sure, there are important verbal and thematic points of contact between the two texts that show them to be drawing on similar biblical traditions. These similarities alone make the two texts worthy of comparison. Crucially, however, when the respective theologies of Paul and Ben Sira are examined closely, it becomes clear that they have quite distinctive perspectives on the relationship between the human, the law, and sin.

For the sake of his argument, Paul adopts the two-ways paradigm. This is apparent from Paul's use of the terms "life," "death," "good," and "evil," which are borrowed from **LXX** Deut 30:15. For Paul, as with Moses and Ben Sira, "life" and "death" are contrasting destinies, while "good" and "evil" are the contrasting modes of conduct specified in the law.

Choosing Life or Death. The three features noted above about Ben Sira's view are also found in Paul's narrative. First, as with Ben Sira, Paul describes a symmetrical relationship between Torah observance and life: the one who obeys the Torah lives, but the one who disobeys dies. In 7:10, Paul identifies the purpose of the law as being for life. Throughout the account, however, Paul focuses on the human's failure to obey the Torah, and he stresses that death is the result of such disobedience.

The Autonomy of the Human. Second, although in the narrative as told by Paul the speaker's pessimism dominates Rom 7, one must not miss that he views himself, with Ben Sira, as morally capable of keeping the Torah. When the narrative begins, he is ignorant of sin and disobedience (7:7c) and claims to possess life prior to the arrival of the law (7:9a). Moreover, while 7:15–20 describes the failings of the speaker, the twice-repeated pattern of desiring and attempting good and yet performing evil (7:15–17, 18–20) reveals the speaker's initial, mistaken optimism: he thinks he can be obedient, if only he keeps trying.

The Absence of God. Third, nowhere in Rom 7 does Paul describe God as coming to the assistance of the failing speaker. God is absent from the scene. The speaker of Rom 7 stands exactly where Ben Sira's human stood: endowed by God with the ability to obey and, given the Torah that is "unto life," he stands at a fork in the road, with one path leading to life and the other to death. Paul's speaker chooses life and journeys down that path as a lone figure.

The Power of Sin. Despite these similarities to Sirach's portrayal, Paul introduces an important twist, one that in the end invalidates the two-ways paradigm advocated by Ben Sira. For Ben Sira, only two agents are present in the quest for life: the human and God. Paul, however, describes a third agent, namely, Sin. For Paul, Sin is not merely disobedience; Sin is an active agent, a cosmic power, whose goal is to bring death to the human being.[5] Sin works by deceiving the human (7:11) and utilizes the law to cause the human to do the opposite of the good that he or she desires (7:8, 11, 15–20).

With the introduction of this third agent, the positive portrait of the human agent fades. Paul's speaker is left dead (7:10) and with only a single cry: "What a wretched man I am! Who will rescue me from this body [of] death?" (7:24). The negative portrait of the dying human is described in 7:15–20 as the repetitive cycle of one who, despite desiring to do good, always does evil. This cycle is expressed as a general rule in 7:21: "So then I find the 'law' that, when I will to do the good, evil is present with me" (my translation).

Getting a little ahead of his argument, Paul interjects in 7:25a that the solution to the human dilemma is to be found in "Jesus Christ our Lord." This is further developed in 8:1–13, where Paul describes both the deliverance accomplished through Christ's obedient life and death and the constitution of the human as an agent through the empowerment of the Holy Spirit.

Reading Rom 7 in the light of Sirach 15:11–20 provides a unique insight into the argument that Paul was making at this point in the letter. In Rom 6–8, Paul primarily seeks to show how his law-free gospel can produce an obedient people. In 7:7–25, he demonstrates that one popular understanding of the Torah, life, and human ability is actually mistaken. This perspective, clearly articulated in Sirach, believes that the human is a competent agent and the Torah is the source of life for those who obey it. Paul levels a devastating critique of this understanding of the human agent and Torah in Rom 7. Here the agent is declared incompetent, even enslaved to the power of Sin. And the law that should have brought life now, in fact, brings death. Within Paul's developing argument, he has demonstrated that a life still oriented around the law as a moral guide will not ensure obedience. In the next stage of his argument (8:1–13), Paul shows that his gospel of God's redemption in Jesus Christ does create an obedient people, precisely because God sends his own Spirit to empower believers.

---

5.   For more on Paul's view of Sin, see chapter 9 (Dodson).

For Further Reading

Additional Ancient Texts

One might compare the following Jewish texts for similar presentations of the two-ways paradigm: *1 Enoch* 94:1–5; *Psalms of Solomon* 9:1–5; *4 Ezra* 7:3–24, 127–129. Galatians 5:13–126 presents similar ideas and can be profitably compared with these Jewish texts and Rom 7:7–25.

English Translations and Critical Editions

NETS

Beentjes, Pancratius C. *The Book of Ben Sira in Hebrew: A Text Edition of All Extant Hebrew Manuscripts and a Synopsis of All Parallel Hebrew Ben Sira Texts*. Leiden: Brill, 1997.

Ziegler, Joseph. *Sapientia Iesu Filii Sirach*. 2nd ed. Septuaginta 12.2. Göttingen: Vandenhoeck & Ruprecht, 1980.

Secondary Literature

Barclay, John M. G., and Simon J. Gathercole, eds. *Divine and Human Agency in Paul and His Cultural Environment*. LNTS 335. London: T&T Clark, 2006.

Collins, John J. *Jewish Wisdom in the Hellenistic Age*. Edinburgh: T&T Clark, 1998.

Maston, Jason. *Divine and Human Agency in Second Temple Judaism and Paul: A Comparative Study*. WUNT 2.297. Tübingen: Mohr Siebeck, 2010.

Skehan, Patrick W., and Alexander A. Di Lella. *The Wisdom of Ben Sira: A New Translation with Notes*. AB 39. Garden City, NY: Doubleday, 1987.

CHAPTER 11

4 *Ezra* and Romans 8:1–13:
The Liberating Power of Christ
and the Spirit

————— ∞ —————

KYLE B. WELLS

Romans 8:1–13 begins a chapter that is arguably one of the high-water marks in Paul's letters. The feeling that we have reached such heights is due in no small part to the depths from which we have just climbed in 7:7–25. As was pointed out in the previous chapter, 8:1–13 is part of a unit that runs from 7:5 until at least 8:13 and is divided into two sections (7:7–25 and 8:1–13). Romans 7:5 and 7:6 provide the respective thesis statements for each section.[1] Here Paul juxtaposes two modes of human existence: existence in the flesh, which leads to death, versus existence in the Spirit, which leads to eternal life. This chapter focuses on the second of those modes—life in the Spirit as seen in Rom 8:1–13.

Having described the bondage of humanity under the power of sin in 7:7–25, Paul issues an emancipation proclamation: "Therefore, there is now no condemnation for those who are in Christ Jesus, because through Christ Jesus the law of the Spirit who gives life has set you free from the law of sin and death" (8:1–2). From there Paul goes on to describe the Christian life as one that has been liberated from both sin and death (8:3–11). But what, if anything, is unique about Paul's outlook on humanity's liberation from sin? And how do Christ and the Spirit contribute to the uniqueness of his outlook? To sharpen our answers to these questions, we will look at Rom 8:1–13 alongside another ancient Jewish text that considers the need for humans to be released from bondage to sin—*4 Ezra*.

---

1.   See figure 10.1 in chapter 10 (Maston).

4 Ezra

"THE HEART OF THE INHABITANTS OF THE WORLD SHALL BE CHANGED"

Fourth Ezra is a piece of **apocalyptic** literature that dates from sometime near the end of the first century AD.[2] The book uses the fictional setting of the Babylonian exile to address the situation posed by the destruction of the Jerusalem temple in AD 70. In this unique setting, age-old theological questions are given a fresh hearing. These questions are addressed in the form of a dialogue between the biblical character Ezra and the angel Uriel. While Ezra's questions probably represent the concerns of many Jews living at the end of the first century, Uriel's responses relay the divine perspective on the matter.

The Problem of the Evil Heart. Among other things, Ezra wants to know how his people can be held responsible for keeping God's law when God did not remove the evil heart from within them. At one point, Ezra complains that the very gift of the law was undermined by the fact that God failed to remove the evil nature that Israel shares with the rest of humanity.

> [18] You bowed down ... to give the law to Jacob's seed and the commandment to the posterity of Israel. [20] And yet you did not take away from them the evil heart, that your law might bring forth fruit in them. [21] For the first Adam, clothing himself with the evil heart, transgressed and was overcome; and likewise also all who were born of him. [22] Thus the infirmity became permanent; the law indeed was in the heart of the people, but in conjunction with the evil root; so what was good departed, and the evil remained.
>
> *4 EZRA 3:18–22*[3]

Note that Ezra presents a conflict within humanity that keeps humans from achieving righteousness and receiving life. The opponent to human righteousness is "the evil heart" (see figure 11.1). The evil heart defeated Adam and has defeated his descendants ever since (cf. 4:30–32). In the battle between the evil heart and humanity, the evil heart proves indomitable. But God sends Israel a divine helper, the law, so that his chosen people might achieve righteousness.

---

2. *Fourth Ezra* is also found under 2 *Esdras* 3–14.
3. All *4 Ezra* translations are adapted from R. H. Charles, ed., *The Apocrypha and Pseudepigrapha of the Old Testament in English* (Oxford: Clarendon, 1913).

Figure 11.1: The Problem of the Evil Heart in 4 Ezra

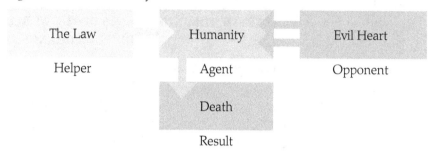

With the giving of the law there is now a battle within the hearts of the people of Israel between the good law and the evil root, or desire. The outcome is somewhat surprising: the "good departed, and the evil remained" (3:22). In other words, the law was insufficient to aid humanity in its quest for righteousness. Thus, Ezra cannot understand how God could hold his people responsible when he failed to eradicate their powerful opponent, the evil heart.

The Eschaton and Heart Transformation. Importantly, Uriel never denies the great problem the evil heart presents for achieving righteousness. However, he promises that one day God will defeat it.

> [25] And it shall be whosoever shall have survived all these things that I have foretold to you shall be saved and shall see my salvation and the end of my world … [26] [T]he heart of the inhabitants of the world shall be changed, and be converted to a different spirit. [27] For evil shall be blotted out, and deceit extinguished; [28] faithfulness shall flourish, and corruption be vanquished; and truth, which for so long a time has been without fruit, shall be made manifest.
>
> 4 EZRA 6:25–28

In language reminiscent of the prophet Ezekiel,[4] Uriel describes how God will resolve the problem of the evil heart by transforming the heart of humanity into a different spirit. At that time "faithfulness shall flourish."

Willpower and Law Observance. Notably, those who are transformed are described by Uriel as "being received." In 4 Ezra, "being received" denotes vindication at the judgment and is associated with resurrection to everlasting life (cf. 7:31–33a; 5:42–45; 14:35). A reasonable question to ask at this point is: Who are these people? If all of humanity is plagued by the evil heart, then

---

4.   *Fourth Ezra* 6:26 resembles Ezek 11:19 and 36:26 and is most likely related to them. See further, Michael E. Stone, *Fourth Ezra: A Commentary on the Book of Fourth Ezra* (Hermeneia; Minneapolis: Fortress, 1990), 124.

who could possibly "be received"? As the dialogue progresses, Uriel gives us an answer:

> [88] Of those ... who have *kept the ways* of the Most High, this is the order, when they shall be separated from this vessel of mortality. [89] What time they dwelt therein they *painfully served* the Most High, and were in jeopardy every hour, that they might *observe the law of the lawgiver perfectly* ... [91] [T]hey shall see with great joy the glory of him who *receives* them.
>
> 4 EZRA 7:88–89, 91, italics added

Uriel assumes there are people who with intense determination can keep God's law and achieve righteousness. He goes on to say that these people "have striven much and painfully to overcome the innate evil thought, that it might not lead them astray from life unto death" (7:92). Here we find a corrective to the position held earlier by Ezra. In the conflict that rages within humanity, Israel has not one aid but two: willpower and the law. When these two powers are fully engaged, humanity can overcome the evil heart (see figure 11.2).

Figure 11.2: The Solution to the Evil Heart in 4 Ezra

Thus, while in agreement with Ezra that humanity is plagued by an evil heart that will only be cured at the **eschaton** (6:26), Uriel nevertheless maintains that, with great effort and with the law, humans can achieve the righteousness required for life in the new world. Ezra eventually comes to this position as well. At the end of the book, he reminds his contemporaries, "If you, then, will rule over your own understanding and will discipline your heart, you shall be preserved alive and after death obtain mercy. For after death shall the judgment come, when we shall once more live again: and then shall the names of the righteous be made manifest, and the works of the godless declared" (14:34–35).

Fourth Ezra thus gives hope to Jews living in a post-temple world by assuring them that the evil that led to their current plight does not have to have the final word in an Israelite's life. To be sure, the evil heart is a formidable opponent. Nevertheless, commitment to the law in this present age is possible and will lead to eternal life. In the age to come, God will change the hearts of those who have been unflagging in their efforts to keep his law.

Romans 8:1–13
"WHAT THE LAW WAS POWERLESS TO DO ... GOD DID"

Reading Rom 8:1–13 alongside *4 Ezra* is illuminating in many respects. Along with *4 Ezra*, Paul believes that Adam's progeny are kept from achieving righteousness due to a condition he calls being "in the flesh."[5] As Rom 7:7–25 painfully details, in this condition human obedience is opposed by the power of sin (see figure 11.3). Paul even shares Ezra's initial position on the impotence of the law (8:7). The good law that should assist people in their struggle with sin has itself been "possessed by the powers of sin and death" (8:2; cf. 7:8, 11, 13).[6] "Weakened by the flesh," the law proves "powerless" to help anyone (8:3). Not only does the mind governed by the flesh fail to submit to God's law; it *cannot* submit (8:7). When Paul says that a "mind governed by the flesh" cannot please God, he is not referring to the mental capacity to reason. Neither is he here speaking of the determination to make certain moral choices. More than ethics, Paul is referring to **ontology**—those whose being is "in the realm of the flesh" (8:8–9). And Paul goes so far as to say that human nature "in the realm of the flesh cannot please God" and is hostile to God—and that this hostility leads to death (8:6–8).

Figure 11.3: The Problem of Flesh and Sin in Romans

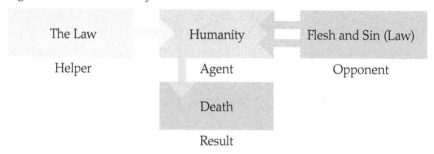

The Law	Humanity	Flesh and Sin (Law)
Helper	Agent	Opponent
	Death	
	Result	

The author of *4 Ezra*, when he described Ezra's initial outlook, seems to have in mind someone very similar to the one whom Paul envisions. Though

---

5. For Paul, "flesh" is broader than sinful human nature and can even take on connotations of being a suprahuman power.

6. My translation of the ambiguous genitive construction "law of sin and death." That the law is "possessed" by the powers of Sin and Death can be seen from how sin acts on and through the law, making it sinful (7:8, 11, 13).

Paul uses different terms, like "flesh" and "sin," the basic structure of his thought is nearly identical. We must remember, however, that Paul's position finds resonance with Ezra's *initial* outlook and not with the position of the book as a whole. Uriel corrects Ezra's pessimism, suggesting that when coupled with human determination the law can achieve its goal and bring forth righteousness. When God brings this world-age to a close, those who with much effort have achieved righteousness will finally be set free from the evil heart.

Liberation through Christ and the Spirit. In Rom 8:1–3 Paul also describes a liberation from the powers that oppose human obedience, righteousness, and life. Only for Paul this liberation happens "now" and is due neither to the power of the law nor to any power within human beings themselves (8:3, 5–8). Rather, the newfound freedom Paul describes comes from God's sending Christ and the Spirit (8:2–3). Through the **Messiah**'s own sacrificial death, sin has been condemned. Sin can therefore no longer bring condemnation on anyone in Christ (8:1). What is more, the law that was formally co-opted by sin and death has now been placed in the possession of the Spirit, who gives life (8:2–3). It is thus not ultimately the law that is liberating humanity in 8:2; rather, it is Christ and the Spirit who now possess and use the law for their redeeming purposes. The Spirit now produces in humans the righteousness that the law had always intended but could never achieve. Such righteousness is now able to be "fully met in us," who live "according to the Spirit" (8:4). Notably it is those who actively walk according to the Spirit that have "the righteous requirement of the law" passively fulfilled in them. Unlike *4 Ezra*, what Paul describes is far from a matter of the human will exerting itself independently. Human action is bound up with and founded on God's own Spirit working in human lives (see figure 11.4).

Figure 11.4: The Solution to Flesh and Sin in Romans

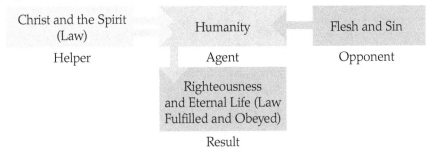

Christ and the Spirit (Law)	Humanity	Flesh and Sin
Helper	Agent	Opponent
	Righteousness and Eternal Life (Law Fulfilled and Obeyed)	
	Result	

The Eschatological Spirit and Heart Transformation. When Paul says this liberation happens "now," one must be careful to tease out just how he differs from the perspective of the author of *4 Ezra*. As in *4 Ezra*, Paul's description of the Spirit borrows language and concepts from the prophet Ezekiel. And like the author of *4 Ezra*, Paul reads Ezekiel eschatological-ly. Only for Paul a new world-age has already been inaugurated with the events surrounding the sending of Christ and the Spirit. These two agents bring God's future salvation into the present. To be in Christ and to have the Spirit in you is to enter the Spirit's "realm," a realm that is governed by the power of God's future (Rom 8:9). Just as living in the realm of the flesh has implications for human nature, so too does living in the realm of Christ and Spirit. In this realm, humans are given new life, and this life is shaped by Christ's own likeness (7:6; 8:29).[7]

Here we come upon another significant difference between the perspec-tives of Paul and those of *4 Ezra*. Whereas *4 Ezra* understands the Spirit prom-ised in Ezekiel as the transformed *human* spirit given after the resurrection of the body, for Paul the Spirit given is fundamentally the Holy Spirit, who is also the Spirit of the resurrected Christ (8:9–10). This Spirit in turn transforms the human spirit before a person is bodily raised (8:10) and gives those in Christ confidence that God will eventually give life to their "mortal bodies" at the resurrection (8:11). For Paul, it is the Spirit and not the law that ultimately grants to humans righteousness and eternal life (8:10–11).

The perspectives and concerns of Paul and the author of *4 Ezra* are sim-ilar in many respects. Both writers are concerned with questions of sin, law, righteousness, eternal life, human agency, and God's faithfulness. Though Paul writes before the fall of the Jerusalem temple, he has had his own crisis on the Damascus road that forced him to consider these questions anew (Gal 1:11–17; Phil 3:4–11; cf. Acts 9:1–19). And yet while both Paul and the author of *4 Ezra* ask similar questions, each presents his own unique answers. Whereas the view presented in *4 Ezra* maintains that the law and human effort are sufficient to achieve righteousness and eternal life, Paul's experience of Christ and the Spirit has pushed him to deny humans any ability to achieve these things. Moreover, for Paul the law is not so much an aid or a means to life but a by-product of the Spirit's work in those who belong to Christ. There-fore, believers have an obligation, but it is not to the law; it is to keep in step with the Spirit (8:13).

---

7.   See also 2 Cor 3:18; 5:17; Gal 2:20.

For Further Reading

Additional Ancient Texts

In addition to *4 Ezra,* one could fruitfully read Rom 8:1−13 alongside the *Damascus Document* 1:1−11; 3:12−16; *Community Rule* 5:1−9; *Jubilees* 1:19−23; *2 Baruch* 78:6−7; 85:3−15. It would also be worth comparing Paul's thought here to Rom 2:25−29; 2 Cor 3; Gal 5−6.

English Translations and Critical Editions

NRSV

Bidawid, R. J. "4 Esdras." In vol. 4.3 of *The Old Testament in Syriac according to the Peshitta Version.* Edited by M. Albert and A. Penna. Leiden: Brill, 1973.

Klijn, A. Frederik J. *Der lateinische Text der Apokalypse des Esra.* TUGAL 131. Berlin: Akademie, 1983.

Metzger, B. M. "The Fourth Book of Ezra." Pages 517−59 in vol. 1 of *The Old Testament Pseudepigrapha.* Edited by James H. Charlesworth. Garden City, NY: Doubleday, 1983.

Stone, Michael E. *The Armenian Version of IV Ezra.* UPATS 1. Missoula, MT: Scholars Press, 1978.

Secondary Literature

Bauckham, Richard. "Apocalypses." Pages 135−87 in vol. 1 of *Justification and Variegated Nomism.* Edited by D. A. Carson, Peter O'Brien, and Mark A. Seifrid. Tübingen: Mohr Siebeck, 2001.

Deidun, T. J. *New Covenant Morality in Paul.* AnBib 89. Rome: Biblical Institute Press, 1981.

Fee, Gordon D. *God's Empowering Presence: The Holy Spirit in the Letters of Paul.* Peabody, MA: Hendrickson, 1994.

Longenecker, Bruce W. *2 Esdras.* GAP. Sheffield: Sheffield Academic, 1995.

Moo, Jonathan. "The Few Who Obtain Mercy: Soteriology in 4 Ezra." Pages 98−113 in *This World and the World to Come: Soteriology in Early Judaism.* Edited by Daniel M. Gurtner. LSTS 74. London: T&T Clark, 2011.

Wells, Kyle B. *Grace and Agency in Paul and Second Temple Judaism: Interpreting the Transformation of the Heart.* NovTSup 157. Leiden: Brill, 2014.

CHAPTER 12

The *Greek Life of Adam and Eve* and Romans 8:14–39: (Re-)creation and Glory

BEN C. BLACKWELL

In Rom 8:14–39 Paul's argument for the first eight chapters reaches a climax when he emphasizes that believers, though they suffer in this life, will ultimately be glorified. Many see this passage as closing out the section begun in 5:1–5, where the themes of justification, the Spirit, God's love, suffering, and glory are also present. In 8:14–39, the Spirit's presence establishes believers as God's adopted children, and these beloved sons and daughters are transformed into the image of the Son, who suffered but was glorified. Thus, God's love for his children is manifested in the work of Christ and the Spirit, so that even in the midst of their own suffering, believers are assured of eternal life. Importantly, Paul describes this hope in terms of being glorified with Christ (8:17–18) and sets it within the context of the restoration of corrupted creation, a corruption arising from the original advent of sin (8:19–23). But what does the glorification of humans have to do with the restoration of the created world? Does Paul have the creation account from Genesis in mind here, where sin is introduced into the world?

The advent of sin is narrated in Gen 3 as a pivotal point in the life of Adam and Eve and thus the narrative of the whole world, but curiously "the narrative of Adam and Eve in the Garden of Eden receives no attention in the Hebrew Bible outside of Gen 2–3."[1] However, Jews in the **Second Temple Period** became increasingly interested in the people and themes from the early parts of Genesis (cf. *1 Enoch*). Besides *Jubilees*, which does little more

---

1. Eibert J. C. Tigchelaar, "Eden and Paradise: The Garden Motif in Some Early Jewish Texts (1 Enoch and Other Texts Found at Qumran)," in *Paradise Interpreted: Representations of Biblical Paradise in Judaism and Christianity* (ed. G. Luttikhuizen; Leiden: Brill, 1999), 37–62, at 37.

than restate this portion, the *Life of Adam and Eve* is one of the first robust explanations of the earliest chapters of Genesis.[2] Importantly, both the notion of glory and the association between the fate of humanity and the created world play significant roles in the narrative. Thus, exploring this early Jewish account of the advent of sin, suffering, and glory will illuminate why Paul discusses the glorification of believers together with the restoration of creation as a reflection of the early chapters of Genesis.

Greek Life of Adam and Eve
"YOU HAVE SEPARATED ME FROM THE GLORY OF GOD"

The *Greek Life of Adam and Eve* (GLAE, also known as the *Apocalypse of Moses*) is one of a number of translations of the *Life of Adam and Eve*. Each version of the *Life of Adam and Eve* adds, subtracts, and rearranges different parts of the story, while sharing a common core. The assumed Hebrew original is no longer extant, but this Greek version is likely the earliest translation and is possibly contemporaneous with Paul. The *GLAE* is a testamentary document in which Adam and Eve, near the time of Adam's death, recount to their progeny their fall and the hope of resurrection. The central core of the story is an expansion of Gen 2–3. Adam gives a brief retelling of the Genesis narrative in *GLAE* 7–8, but Eve gives a much fuller account in *GLAE* 15–29. Our focus will be on the effects of their fall and the nature of the restoration.

Unrighteousness, Death, and the Loss of Glory. After being seduced by the serpent, Eve recounts how death was introduced and connects that to a loss of her experience of God's glory: "At that moment my [Eve's] eyes were opened, and I knew that I was stripped of *the righteousness with which I had been clothed*, and I wept and said to him [the serpent]: 'Why have you done this to me? You have separated me from *the glory with which I was clothed*'" (20:1–2, italics added). Notice how her loss of glory is parallel to her loss of righteousness.

Later, Eve continues: "And I cried out in that very hour, 'Adam, Adam, where are you? Get up, come to me, and I will show you a great mystery.' But when your father came, I spoke to him evil words which brought us down from our great glory ... And he said to me, 'O wicked woman! What have you done to us? *You have separated me from the glory of God*'" (21:1–2, 6, italics added). Adam, too, focuses on losing glory.

---

2. Many place this as a Jewish document in the late first century AD, but some have argued that the text originates as a second- or third-century Christian document.

What does it mean to lose or be "separated from" God's glory? The concept comes more clearly into view in a parallel statement in 14:2 (italics added): "O Eve, What have you done to us? *You have brought the great wrath of death upon us,* which will rule over our entire race."

Here Adam asks Eve the same question as he does in 21:6 ("What have you done to us?"), but he speaks of the consequence of Eve's transgression in different terms—as "death." The narratival juxtaposition of death and the loss of glory suggests that *the loss of glory entails death, and the experience of glory is to be equated with the experience of life, even immortality.* Thus, when Adam and Eve lost their glory, they lost righteousness and became mortal.[3] This association of righteousness, glory, and life will illuminate our discussion of Romans below.

Righteousness, Resurrection, and Glory. This characterization of death as a loss of glory is important because a major focus of the work is God's solving the problem of suffering and death through resurrection. Indeed, the *Greek Life of Adam and Eve* was written to give Adam's progeny the hope of righteousness and eternal life at the end of times. As Michael the angel tells Eve:

> [Comfort] will not be yours now, but at the end of the times all flesh from Adam until that great day will be raised up, all who are the holy people. Then the delights of paradise will be given to them, and God will be among them. And they will no longer sin before him, for their evil hearts will be taken away, and they will receive hearts that understand the good so that they only serve God.
>
> GREEK LIFE OF ADAM AND EVE 13:3–5

The problem of death and loss of glory caused by their transgression will be finally remedied through bodily resurrection and renewed access to God's presence and the Tree of Life (*GLAE* 28:2–4; 41:1–3; 43:2).

Re-creation. Besides the future provision of resurrection life, God's redemptive work involves the restoration of the world and the created order. As Adam suffers on his deathbed, Eve and Seth attempt to retrieve some oil from Eden to sooth his pain. On the way, Seth and Eve have an exchange with a beast that is attacking Seth (*GLAE* 10–11). Though the beast should have been subject to Seth as "the image of God" (10:3), it is no longer because of Eve's sin (11:1). God explains this as part of the curse: "The beasts, over whom you ruled, will rise up in rebellion against you, for you did not keep my

---

3. This connection between sin and death (or mortality) is not surprising since death as the result of sin is the basic moral of Gen 2–3.

commandment" (24:4). The humans, as "the image of God," should have ruled over or subjected creatures, but sin inverted the created order. Ultimately, God comforts Adam by telling him that he (Adam) will be returned to his place of authority (39:2 – 3).

Though the *GLAE* details the loss of glory and the death and corruption that Adam and Eve brought upon the world, the story is also one of hope, explaining that they and their progeny will be restored to life and to a proper status over creation. Likewise, we will see in Rom 8 how Paul speaks of believers being restored to glory and of creation being restored along with them (see figure 12.1).

Figure 12.1: Aspects of Corruption and (Re-)Creation in GLAE and Romans

Corruption from Sin	(Re-)Creation by God
Loss of Glory	Glory/Restored Glory
Death	Life/Resurrection
Separation from God	God's Presence
Inversion of Created Order	Proper Created Order

Romans 8:14 – 39

"THE CREATION WAITS ... FOR THE CHILDREN OF GOD TO BE REVEALED"

Though Paul likely did not read the *GLAE*, he probably knew some of the traditions it represents. Thus, when we consider that Romans reflects a wider, growing interest in Gen 1 – 3 shared by other Second Temple texts like the *GLAE*, we can better see the depth of Paul's argument. Creation themes are clear, but might we also find echoes of Adam's story?

In Rom 8:14 – 39, Paul explains the hope of the future age while reminding believers that the current age will remain one of suffering. Further explaining the life-giving presence of the Spirit (8:1 – 13), Paul clarifies that God's adopted sons and daughters through the Spirit will continue to experience suffering, as did their co-heir Christ. He is the Son who suffered (8:17, 32), yet his suffering was not in vain or absent of the Father's love (8:33 – 39). Thus, Rom 8, like the *GLAE*, offers the hope of life in the midst of suffering and death. In this respect, the passage points to an **inaugurated (already/not yet) eschatology**. Life and restoration are truly present in this current age (see esp. 8:1 – 17), but death and suffering still remain until the final restoration (8:17–39), a restoration characterized by hope (8:20, 24–25). Paul is assured that at Christ's return, God will both glorify believers (8:17–18, 21, 30) and restore the created world in which they live (8:19–22), as a fulfillment of the current work of the Spirit.

Unrighteousness, Death, and the Loss of Glory. Since Rom 8:14–39 serves as the climax of Paul's argument to this point, we need to draw in a few key points from the previous chapters. In particular, Paul has framed humanity's problem as one of death resulting from unrighteousness, and humanity's salvation as the restoration of life (e.g., 5:12–21; 6:23). However, he has also framed this experience of death as a loss of God's glory (1:18–32; 3:23), and life as a return to glory (2:6–11; cf. 9:19–24). Paul directly sets the problem of sin at Adam's feet (5:12–21). The direct parallel between 5:12 and 3:23 is striking: "death came to all people, because all sinned" as Adam, and "all have sinned and fall short of the glory of God." This strongly suggests that Paul holds the same perspective as that of the *GLAE*: Adam originally experienced glory, but his loss of glory signaled the introduction of mortality, or death (cf. Rom 1:18–32).[4]

Righteousness, Resurrection, and Glory. As we come to Rom 8, Paul describes the climax of human restoration as the hope for life, which is experienced as bodily resurrection: "we wait eagerly for our adoption to sonship, the redemption of our bodies" (8:23; cf. 8:10–11). At the same time, a number of creational and Adamic motifs are employed to explain this resurrection. It is none other than a recovery of God's glory through Christ as we "share in [Christ's] glory" (8:17) and are "conformed to the image of [God's] Son," such that "those he justified, he also glorified" (8:28–30).[5] Just as in the *GLAE*, we see here the collocation of glory, life, righteousness, and "image of God" language all together, showing that Paul also saw these as interrelated motifs.

Through his sin Adam perverted human nature by causing humanity to lose the "glory of God," which corrupted our reflection of God's image. Salvation is not a further diminution of human nature, for we do not simply leave our bodies behind as our souls float up to heaven. Rather, salvation is a restoration of human nature as God intended it. He raises believers from the dead *bodily*, just like Christ, by restoring their participation in divine glory with Christ.

---

4. Cf. Ben C. Blackwell, "Immortal Glory and the Problem of Death in Romans 3:23," *JSNT* 32 (2010): 285–308.

5. Note how "decay" and "glory" are contrasted in 8:21, which demonstrates the glory-death contrast here in our passage.

Re-creation. At the same time, this restoration is not just for believers. Like the *GLAE*, Paul points out that sin has corrupted creation as well as humans. Creation has been *subjected* to decay and frustration (8:19–22), which is a clear reference to the curses because of Adam's sin in Gen 3:14–19 and which signals an inversion of the original created order. Just as Adam's sin introduced **anthropological** *and* creational problems, Christ's redemption will bring restoration not only to humans but to all creation. As C. Clifton Black writes, "Redemption is not confined to our *soma* [body] but is operative with respect to *the whole* of the Creator's work. The lordship of Christ, sealed by his resurrection from the dead, functions as nothing less than the universal reclamation of God's sovereignty over everything that has been created."[6]

Human creation and nonhuman creation stand in solidarity as both suffer and groan together and look forward to a common restoration. That is, "creation waits in eager expectation for the children of God to be revealed" (Rom 8:19). Even now, through Christ, the creational order is being reconstituted and believers stand over creation, such that nothing "in all creation will be able to separate us from the love of God" (8:39).

Paul does reflect the narrative in Genesis, but not merely Genesis by itself but Genesis as understood through Second Temple traditions in which Adam fell from glory and experienced death. As a Christian, Paul proclaims that believers will share in Christ's glory, being restored as the image of God, and will take their rightful place in God's created order. This passage shows that Paul takes seriously the problem of suffering and corruption in the present age, but he also takes seriously the resurrection of the body and the restoration of the future world, a narrative not dissimilar to the GLAE (see figure 12.1).

For Further Reading

Additional Ancient Texts

For other texts that explore the hope of glory, you might compare *Targum Pseudo-Jonathan: Genesis* 2:25; 3:7; *4 Ezra* 7:116–31; *2 Baruch* 15:1–19:8; 54:13–21; 1QS 4:22–23; CD 3:19–20; 1QH[a] 4:14–15. For related Pauline texts, see 1 Cor 15:35–57; 2 Cor 3:6–5:10; Phil 3:7–11.

---

6. C. Clifton Black, "Pauline Perspectives on Death in Romans 5–8," *JBL* 103 (1984): 413–33, at 428, emphasis original.

English Translations and Critical Editions

Johnson, M. D. "Life of Adam and Eve: A New Translation and Introduction." Pages 249–94 in vol. 2 of *The Old Testament Pseudepigrapha*. Edited by James H. Charlesworth. Garden City, NY: Doubleday, 1985.

Levison, John R. *Texts in Transition: The Greek Life of Adam and Eve*. SBLEJL 16. Atlanta: Society of Biblical Literature, 2000.

Miller, David M., and Ian W. Scott, eds. "Life of Adam and Eve." Edition 1.1. In *The Online Critical Pseudepigrapha*. Edited by Ian W. Scott, Ken M. Penner, and David M. Miller. Atlanta: Society of Biblical Literature, 2006. Online: http://ocp.stfx.ca/.

Tromp, Johannes. *The Life of Adam and Eve in Greek: A Critical Edition*. PVTG 6. Leiden: Brill, 2005.

Secondary Literature

Blackwell, Ben C. "Immortal Glory and the Problem of Death in Romans 3:23." *JSNT* 32 (2010): 285–308.

———. *Christosis: Pauline Soteriology in Light of Deification in Irenaeus and Cyril of Alexandria*. WUNT 2.314. Tübingen: Mohr Siebeck, 2011.

Hahne, Harry Alan. *The Corruption and Redemption of Creation: Nature in Romans 8.9–22 and Jewish Apocalyptic Literature*. LNTS 336. London: T&T Clark, 2006.

Levison, John R. "Adam and Eve in Romans 1.18–25 and the Greek *Life of Adam and Eve*." *NTS* 50 (2004): 519–34.

Sprinkle, Preston. "The Afterlife in Romans: Understanding Paul's Glory Motif in Light of the *Apocalypse of Moses* and *2 Baruch*." Pages 201–33 in *Lebendige Hoffnung—ewiger Tod?!* Edited by Michael Labahn and Manfred Lang. Leipzig: Evangelische Verlagsanstalt, 2007.

CHAPTER 13

Philo of Alexandria and Romans 9:1–29: Grace, Mercy, and Reason

ORREY McFARLAND

Romans 9 begins with an expression of grief. Paul declares that he could wish himself to be "cursed and cut off from Christ" for the sake of his fellow Jews who have not believed in the gospel (9:3). Such unbelief is troubling for Paul because the Jews were supposed to be the recipients of God's blessing. As he explains, they are "the people of Israel. Theirs is the adoption to sonship; theirs the divine glory, the covenants, the receiving of the law, the temple worship and the promises. Theirs are the patriarchs, and from them is traced the human ancestry of the Messiah" (9:4–5). Despite these divine privileges, however, many Jews have rejected the gospel. What, then, does this suggest about God's faithfulness to his promise?

In Rom 9 Paul seeks to show that the present unbelief of the Jews does not mean God's promise has failed (9:6). To establish this point Paul makes a paradoxical claim: "Not all who are descended from Israel are Israel" (9:6). This distinction allows Paul to explain why some Jews have received the promise and others (despite being "from Israel") have not. Paul subsequently works through the early parts of scriptural history to show the constancy of God's promise to Israel. Moreover, Paul is concerned to show that God's decisions to bless some but not others are entirely just. As he concludes concerning God's elective purposes, "Is God unjust? Not at all!" (9:14). But what is the basis for Paul's understanding of God's justice as it relates to election? The distinctiveness of Paul's view on the relationship between divine righteousness and election can be illuminated through a comparison with one of the most prolific Jewish authors of the **Second Temple Period — Philo** of Alexandria. As we shall see, in Rom 9 Paul was engaged in a lively conversation about the character of God's faithfulness, a conversation that revolved around two interrelated questions: To whom is God gracious, and why to those people and not others?

Philo of Alexandria

"TWO NATURES HAVE BEEN CREATED ... BY GOD"

Philo came from a wealthy family and was well educated in Greek philosophy and the Jewish Scriptures. He was also a devout member of his Jewish community and wrote to help others understand and live out Scripture. Thus, the majority of Philo's treatises are devoted to **allegorical** interpretation of the Torah. Philo searched for truth by penetrating the surface meaning of Scripture to see what its words, phrases, and characters *symbolize*. Now, the Torah is not straightforwardly philosophical; moreover, many of its stories seem to portray God in unseemly ways. Through allegory, however, the philosophically astute Philo discovered a level of scriptural meaning where God's actions were sensible, the universe was orderly, and historical figures pointed to philosophical truths about human nature and virtue.

Blessings Based on Natures. In one of his writings—the third book of his allegorical interpretation of Genesis (*Legum allegoriae*)—Philo (interpreting Gen 3:8–19) addresses some of the same theological questions as Paul does in Rom 9—why some people receive blessings and not others. Philo, however, reaches quite different conclusions. He was quite unsettled by the fact that the biblical text often depicts God blessing or cursing people for no obvious reasons. For example, Philo protests that God "slays Er [Judah's son] without any visible cause" (*Leg.* 3.69; cf. Gen 38:7). Moreover, it strikes Philo as odd that in Gen 3 God did not allow the serpent to defend himself as he had allowed Eve (*Leg.* 3.65–68). For Philo, God's actions cannot be unreasonable or inexplicable. Philo thus provides an ingenious solution to these otherwise baseless judgments: "God has made natures in the soul that are *in themselves* faulty and blameworthy" and others that are "excellent and praiseworthy" (*Leg.* 3.75, italics added). It is therefore the inherent goodness or badness of a person's *nature*—rather than one's explicit *actions*—that leads God to bless or curse them: "As God has hated [the Serpent] and [Er] without [giving] reasons, so also has he elevated excellent natures without clear reasons" (*Leg.* 3.77).

Natures Revealed through Names. How, then, is a person's nature revealed? Because God cannot bless or curse people inexplicably, Philo finds in the text a basis for divine blessing and cursing perceived solely through a person's *name*. For Philo, behind every *unmentioned action* is a *name*, and behind the name is a *nature*—whether praiseworthy or blameworthy—and this provides the warrant for God's decisions to bless or to curse (see figure 13.1).

Figure 13.1: Philo's Allegorical Interpretation of God's Actions in Genesis

Biblical figure with no listed works	Name	Nature	The vindication of God's actions

Noah. In his discussion of Noah, for example, Philo observes how "Noah found favor before the Lord God" (*Leg.* 3.77//Gen 6:8). However, no specific works are attributed to Noah that would justify God having blessed him. Philo thus reasons that Noah's favor was due to his praiseworthy *nature*, which is revealed through his *name*. As Philo explains, if "anyone asks why [Moses] says that Noah found favor before the Lord God although he had not, so far as our knowledge goes, done anything good, we shall properly answer that he was proven to have a praiseworthy nature from birth, for Noah means 'rest' or 'righteous'" (*Leg.* 3.77).

Abram. Philo discerns a similar rationale for God's blessing of Abram. Although Abram in Gen 12 does nothing to deserve God's calling, Philo finds the key to God's actions in the patriarch's name: "God produced this character having an image worthy of zeal, for 'Abram' means 'father high-soaring'" (*Leg.* 3.83). As Philo reasons, a guiding *father* is better for the soul than a threatening master; and *soaring* in contemplation of divine things is better than thinking on mortal things. Thus, both aspects of Abram's name are "praiseworthy" (3.84) and reflect his nature.

Isaac and Ishmael. By recourse to a figure's name, Philo explains why God has blessed them. How, then, does Philo explain God's blessing or cursing of those (like Isaac and Ishmael, Jacob and Esau) whose destinies were announced prior to birth, and thus before they had done anything virtuous or unvirtuous? Philo presses his logic further: "But even *before birth* God molds some people and arranges things in their favor and chooses for them to have an excellent portion" (*Leg.* 3.85). For Philo, God cannot bless or curse arbitrarily; therefore, Philo finds a rationale for God's actions rooted in the person even before birth. Such prenatal favor was granted to Isaac, about whom God promised to Abraham, "Sarah your wife shall bear you a son and you shall call his name Isaac, and I will establish my covenant with him to be an everlasting covenant" (*Leg.* 3.85//Gen 17:19). Philo raises the necessary question: "What is it, then, that has made this one also to be praised before birth?" (3.86). He answers by distinguishing between those things that are good "not only when they *have* come, but also when it is foretold that they *will* come" (3.86, italics added). Isaac is an example of the latter: because "joy, not only when present but when *hoped for*, causes the soul to overflow with rejoicing, God rightly considered Isaac before he was born worthy of his name and a great gift: for his name means 'laughter of soul' and 'joy' and 'gladness'" (3.87, italics added). Thus, Isaac's name reveals his worthiness of God's blessing, even before his birth.

Jacob and Esau. Philo offers a different explanation for God's choice of Jacob over Esau, one based on God's foreknowledge. Philo explains: "God the creator of living beings knows his own handiwork well, *even before he has thoroughly chiseled them,* both their faculties ... and their works and passions" (*Leg.* 3.88, italics added). According to Philo, even the "slightest breeze of virtue points to leadership and authority," while the beginnings of wickedness "enslave reason," which leads to a base and irrational life (3.89). Therefore, although Esau was the older son and thus Isaac's rightful heir, God's decision that "the older will serve the younger" (*Leg.* 3.88//Gen 25:23) was based on God's foreknowledge of how the twins would live out their respective lives.

Accordingly, there are "two natures created and molded and chiseled fully by God," one blameworthy and one praiseworthy (*Leg.* 3.104). This distinction clarifies what the biblical text leaves unsaid and, to Philo's mind, vindicates God's actions. Philo is not interested in determinism—in relating one's ultimate fate to their God-molded nature—but in explaining how those natures relate to God's actions in bestowing blessings and curses. Thus, the one true God is a logical God who acts wisely—which, for Philo, means that God's actions make sense.

Figure 13.2: Philo's Allegorized Names in Genesis

Figure's Name	Name's Meaning	God's Action
The Serpent	Pleasure	Condemns
Eve	Sense Perception	Allows for defense
Noah	Rest or Righteous	Gives favor
Abram	High-Soaring Father	Calls and blesses
Isaac	Joy	Establishes covenant
Jacob and Esau	N/A	Chooses based on foreknowledge

Romans 9:1–29

"I WILL HAVE MERCY ON WHOM I HAVE MERCY"

In Rom 9, Paul insists that "God's word" (his promise) has not "failed" (9:6). He therefore traces God's electing activity through fundamental points in scriptural history to prove how a chosen people has always been constituted by that promise. Paul analyzes several of the same patriarchs as Philo does, yet in his argumentation, Paul deconstructs the kinds of rational explanations that Philo was insistent on finding in the Genesis narratives. Indeed, Paul recognizes *none* of the qualities that, according to Philo, had made these figures praiseworthy. Instead, Paul concludes that receipt of the promise is based entirely on God's merciful choice.

Isaac and Ishmael. Paul's defense of God's faithfulness begins with an apparent contradiction: "Not all who are descended from Israel are Israel" (9:6). This shows that receipt of the promise is not dependent strictly on ethnicity. Rather, Abraham's family is constituted by God's choice. This, Paul demonstrates, is how God has operated since the beginning: "It is through Isaac that your offspring will be reckoned" (Rom 9:7//Gen 21:12). Paul's point is that, even in the first generation, God chose to fulfill his covenant promises through *Isaac's* lineage rather than that of *Ishmael*, Abraham's firstborn son. As Paul explains, "It is not the children by *physical descent* who are God's children, but it is the children of the *promise* who are regarded as Abraham's offspring. For this was how the promise was stated: 'At the appointed time I will return, and Sarah will have a son'" (Rom 9:8 – 9, italics added//Gen 18:14). In other words, Isaac is a child of the promise neither because of his "physical descent" (ethnicity/birthright) nor even because of his praiseworthy nature (as Philo argued), but due solely to the promise God made to Abraham that it would be Sarah, not Hagar, who would produce an heir (Rom 9:9; cf. 4:18 – 21; Gal 4:22 – 23).[1]

Jacob and Esau. Paul reasons similarly with regard to God's choice of Jacob. For Paul, God chose Jacob over his twin brother Esau *prior to birth* so that his election would take place before they had "done anything good or bad" (9:11). Election occurs "not by works but by him who calls" (9:12). Jacob's election, therefore, is based not on his future actions (as for Philo) but solely on the initiative of the God "who calls"—having declared, "The older will serve the younger" (Rom 9:12//Gen 25:23) and "Jacob I loved, but Esau I hated" (Rom 9:13//Mal 1:2). Thus, any presumption based on works or birthright is undercut.

Gentiles. The counterintuitive election of Jacob also helps to explain God's calling of Gentiles. Paul, seeking to show God's freedom in extending the promise to those outside of Israel (9:24), reworks a citation from Hosea

---

1. Paul also stresses Abraham's unworthiness when he says he was justified while ungodly (Rom 4:5).

to apply it to Gentiles: "I will call them 'my people' who are not my people; and I will call her 'my loved one' who is not my loved one" (Rom 9:25//Hos 2:23). Gentiles are now *called* and *loved* despite their prior exclusion ("not my people") and inherent unworthiness ("not my loved one"). Indeed, God declares that "you are my people" (Hos 2:23) and promises that "they will be called 'children of the living God'" (Rom 9:26//Hos 1:10). Thus, both Jews *and* Gentiles are God's people because of God's electing mercy, and the same inexplicable mercy that was at work in Israel's early history (9:6–18) remains operative in the present (9:24–33; 11:1–6).

Election Based on Mercy. Thus, where Philo found in Genesis a logic for God's actions that was based on a person's name, character, or future behavior, Paul finds no such logic. Neither virtuous acts nor physical descent nor social status are determinative of God's grace and mercy. For Philo, God cannot be merciful arbitrarily; for Paul, however, God's mercy seems arbitrary, because it works with no reference point in any human criteria. Paul understands that his argument seems to cast God in a capricious light, so he asks, "What then shall we say? Is God unjust?" (9:14). Paul answers with an emphatic "Not at all!" (9:14). He bases his assertion in God's declaration to Moses following the golden calf incident: "I will have mercy on whom I have mercy, and I will have compassion on whom I have compassion" (Rom 9:15//Exod 33:19). God's mercy is issued in accordance with God's will alone (9:16–18), and nobody has the right to challenge the Creator's decisions (9:19–23). But God is neither arbitrary nor unjust. Paul's understanding of God's mercy is founded on his understanding of Christ's death and resurrection for the ungodly (3:21–26; 5:6–8; 10:1–17). Because God has fulfilled his promise to Abraham, and thus to Israel, by giving Jesus Christ for sinners (those who do not deserve the gift), this event has reshaped how Paul reads the history of God's faithfulness to the promise; and this is what creates the distance between Paul's and Philo's views on why and to whom God is merciful.

Philo's and Paul's use of similar characters and probing of similar questions is met by equally dissimilar understandings of God's generosity. It is not questioned *whether* God is gracious, but *why*. Paul's explanation would be unsettling to Philo, because, for Philo, the universe depends on a God whose ways are rational and justifiable. For Paul, however, God's merciful election is logically inexplicable because it is dependent solely on God's willingness to be merciful. And this understanding of divine favor is, for Paul, the key to tracing the thread of God's merciful election within Israel, as well as the basis for God's establishment of the multiethnic church.

FOR FURTHER READING

Additional Ancient Texts

See also Wisdom of Solomon 11; Pseudo-Philo's *Liber Antiquitatum Biblicarum*; 1QH (*Thanksgiving Hymns*); the *Epistle of Enoch* (*1 Enoch* 92:1–5; 93:11–105:2). Within Paul, see also Rom 3–5; 2 Cor 5–6; Gal 2.

English Translations and Critical Editions

Philo. Translated by F. H. Colson et al. LCL. 12 vols. Cambridge, MA: Harvard University Press, 1929–1962.

Secondary Literature

Barclay, John M. G., and Simon J. Gathercole, eds. *Divine and Human Agency in Paul and His Cultural Environment*. LNTS 335. London: T&T Clark, 2006.

Barclay, John M. G. "Grace Within and Beyond Reason: Philo and Paul in Dialogue." Pages 9–21 in *Paul, Grace and Freedom: Essays in Honour of John K. Riches*. Edited by P. Middleton et al. London: T&T Clark, 2009.

Gaventa, Beverly R. "On the Calling-Into-Being of Israel: Romans 9:6–29." Pages 255–69 in *Between Gospel and Election: Explorations in the Interpretation of Romans 9–11*. WUNT 257. Edited by F. Wilk and J. R. Wagner. Tu"bingen: Mohr Siebeck, 2010.

Harrison, James R. *Paul's Language of Grace in Its Graeco-Roman Context*. WUNT 2.172. Tübingen: Mohr Siebeck, 2003.

Kamesar, Adam, ed. *The Cambridge Companion to Philo*. Cambridge: Cambridge University Press, 2009.

Sandmel, Samuel. *Philo of Alexandria: An Introduction*. Oxford: Oxford University Press, 1979.

CHAPTER 14

Philo of Alexandria and Romans 9:30–10:21: The Commandment and the Quest for the Good Life

DAVID LINCICUM

In Rom 9–11 Paul addresses the problem of Jewish unbelief in the gospel and the resultant problem of Gentile Christian boasting. In chapter 9, after first confessing his sorrow at the situation and stressing the divine privileges his compatriots have received (9:1–5), Paul develops a sustained argument contending that there has always been a process of election *within* historical Israel, and so the fact that some have not believed is entirely consistent with God's electing purposes rather than indicating that "God's word had failed" (9:6–29). These electing purposes have, moreover, been extended in a surprising way to the Gentiles. But how can it be that God's chosen people, Israel, have only partially believed, while the Gentiles, who had no claim on the **covenant**, have now been included in the people of God? In Rom 9:30–10:21, Paul moves beyond his initial argument about election to explain further this state of affairs.

Part of Paul's argument is the claim that Israel failed to grasp the **Messiah** they had awaited, not simply because of divine hardening, but because Israel had not pursued righteousness in the correct manner. The law should have led Paul's fellow Jews to faith in Jesus as the Messiah, but — Paul alleges — they failed to reach this goal because they approached the law in the wrong way. In this manner, the inclusion of Gentiles in the righteousness of the **covenant community** is closely (and unexpectedly) bound up with the failure of most Jews to recognize the goal of the law in the Messiah (9:30–10:4). The "righteousness" that Israel unsuccessfully sought and the Gentiles unintentionally found, Paul goes on to argue, is available to all indiscriminately on the basis of faith in the Messiah (10:5–13). And the divine election that Paul has described at length in Rom 9:6–29 cannot be taken to excuse Israel for their unbelief, since messengers who proclaimed an intelligible message to Israel had announced the gospel to them, leaving them without excuse (10:14–21).

In what is perhaps the most puzzling element of a passage that could by no means be called straightforward, Paul apparently contrasts two kinds of righteousness in 10:5–8: the "righteousness that is by the law" and the "righteousness that is by faith." In support of the first, he cites Lev 18:5, while the second is personified and speaks words that sound reminiscent of Deut 30:11–14. But the Deuteronomy quotation differs from the original **Septuagint** version, from which it was ultimately taken, in some intriguing ways. A comparison with **Philo** of Alexandria helps elucidate this point.

Philo of Alexandria
"A PRAISEWORTHY AND PERFECT LIFE"

We have already encountered Philo, the urbane Alexandrian Jewish philosopher and exegete from the first century who wrote voluminously on the Pentateuch, combining his interpretative interests with his fascination with the tradition of **Plato's** philosophy. Philo's vast writings are remarkable for the intellectual restlessness with which he tries to square biblical faith and philosophical thought. He was not hesitant to employ **allegorical** reading strategies to achieve this resolution, and generations of scholars have praised or blamed him for that choice. But more recent scholarship has emphasized Philo's Jewish identity and taken more seriously his claim to be an interpreter of Israel's Torah.

The way Philo uses Deut 30:11–14 sheds some interesting light on Paul's usage of the same verses in Rom 10:6–8. Philo paraphrases Deut 30:11–14 a number of times in his works. For example, in his treatise *On the Virtues* (*De virtutibus*), which is an extended meditation on the biblical evidence for some philosophical virtues, he uses Deut 30:14 to speak of three ways of repentance—in thoughts, intentions, and actions, corresponding to the Septuagint's heart, mouth, and hands. It is worth pausing to consider in greater detail Philo's interpretation of Deut 30:14.

> [Moses] has also certainly offered very good instructions for repentance, by which we are taught to change our way of life from a discordant one to a better and improved one. For he says that this thing is not excessively great nor too far away, neither is it in the atmosphere high above nor at the ends of the earth or beyond the

great sea, so that we are unable to receive it, but it is very near, dwelling in three parts of our own selves, in mouth and heart and hand, which symbolize words and intentions and actions. For "mouth" is the symbol of the word, "heart" of intentions, and "hands" of actions, and in all of these is well-being. For whenever thought aligns with word and intention aligns with action, then such a life is praiseworthy and perfect; but when these are at odds with each other, then one is imperfect and blameworthy. Unless someone forgets this harmony, they will be pleasing to God, both God-loving and God-loved.

ON THE VIRTUES 183–184

Holistic Acceptance of the Law. Philo here offers a reflective unfolding of the Deuteronomy citation. The Greek translation mentions that the commandment is neither excessive nor far-off, but rather, "the word is very near you, in your mouth and in your heart and in your hands, so that you may do it" (**LXX** Deut 30:14). Philo asks the natural question: Why is there a threefold repetition here? Is the adding up of body parts—mouth, heart, hands—merely rhetorical flourish, or do the individual elements mentioned signify different emphases? To these questions he offers an attractive answer: the biblical text is speaking of the *holistic* acceptance of the law, in words and intentions and actions. Philo suggests this indicates a situation in which "thought aligns with word and intention aligns with action." Keeping the law is a matter of personal integrity and being free from inner conflict: rather than being merely a matter of external obedience, truly obeying means that what one says is a clear reflection of what one thinks, and what one does is not in disagreement with what one wishes or intends to do. This *total obedience* is the way to the good life.

The Benefits of Obedience. Thus, the overall thrust of Deut 30:11–14 is (1) to deny that keeping the law is difficult—it is, as Philo states, neither "excessively great nor too far away"—as well as (2) to stress the benefits of obeying God's command. For Philo, doing the law is beneficial, since obeying God leads one to a healthy and well-rounded life, free from inner conflict and full of well-being and peace. In the broader context (*Virt.* 175–187), Philo also mentions benefits such as bodily health and safety during travel, ideas adapted from the catalog of blessings and curses in Deut 27–28. If some of the terminology Philo uses to express this seems philosophically inflected, his basic point is not obscured by it.

One could say Philo offers a fairly straightforward, if expansive, paraphrase of these verses. If Philo is known for his interest in **allegory**, that interest does not seem to be very much in evidence here — or at least the allegorical elements seem not to distort the basic message of Deut 30:11 – 14. Philo looks to these verses in order to urge obedience to God's commands, by using them to stress how possible and beneficial such obedience really is. Philo is far from any sort of wooden legalism that implies a commercial exchange of goods between God and humanity in a strict tit-for-tat manner. Rather, he paraphrases Deuteronomy's message, even while avoiding the term "commandment," to present obedience as being in the human subject's best interests, a way to "well-being" and internal peace. In this sense, Philo riffs on the original context of Deut 30:11 – 14, which also functions to urge obedience to the law, and even though he uses philosophical vocabulary to enumerate the benefits of obedience, his basic construal of the passage seems to be more or less in line with the Deuteronomic original.

Romans 9:30 – 10:21

"THE WORD IS NEAR YOU"

Paul's rendering of Deut 30:12 – 14 in Rom 10:6 – 8, by contrast, seems much less straightforward. In his quotation of Deuteronomy, Paul has made three substantial interpretative judgments that are expressed in his presentation of the text.

Renouncing Self-Reliance. First, Paul introduces the text with words drawn from Deut 8:17 or 9:4 (where they occur identically in similar contexts): "Do not say in your heart." In both Deut 8 and 9, Israel is warned not to grow proud after they have entered the land of promise and say in their hearts, "My power and the strength of my hands have produced this wealth for me" (Deut 8:17), or "The LORD has brought me here ... because of my righteousness" (9:4). Paul invokes this stress against self-reliance as the lens through which his reading of Deut 30:12 – 14 is to be seen.

Erasing the "Doing." Second, Paul edits out any notion of "doing" the commandment from the original. The following presentation of the text shows what Paul has omitted in underline:

LXX Deuteronomy 30:12–14 (my translation)	Romans 10:6–8
[The command] is not in heaven that one should say,	But the righteousness that is by faith says: "Do not say in your heart,
"Who will ascend for us into heaven and take it for us? <u>And once we have heard, we will do it.</u>"Nor is it on the other side of the sea that one should say,	'Who will ascend into heaven?'" (that is, to bring Christ down) "or
"Who will cross over to the other side of the sea for us and take it for us? <u>And when he has caused us to hear it, we will do it.</u>"	'Who will descend into the deep?'" (that is, to bring Christ up from the dead). But what does it say?
The word is very near you, in your mouth and in your heart <u>and in your hands, in order for you to do it.</u>	"The word is near you; it is in your mouth and in your heart," that is, the message concerning faith that we proclaim.

This, in turn, prepares the way for Paul's third change.

Replacing the Commandment with Christ. Paul intersperses comments in his citation of the text that specify *Christ* as the object of the actions (as opposed to "the commandment"). Here also one can observe a progression by which Deuteronomy's *commandment* is replaced with *Christ*, who, in turn, is elided into the message about him, the word of faith. The specific content of Paul's interpretation might have been surprising to a Jewish audience, but this way of rewriting a scriptural citation as a means of conveying one's interpretation of the text was not uncommon in **Second Temple Judaism**.

Paul's formal method can be paralleled in part from both the **Qumran** *pesharim*—commentaries that cite Scripture and identify the fulfillment of prophecy in contemporary events—and elsewhere in Philo's writings. While Philo seeks a certain deeper identification for the three terms in Deut 30:14 (mouth, heart, hand), Paul seeks a deeper identification of the commandment itself, finding it in Christ. But while Philo's allegorical hermeneutic operates with a sense of the divine fullness of Scripture, he does not seem to have had the same sense of living in the last days that we find in Paul. Both Paul and Philo have in common a desire to explain elements in the Deuteronomic text by means of realities outside the text, but their explanations naturally differ because of the concrete aims with which they approach the task of under-standing Scripture.

These clear contrasts in intention help explain the most striking difference between Paul and Philo in their interpretation of Deut 30:11–14. Philo has sought to understand and exposit the ways in which obedience to the Torah's commands is achievable and worthwhile, but Paul has erased any hint of "doing" the commandments, instead placing emphasis on confessing and trusting Jesus as the Messiah. So, in Rom 10:5–8, Paul offers a discussion of two types of righteousness: the righteousness from the law and the righteousness from faith, each with its own witness in the law. Leviticus 18:5 serves as a witness to righteousness from the law and speaks of "the person who obeys [the commandments]" ("the person who does [them]," Rom 10:5), while Paul has, by way of contrast, extensively rewritten Deuteronomy to expunge any notion of doing.

Arguably, Paul invokes Leviticus not as a witness to any sort of merit theology whereby one might "earn" one's way to heaven, but rather as an example of the conditional logic of the covenant: human behavior in accordance with the terms of the covenant will meet with life, the promised end of that covenant. To this scenario of human obedience that leads to life, Paul opposes his interpretation of Deuteronomy, according to which the Messiah is the ultimate aim of Torah, and so has achieved the conditions for righteousness for Gentile and Jew alike.

While Philo uses Deut 30:11–14 to express the very real attainability of obedience to the law and to stress the benefits such obedience renders, for Paul, the Messiah has in some sense taken the place of the command. Both Philo and Paul might be said to have offered contextual interpretations of Deuteronomy, but their basic construal of that book differs in significant ways. Philo's exhortations approximate the tone and content of the original Deuteronomic elements in a relatively straightforward way, but Paul has offered a surprising interpretation of Deuteronomy from his perspective as an apostle to the Gentiles. He views the book retrospectively from his perception of **the Christ event**, and so gives a radical clarification of the true referent of the "commandment," ultimately identifying this as Jesus Christ. Paul, like Philo, may be seen to offer a proposal for how Deut 30:11–14 leads to the good life, but the precise content of that good life clearly differs.

In Rom 9:30–10:21, then, Paul's argument serves to undercut any suggestion that Israel might find an excuse for unbelief in the nature of the law God gave them or in the way the message was announced to them. Having already established divine election in Rom 9:6–29, Paul now firmly lays the emphasis on human responsibility. In this context, Paul's appeal to Deuteronomy allows him to give substance to his claim that "Christ is the culmination of the law" (10:4), and so to emphasize that God's gracious provision has always been sufficient for his people.

FOR FURTHER READING

Additional Texts

Philo also interacts with Deut 30:11–14 in *On the Change of Names* 236–238; *On Rewards and Punishments* 79–84; *That Every Good Person Is Free* 66–70; *On Dreams* 2.179–180; and *On the Posterity of Cain* 84–86. Cf. further Baruch 3:29–30. Paul also seems similarly to rewrite Deut 6:4 in 1 Cor 8:4–6.

English Translations and Critical Editions

Philo. Translated by F. H. Colson et al. 12 vols. LCL. Cambridge, MA: Harvard University Press, 1929–1962.

Secondary Literature

Bekken, Per Jarle. *The Word Is Near You: A Study of Deuteronomy 30:12–14 in Paul's Letter to the Romans in a Jewish Context*. BZNW 144. Berlin: de Gruyter, 2007.

Hays, Richard B. *Echoes of Scripture in the Letters of Paul*. New Haven: Yale University Press, 1989.

Henze, Mattias, ed. *A Companion to Biblical Interpretation in Early Judaism*. Grand Rapids: Eerdmans, 2012.

Lincicum, David. *Paul and the Early Jewish Encounter with Deuteronomy*. Grand Rapids: Baker Academic, 2013.

Sprinkle, Preston M. *Law and Life: The Interpretation of Leviticus 18:5 in Early Judaism and in Paul*. WUNT 2.241. Tübingen: Mohr Siebeck, 2008.

Watson, Francis. *Paul and the Hermeneutics of Faith*. London: T&T Clark, 2004.

CHAPTER 15

Tobit and Romans 11:1–36: Israel's Salvation and the Fulfillment of God's Word

JOHN K. GOODRICH

In Rom 9–11 Paul explains that even though "not all the Israelites accepted the good news" (10:16), "it is not as though God's word had failed" (9:6). For Israel's unbelief, Paul reasons, is due to two factors. First, God's promises to Israel are and have always been restricted to the elect (9:6–29); indeed, God would remain righteous even should he not save every Israelite, for it is his prerogative to extend mercy and compassion only to those he chooses (9:14–15). Second, the Jewish people are to blame for their own unbelief (9:30–10:21), for while they have both heard and understood the gospel (10:18–19), they have rejected God's righteousness and instead sought their own (9:30–10:4).

Paul, however, does not leave Israel's story with such a bleak ending. He continues to address the matter of God's faithfulness in relation to Israel's fate, insisting that "God did not reject his people, whom he foreknew" (11:2). This he shows by observing that there are in fact Jewish believers within the church, including himself (11:1). For just as God reserved seven thousand obedient Israelites in the time of Elijah (11:2–4, citing 1 Kgs 19:18), "so too, at the present time there is a remnant chosen by grace" (Rom 11:5). But even those who remain hardened are not beyond the pale of grace, for they did not "stumble so as to fall beyond recovery" (11:11). In fact, as this important passage goes on to show, Paul asserts that, in due course, "all Israel will be saved" (11:26). But whom does Paul mean by "all Israel," and when and how will they "be saved"? Furthermore, why is it that God hardened so many Israelites only to extend salvation to Israel at a later time? Although these questions have confounded interpreters for centuries, the meaning and logic of Paul's discourse come more clearly into view when read within the context of **Second Temple Jewish** views on the restoration of Israel, especially the farewell speech in the book of Tobit.

Tobit

"THEY ALL WILL RETURN FROM THEIR CAPTIVITY"

The book of Tobit is a fictional, **apocryphal** narrative (before 100 BC) involving a Jewish man (Tobit) and his family, including his wife, Sarah, and his son, Tobias. The book narrates the life of this faithful Naphtalite during the Assyrian exile (after 722 BC) and demonstrates, in Job-like fashion, how a person who undergoes tragedy is eventually blessed by God. Beyond employing an interesting story line, however, the book is rich in its presentation of Jewish **eschatology**, particularly with regard to how the Jewish people perceived their state of exile and eventual restoration at the hand of God.

Eschatological insights can be inferred throughout the narrative—Tobit's own life (from tragedy to triumph) probably represents the fate of the entire northern kingdom. But the final two chapters (Tob 13–14) contain the book's clearest presentation of Israel's eschatological story line. Particularly relevant for our study is Tobit's farewell speech in 14:3–7.

> [3] When he [Tobit] was about to die he called his son Tobias and instructed him saying, "Child, take your children [4] and hurry off to Media, for I believe the word of God that Nahum spoke about Nineveh, that all these things will occur and happen to Assyria and Nineveh. And whatever the prophets of Israel, whom God sent, spoke, all of it will happen. And none of all their words will be lacking and all things will transpire in their times. And there will be more salvation in Media than among the Assyrians and in Babylon. For I know and believe that all that God said will be fulfilled and will occur, and the word from the prophecies will in no way fail. And all our brothers who are dwelling in the land of Israel will be scattered and exiled from the good land. And the entire land of Israel will be a desert: both Samaria and Jerusalem will be a desert. And the house of God will also burn in grief for a time.
> [5] But again God will have mercy on them. God will return them to the land of Israel and again they will rebuild the house—but it will not be like the first one, until the time when the time of seasons is fulfilled. And after these things, they all will return from their captivity and will rebuild Jerusalem gloriously, and the house of God

in it will be rebuilt just as the prophets of Israel said about it. [6] And all the nations in the entire earth, everybody will turn and truly fear God: everybody will abandon their idols which have falsely led them astray and will bless the eternal God in righteousness. [7] All the sons of Israel who are saved in those days and are truly mindful of God will be gathered together, go to Jerusalem, and dwell eternally in the land of Abraham with safety, which will be handed over to them. And those who truly love God will rejoice and those who do sin and injustice will depart from all the earth.[1]

Four aspects of this passage deserve attention for the sake of our comparison with Romans.

The Fulfillment of God's Word. First, it is significant that Tobit begins the speech by declaring his trust in "God's word." After insisting that Tobias take his family to Media, Tobit provides a theological basis for his instructions: God's judgment is coming upon Nineveh (Assyria). Within the setting of the narrative, Israel's northern kingdom ("Samaria") had already been exiled by Assyria, while Israel's southern kingdom ("Jerusalem"/Judah) was soon to be taken captive by Babylon. Tobit, however, was convinced that God would keep his promises to his **covenant** people by deposing those nations that had besieged them and by restoring Israel to its former glory. Tobit clings especially to those restoration-from-exile promises recorded in the Song of Moses (Deut 32).[2] Therefore, Tobit brackets 14:4a with affirmations of his confidence in God's word ("I believe … I know and believe"), while emphasizing the unqualified nature of his trust in God through the repetition of absolute terms ("all,""whatever,""none"). While Joseph Fitzmyer is perhaps correct to observe how in 14:4 "[t]he dying Tobit's discourse has become long-winded and repetitious,"[3] the speech's recurring affirmation of trust in God's word serves to underscore Tobit's principal and unmistakable message: *God will fulfill his promises to Israel*.

Three-Stage Fulfillment. Second, in order to show how he believed God's promises would come to fruition, Tobit presents a salvation history of Israel occurring in three stages: (1) exile; (2) partial restoration; (3) full restoration. First, because of its iniquities (13:5), all Israel will be taken into captivity; indeed, even the Jerusalem temple ("house of God") will "burn in grief for a

---

1.   My translation, based on the Greek text of Codex Sinaiticus.
2.   Alexander A. Di Lella, "The Deuteronomic Background of the Farewell Discourse in Tob 14:3–11,"*CBQ* 41 (1979): 380–89; Steven Weitzman, "Allusion, Artifice, and Exile in the Hymn of Tobit,"*JBL* 115 (1996): 49–61.
3.   Joseph A. Fitzmyer, *Tobit* (CEJL; Berlin: de Gruyter, 2003), 327.

time" (14:4b; cf. Isa 64:10–11). Tobit is assured, however, that the Lord will not forsake his promises to Israel and will eventually restore the nation, though this will occur in two phases.

In the first phase of restoration, in what Tobit considers to be an act of divine "mercy," "God will return them to the land of Israel and again they will rebuild the house" (Tob 14:5). However, this initial return—though already inaugurated (from the perspective of the author) in the decree of Cyrus (539 BC) and the rebuilding of Jerusalem under Ezra and Nehemiah (516 BC)—will neither involve every Israelite tribe nor result in the final rebuilding of the temple anticipated by the prophets. Indeed, the book's author undoubtedly knew what several postexilic texts had already lamented—that Jerusalem's second temple was anything but "like the first one" (14:5; cf. Ezra 3:12; Hag 2:3).

Nevertheless, Tobit knows that the inglorious state of this temple—together with the partial nature of Israel's initial return from exile—will only last "until the time when the time of seasons is fulfilled" (14:5). For "after these things," in a third and final stage of Israel's story line, "*all* will return from their captivity and will rebuild Jerusalem gloriously, and the house of God in it" (14:5, italics added; cf. 13:5). Tobit even refers to God's restoration of Israel with *salvation* language ("All the sons of Israel who are *saved*," 14:7, italics added) and understands Israel's deliverance to have resulted in their permanent reoccupation of the land (14:7; cf. 13:10). In the light of this climactic ending to Israel's story, Tobit's declaration that "the word from the prophecies will in no way fail" (14:4) shows that he had the consummation of the process in view from the outset of the speech, and that the author's purpose in recording it was to generate among his stage-two contemporaries faith and hope in the fact that God would complete the restoration process already underway.

Figure 15.1: Tobit's Eschatological Story Line

Israel's Exile (14:4)	Israel's Partial Restoration (14:5)	Israel's Full Restoration (14:5, 7)	Conversion of the Gentiles (14:6)

Gentile Inclusion. Third, Tobit's speech shows that he believed the scope of God's mercy would not be limited to Israel alone, for participation in God's kingdom would also be extended to the Gentiles. Tobit reports that, after Israel's full restoration, "all the nations in the entire earth, everybody will turn and truly fear God" (14:6; cf. 13:11). The order of events here is significant: Israel will be restored; the nations will "abandon their idols"; and only then will the nations direct their worship to Yahweh.

Salvation for Many, Not All. Fourth, Tobit is aware that not every person (even every Israelite) will be saved, for repentance is a critical condition of participation in God's kingdom. God requires that his people "turn to him with all [their] heart and with all [their] soul to do what is true before him" (13:6), such that only those who are "truly mindful of God will be gathered together, go to Jerusalem, and dwell eternally in the land of Abraham with safety" (14:7). Similarly, Gentiles are required to "abandon their idols" and to "turn and truly fear God" (14:6; cf. 13:11). Thus, while all "those who truly love God will rejoice," "those who do sin and injustice will depart from all the earth" (14:7).

Romans 11:1–36

"ALL ISRAEL WILL BE SAVED"

God's Word Fulfilled in Three Stages. Tobit's farewell address in many ways mirrors Rom 11, Paul's lengthiest treatment of the status and future of Israel. First, like Tobit's speech, Paul's discussion of Israel's fate is introduced by a declaration of confidence in the fulfillment of God's word: "It is not as though God's word had failed" (9:6). This affirmation, though occurring two chapters earlier, serves as Paul's thesis statement for all of Rom 9–11. The thesis is unpacked in a series of arguments that unveils, in a manner similar to Tobit 14:3–7 and through a shared reliance on the Song of Moses,[4] a three-stage story line for the people of Israel: (1) exile; (2) partial restoration; (3) full restoration.

Paul, however, does not consider Israel's exile primarily in a *geographical* sense (deportation from the land), but in a *spiritual* sense (separation from God). Thus, while Paul describes unbelieving Israel's status in various ways (e.g., "hardened," 11:7; "transgression," 11:11–12; "broken off," 11:17–22; "disobedience," 11:30–32), he does so without explicit mention of temple or territory (cf. 4:13). Nevertheless, Paul's use of the OT throughout Rom 9–11 shows that he understands Israel's predicament as a kind of *metaphorical exile*.[5]

Not all Israelites, however, have rejected the **Messiah** and remain separated from God. Paul finds proof of God's faithfulness to Israel in the fact that "at the

---

4. Paul quotes Deut 32:21 in Rom 10:19 and alludes to it in 11:11, 14; cf. Richard H. Bell, *Provoked to Jealousy: The Origin and Purpose of the Jealousy Motif in Romans 9–11* (WUNT 2.63; Tübingen: Mohr Siebeck, 1994).
5. J. Ross Wagner, *Heralds of the Good News: Isaiah and Paul "in Concert" in the Letter to the Romans* (NovTSup 101; Leiden: Brill, 2002), 353.

present time there is a remnant chosen by grace" (11:5); he even points to himself as one of "the elect" already participating in Israel's initial phase of restoration (11:1, 7). But will this restoration remain only partial? "Not at all!" (11:11), declares Paul, for if the "*firstfruits* is holy, then the *whole batch* is holy" (11:16, italics added). In other words, Paul, like Tobit, assures his readers that there will come a time when God will fully restore Israel, that is, when "*all* Israel will be saved" (11:26, italics added). Just as assuredly as God has saved a *remnant* within Israel, so God will fulfill his covenant promises by saving the *rest* of Israel as well (9:5–6; 11:27–28): "for God's gifts and his call are irrevocable" (11:29).

Salvation for Many, Not All. Paul here understands "all Israel" in a collective sense, as referring to a large number of Israelites at a given moment in time, not necessarily to every member of the Jewish people (cf 1 Sam 7:5; 25:1; 2 Sam 16:22; Dan 9:11). The salvation he anticipates will be a future mass conversion at, or just before, the return of the Messiah—a conversion, like that of all Christians, predicated on faith. For Israel will be saved, he says, but only "if they do not persist in unbelief" (11:23; cf. 10:9–13).

Gentile Inclusion. Why, then, is Israel's salvation to be completed in two phases? Paul maintains that God has installed the period of partial hardening among the Israelites to provide an opportunity for extending his mercy to the Gentiles. While Tobit anticipated the conversion of the nations occurring only after Israel's full restoration, Paul understands Israel's current rejection of the gospel as a catalyst for the Gentile mission, which will, in turn, incite Israelites to believe in the Messiah: "because of their transgression, salvation has come to the Gentiles to make Israel envious" (11:11). Israel's envy, magnified no less by Paul's own ministry, is therefore intended also to save more Israelites, as they come to share in the gospel as well (11:14). Thus, Paul envisions an interdependency between the salvation of Israel and that of the Gentiles: "Israel has experienced a hardening in part *until* the full number of the Gentiles has come in, *and in this way* all Israel will be saved" (11:25–26, italics added). This complex salvation-historical scheme, while underscoring the waywardness of all people, ultimately serves to showcase the greatness of "God's mercy" and "the riches of his wisdom" (11:30–33).

Figure 15.2: Paul's Eschatological Story Line

Israel's Exile (11:11–12)	Israel's Partial Restoration (11:5)	Conversion of the Gentiles (11:25)	Israel's Full Restoration (11:26)

FOR FURTHER READING

Additional Ancient Texts

On the restoration of Israel, see Baruch 1:15–3:8 and the *Testaments of the Twelve Patriarchs* (esp. *Testament of Judah* 22:1–3; *Testament of Benjamin* 9:1–2; 10:1–10; *Testament of Zebulun* 9:5–9). Other Pauline passages on Israel include Rom 9:6–29; Gal 6:16; 1 Thess 2:14–16.

English Translations and Critical Editions

NETS

NRSV

Hanhart, Robert. *Tobit*. Septuaginta 8.5. Göttingen: Vandenhoeck & Ruprecht, 1983.

Weeks, Stuart, Simon Gathercole, and Loren Stuckenbruck, eds. *The Book of Tobit: Texts from the Principal Ancient and Medieval Traditions with Synopsis, Concordances, and Annotated Texts in Aramaic, Hebrew, Greek, Latin, and Syriac*. FSBP 3. Berlin: de Gruyter, 2004.

Secondary Literature

Bell, Richard H. *The Irrevocable Call of God: An Inquiry into Paul's Theology of Israel*. WUNT 184. Tübingen: Mohr Siebeck, 2005.

Fitzmyer, Joseph A. *Tobit*. CEJL. Berlin: de Gruyter, 2003.

Hicks-Keeton, Jill. "Already/Not Yet: Eschatological Tension in the Book of Tobit." *JBL* 132 (2013): 97–117.

Moore, Carey A. *Tobit: A New Translation with Introduction and Commentary*. AYBC 40A. Garden City, NY: Doubleday, 1996.

Scott, James M. "'And then all Israel will be saved' (Rom 11:26)." Pages 489–527 in *Restoration: Old Testament, Jewish, and Christian Perspectives*. Edited by James M. Scott. JSJSup 72. Leiden: Brill, 2001.

———. "Paul's Use of Deuteronomic Tradition." *JBL* 112 (1993): 645–65.

CHAPTER 16

4 Maccabees and Romans 12:1–21: Reason and the Righteous Life

BEN C. DUNSON

Although Paul gives various commands throughout Rom 1–11, ethical application becomes much more prominent in chapter 12. These ethical exhortations, which extend through the final chapters of Romans, are to be carried out "in view of God's mercy" (12:1) and on the basis of the "renewing of [the believer's] mind" (12:2). The grace believers have received from God—combined with a Spirit-endowed way of thinking about God, themselves, and the world—is meant to issue forth in a new way of living in the body of Christ (12:3–8). Romans 12:9–21 gives concrete form to how believers must live the life of faith, focusing primarily on the relationships they have with each other and with those outside the believing community.

The key question of this chapter is this: For Paul, how does transformation of the mind lead to transformation of behavior and emotions? In this chapter, Paul's views on these subjects will be compared with 4 Maccabees, a nearly contemporary Jewish text. Fourth Maccabees makes for an interesting conversation partner with Rom 12 for two main reasons: (1) both writings focus on the importance of reason, or "right thinking," and (2) divine enabling plays a more pronounced role with regard to the implementation of right thinking in Rom 12 than in 4 Maccabees.

4 Maccabees

"REASON IS MASTER OF THE EMOTIONS"

Fourth Maccabees was written by an anonymous Jewish author in the first century AD to provide law-observant Jews with the cognitive and philosophical resources to stand firm against any attempt by outsiders to force them to abandon their fidelity to God's law. The work is primarily taken up with recasting a famous scene from the **Maccabean Revolt** against the **Seleucids** and is based on the earlier telling of this story in 2 Maccabees 6–7. Its stated purpose is to expound on the highly "philosophical matter" of whether "devout reason" is "the master of the emotions" (1:1). To do this, the author employs many motifs and terms borrowed from **Stoicism**, although these ideas are set within a Jewish **covenantal** framework. In line with Stoicism, the author sees mastery of the emotions as "necessary for everyone who desires knowledge" and, in fact, as being the "highest form of virtue" attainable by human beings (1:2).

Fourth Maccabees begins with a brief summary of the situation in Palestine during the reign of the Seleucid king **Antiochus IV** (175–164 BC). The narrative then focuses on one particular moment in the Maccabean uprising—the martyrdom of a law-observant Jewish man (Eleazar) and that of an unnamed law-observant Jewish woman and her seven sons. As the story goes, Antiochus systematically attempted to force the Jews in Palestine to "eat polluted foods" and to "renounce Judaism" (4:26), with death as the punishment for those who refused (5:3). To avoid persecution, or for personal gain, many compromised with the Seleucid authorities, including a temple official named Simon (4:1–5; cf. 2 Macc 3) and the Jewish high priest Jason (2 Macc 4:7–22).

Fidelity through Self-Mastery. How does 4 Maccabees attempt to help Jews struggling to maintain their fidelity to God's law? Primarily it does this through its repeated emphasis on the necessity of strictly controlling one's life according to "rational judgment" (1:2), a phrase that appears repeatedly throughout the treatise (e.g., 1:18, 30). *Rational judgments*, while not defined with philosophical precision in 4 Maccabees, are those processes of the mind that result in *mastery of human emotions*, such as anger, fear, and pain (1:3–4). All of these emotions must be quickly suppressed; otherwise they will lead to a morally compromised life in which one surrenders his or her virtue in order to receive the temporary yet sinful satisfaction that comes from various forms of emotional release, such as the expression of frustration in a fit of anger. For the author of 4 Maccabees, if one desires steadfast faithfulness to God, the emotions must be held in check through mental control.

Even emotions that most people would think of positively, like love, empathy, and grief, must be mastered and subdued by rational judgments, because even these emotions can easily overpower one's reason and lead to moral failure. Consider the following excerpt, which describes the mother (who is one of the main characters of the narrative) watching her seven sons undergo torture and eventually die before her eyes:

> [1] O reasoning about children, that tyrant of the emotions; and yet godliness, more desirable to the mother than her children! [2] When two choices were before her — godliness and the temporary preserva- tion of her seven sons according to the tyrant's promise — [3] she loved godliness more, godliness that, according to God, preserves a person for eternal life …
>
> [11] Nonetheless, though so many factors — such as love for her children — drew the mother to sympathy, with none of them were the various tortures strong enough to turn her away from reason. [12] Instead, the mother urged each individual boy, and all of them together, on to a godly death.
>
> *4 MACCABEES 15:1–3, 11–12*

As this passage shows, love and empathy, while inherently good, are nonetheless potentially dangerous because these emotions — if not mastered by reason — can lead one to renounce one's trust in God in order to avoid torture and persecution. The ideal person (in line with Stoic teaching) is one who, through vigorous mental control, is completely free from coercion into action by external circumstances. For this reason, the author presents self-mastery as the necessary foundation for the ethical life. Self-mastery will lead to godliness and virtue, but other (even positive) moral and emotional states are viewed with a certain degree of reserve.

The Law and Rationality. Human emotions, then, are dangerous, and self-mastery is the God-ordained means of avoiding these potential dangers. Just as important, however, is the *way* in which self-mastery is to be accom- plished. Fourth Maccabees assumes that all people (by virtue of creation) are born possessing "the chief virtue"—"rational judgment" (1:2). Although some foolishly choose not to exercise their capacity for rational judgment, this can be overcome simply by turning to the law, which is the guide for properly functioning reason. An example from 4 Maccabees 2:8–9 illustrates this point.

> [8] Thus, as soon as one begins living according to the law, even though one is a lover of money, one is compelled to act differently than nor- mal and to lend without interest to those who seek help and to for- give debts during the seventh year. [9] If one is greedy, one is grabbed ahold of by the law because of reason so that one neither gleans the

harvest nor gathers the last grapes from the vineyard. With other things, too, it is evident: reason rules over the emotions.[1]

Whatever vices one may struggle with, reason will fight against them as their "antagonist," ensuring that virtue prevails (3:5).

In 4 Maccabees 2:21–23, the creational capacity for rationality is set out most clearly: "For when God formed man, he planted in him emotions and customs, and at that time enthroned the mind among the senses as the supernatural governor of them all. To this mind God gave a law by which—if a man lives subject to it—he will rule a kingdom that is self-controlled, just, good, and courageous." Two things stand out here. First, the subduing of human emotions is possible because God has created humans with minds that are "supernatural governors" of the emotions. God did this when he "formed human beings" at creation. In other words, the minds of all people have the inborn capacity for self-mastery. Creation is certainly an act of God, and thus self-mastery is not devoid of divine initiative. However, no postcreational acts of spiritual enlightenment are necessary for one to think rightly, and thus live rightly, before God. Second, God's law is the only guide necessary for the mind to regulate one's conduct properly. All wisdom necessary for the virtuous life is contained in some form within its commands.

In sum, self-mastery is possible because of the mental "equipment" that is inherent in a person by virtue of their having been created by God. With this equipment in place, the law can be obeyed without hindrance, enabling one to live rightly in all circumstances. For this reason, the author of 4 Maccabees can say that "reason ... is master of the emotions" (2:24).

Romans 12:1–21
"BE TRANSFORMED BY THE RENEWING OF YOUR MIND"

Just as right thinking plays an important role in 4 Maccabees, so it does in Rom 12. Here Paul writes of the radical transformation that has occurred in the lives of believers "in view of God's mercy" (12:1), that is, through the comprehensive spiritual change that has come about through the transforming work of the Holy Spirit (see esp. Rom 6–8). This transformation brings with it a new way of living and a new way of treating others, but is founded on a new way of *thinking*, a "renewing of your mind" (12:2). Words relating to this transformation of the mind dominate in 12:1–4: the worship of the believing community is a rational worship (12:1) that flows out of a renewed mind and

---

1. The OT laws mentioned in this passage are found in Exod 22:25; Deut 15:1–3; Lev 19:9–10.

leads to discernment of God's will (12:2). Furthermore, the principle of unity within the body of Christ leads to Paul's command that believers refrain from thinking too highly of themselves, and instead think with self-control (12:3). Only people whose minds are self-controlled will be equipped to recognize that the diversity of gifts within the body of Christ is itself a gift from God rather than grounds for arrogant boasting or covetous desire (12:4–8). Individual members of the single body are to serve God and each other according to the specific gifts that God has given them rather than to compete for personal glory and honor. The only thing in which they should seek to outdo each other is showing honor to their fellow believers (12:10).

Acceptable Emotions. A difference emerges between Rom 12 and 4 Maccabees in that Paul focuses on the *benefits* of rightly ordered emotions, while 4 Maccabees focuses more on their potential *dangers*. Paul, for example, emphasizes that love should not be fake but "sincere" (12:9), and that the believer should "never be lacking in zeal," but should have an intense "spiritual fervor" (12:11). Even more striking, when compared with the emotional restraint of 4 Maccabees, is Paul's command that the believer "rejoice with those who rejoice" and "mourn with those who mourn" (12:15). At a deep level, one should empathize with fellow believers, sharing in both their joy and tears, because of the intimate relationship all believers share in the single body of Christ (12:4–8; cf. Gal 6:2). It is not that 4 Maccabees counsels a person to spurn his or her fellow human beings or merely to pretend to love them. Rather, in 4 Maccabees, human emotions are viewed more from the vantage point of their potential dangers than their benefits, since even good emotions can corrupt one's ability to reason and thereby turn one away from God. Paul would agree that certain emotional states are dangerous (e.g., anger; cf. Rom 12:19), but he is not as concerned with experiencing positive emotional states like love, joy, and sympathy (cf. Gal 5:22–23).

Renewal from Outside of Oneself. While both texts focus on right thinking leading to right living, a more foundational difference emerges when one examines the grounding for ethical action in the two texts. For Paul, a radical transformation from *outside* of oneself is necessary before one can begin to reason rightly. Throughout Romans Paul has emphasized that a person is unable to make movement toward God apart from the total transformation that comes about by the Spirit's working. For example, Paul describes believers in Christ as those who—solely by the working of God—have been brought from a state of total spiritual death to one of spiritual resurrection in Christ (Rom 6; cf. Eph 2:1–10; 4:20–24; Col 3:1–4). Paul also describes life in union with Christ as freedom from sinful bondage, which has been enacted solely by the Holy Spirit (Rom 8:2). Only "those who live in accordance with the Spirit have their minds set on what the Spirit desires" (8:5). It is the Spirit's working that transforms one's mind, enabling one to submit to God's law and, in so doing, to please God (8:7–8). Paul's emphasis on the necessity of radical spiritual transformation focuses very firmly on the mind. Without the renewal of the mind by the Spirit—a renewal that comes to people *from outside of themselves*—one is unable to exercise discernment in a way that is pleasing to God (12:2). The right thinking, or "sober judgment," necessary for life in the body of Christ is founded firmly on "the faith *God* has distributed to each of you" (12:3, italics added). In other words, right thinking is a *gift* (cf. 12:6).

Right thinking and right living, then, are inextricably linked in 4 Maccabees and Rom 12. We would expect nothing less from two authors whose heritage includes the OT Scriptures, where such a connection is common (e.g., Deut 11:18; Ps 26:2–3; Jer 31:33). The main difference between these two writings is that Paul grounds the right thinking that leads to right living firmly in the comprehensive transformation enacted by the Holy Spirit; in other words, it must come to a believer from *outside* of oneself. Fourth Maccabees sees the resources necessary for right thinking and living as being inherent in the human mind as created by God. These differences are instructive because they reveal how two Greek-speaking Jews from around the same point in history can take divergent paths, even when drawing out the implications of a motif they share.

FOR FURTHER READING

Additional Ancient Texts

For further Stoic resonances in Judaism, see Josephus, *Jewish Antiquities* 2.225, 229; *The Life* 12; Philo, *On the Life of Abraham* 201–204; *Allegorical Interpretation* 1.63–64; *On Flight and Finding* 166–167; *On the Migration of Abraham* 67; *Questions and Answers on Genesis* 2.57. On "body of Christ" language in Paul, see 1 Cor 12:4–31; Eph 1:22–23; 2:11–22. On the necessity of a radical spiritual transformation of the mind, see 1 Cor 2:6–16.

English Translations and Critical Editions

NRSV
Rahlfs, Alfred, and Robert Hanhart, eds. *Septuaginta*. Stuttgart: Deutsche Bibelgesellschaft, 2007.

Secondary Literature

deSilva, David A. *4 Maccabees*. GAP. Sheffield: Sheffield Academic, 1998.

———. *4 Maccabees: Introduction and Commentary on the Greek Text in Codex Sinaiticus*. Leiden: Brill. 2006.

Esler, Philip F. "Paul and Stoicism: Romans 12 as a Test Case." *NTS* 50 (2004): 106–24.

Munzinger, André. *Discerning the Spirits: Theological and Ethical Hermeneutics in Paul*. SNTSMS 140. Cambridge: Cambridge University Press, 2007.

Scott, Ian W. *Paul's Way of Knowing: Story, Experience, and the Spirit*. Grand Rapids: Baker Academic, 2009.

Watson, Francis. "Constructing an Antithesis: Pauline and Other Jewish Perspectives on Divine and Human Agency." Pages 99–116 in *Divine and Human Agency in Paul and His Cultural Environment*. Edited by J. M. G. Barclay and S. J. Gathercole. LNTS 335. London: T&T Clark, 2006.

CHAPTER 17

Josephus and Romans 13:1–14: Providence and Imperial Power

DEAN PINTER

N estled within a larger argument about how fellow Christians should treat one another (Rom 12–15) are Paul's words about how believers should relate to non-Christian society (13:1–7) and conduct themselves within it (13:8–14). In fact, many modern Christians label Rom 13 as Paul's "theology of the state," since this passage contains Paul's most explicit thoughts on how a follower of Jesus ought to live in relation to one's government. But some of Paul's instructions here—such as, "Let everyone be subject to the governing authorities" (13:1)—would undoubtedly have surprised many early Christians. Paul, in his original context, was charging the believers in Rome to obey the very rulers and political powers who, he says elsewhere, "crucified the Lord of glory" (1 Cor 2:8). How could Paul grant the Roman government such authority without compromising his allegiance to Jesus Christ? Other ancient Jews faced the same tensions as Paul, and the Jewish historian **Josephus**, in his work *Jewish War* (*J.W.*), gives us a window into how he and others viewed the Roman state. Read in this context, Paul's views on politics will, in some ways, be seen to be quite typical among some of the Jews who lived under Roman rule.

Josephus

"NO ONE COMES TO RULE APART FROM GOD"

In about AD 30, Jesus of Nazareth was brutally beaten and executed by Roman soldiers at the order of Pontius Pilate, the Roman governor of Judea. But despite the importance of Good Friday for the early Christians, the lives of most first-century Jews remained relatively unaffected. The Jewish people were far more disturbed when, several decades later, at the order of the Roman general Titus, the Jerusalem temple was destroyed and hundreds of deserting Jewish rebels were crucified by the Roman army outside the besieged walls of the capital.[1] These horrific events occurred late in the First Jewish-Roman War (AD 66–70), a major turning point in Jewish history reported comprehensively by Josephus in *Jewish War* (c. AD 75–79). How did this Jewish author perceive the empire that so ruthlessly subjugated his people?

Josephus is commonly remembered as the Jewish general who, shortly after the onset of the Jewish War, defected to the Romans. In fact, at the war's end, when Josephus wrote about the conflict he had witnessed, he did so within the walls of Emperor Vespasian's private residence in Rome. Josephus should be understood, then, as a Jew whose political allegiances were with the Roman Empire.

God Establishes Empires. Despite his loyalties to Rome, however, Josephus remained convinced that it is God who establishes empires and uses governing authorities as his agents. This perspective is expressed often in *J.W.*, whether referring to specific rulers like Emperor Vespasian or to empires in general.

> Vespasian came to think that without divine *providence* he would not have seized power, but that some just fate had placed the sovereignty of the world upon him. For as he remembered the other omens which had everywhere foreshadowed his imperial honors, he recalled the words of Josephus, who had ventured, even in Nero's lifetime, to address him as Emperor.
>
> *JEWISH WAR 4.622–623, italics added*

> For it is evident from all sides that fortune has gone over to [the Romans], and God, who went the round of the nations, now rests sovereign power upon Italy.
>
> *JEWISH WAR 5.367*

In these texts Josephus clearly legitimizes Roman rule. Nonetheless, he also counters imperial propaganda about why and how the Romans came to power.

Imperial ideology was articulated in numerous ways, including literature, triumphal processions, victory coins, monuments (e.g., the Arch of Titus), and architecture (e.g., the Colosseum). By these means, the Romans asserted that

---

1. Josephus writes that so many Jews were crucified that "the land was limited for crosses and crosses limited for the bodies" (*J.W.* 5.451).

they ruled the world because their gods were the strongest, their armies the bravest, and their leaders the smartest. Josephus challenges these assertions, proposing instead that the Romans defeated the Jewish nation because God, the God of Israel, had allowed them to do so. Josephus interprets the circumstances leading up to the war and key events within it as directed by God's power and providence.

Josephus's view on divine providence is apparent, for example, in the words he ascribes to Eleazar, the leader of the Jews who retreated to **Masada**: "Do not attach the blame to yourselves, nor the credit to the Romans, that this war against them has brought destruction to us all; for it was not by their might that they have accomplished these things, but the intervention of some more powerful cause has supplied them with an appearance of victory" (*J.W.* 7.360).

Much like Jeremiah did with his prophecies about the role of the Babylonians, Josephus—who likens his role to that of the prophet (3.391–393; 5.392–393)—argues that the Romans functioned as God's instruments to *purge* the temple and *punish* the Jewish people for their foolish decision to allow a few insurrectionists to lead them into an unsanctioned rebellion. It was in accordance with God's purposes—not that of the Romans—that Jerusalem was destroyed. Josephus reemphasizes this principle when commenting on a prophecy foretelling Jerusalem's destruction: "[It was said that Jerusalem] would be taken when someone would begin to slaughter his own countrymen. Are not the city and the whole Temple full with the corpses of your countrymen? Therefore God, God himself along with the Romans, is bringing fire to purge [the Temple] and ravage this city full of such great defilements" (6.109–110).[2]

Josephus makes two important points: (1) God is providentially in control of the whole scene, such that the Romans are working in concert with God as his agents of chastisement, and (2) the purpose of the judgment is to purge, not eradicate, the temple and God's people.

Honoring the Emperor. Another pertinent element in Josephus's perspective on the state involves taxation. Taxes were a sensitive issue for Jews, since after the war—with their beloved temple destroyed and the Jewish spoils used to construct the Colosseum—every Jew in the empire was required to pay a special tax for the building of Roman shrines. This tax was established to replace the annual half-shekel tax paid by adult Jewish men for the maintenance of the Jerusalem temple, and consequently it induced deep humiliation. Josephus repeatedly mentions the issue of tribute in his work. For example, he

---

2. Cf. *J.W.* 1.10; 5.19, 367–368, 378, 408–412, 442–445; 4.233; 6.109–110, 251.

reports how Herod Agrippa once addressed a Jerusalem crowd on the edge of revolt due to the excesses of Florus, the Roman procurator of Judea (AD 64–66). Agrippa warns the crowd that a failure to pay tribute to Caesar would be considered an act of war against the Romans. His counsel is direct: "Pay your taxes" (J.W. 2.403–404). Unfortunately, the Jews did not heed this advice, and Josephus recounts that Agrippa was expelled from Jerusalem shortly afterward.

Closely linked with the failure to pay taxes is a final incendiary act on the part of the Jewish rebels: the cessation of twice-daily sacrifices (2.409) that were customarily offered on behalf of "Caesar and the people of Rome" (2.197). Josephus concludes that the failure to honor the Romans in this way "laid the foundation of the war against the Romans"in AD 66 (2.409). Thus, in Josephus's account, there is a close relationship between paying tribute and honoring the emperor and the Roman people.

Romans 13:1–14

"THERE IS NO AUTHORITY EXCEPT THAT WHICH GOD HAS ESTABLISHED"

Paul's theological perspective on the state is quite similar to that of Josephus. But while Josephus wrote seven *volumes* on the Jewish War, Paul wrote a slim seven *verses* on how Christians should relate to Rome. It is important to realize, however, that Paul's comments about the state in Rom 13:1–7 are embedded within the larger argument of 13:1–14 as well as connected thematically and terminologically to the rest of Rom 12–15.[3] These four chapters are intended to guide the somewhat divided Roman church toward Christian unity as they learn to love one another.

But between his appeals for Christian unity and single-mindedness (12:3–5; 15:5–6), Paul insists the attitudes and actions that believers bring to relationships *within* the church should also characterize their affairs with those *outside* the church. Thus, as they seek to "overcome evil with good" (12:21), believers should be subject to those whom God established to support "good/right"behavior (13:1–4). Moreover, as they aim to "let no debt remain outstanding"(13:8), believers are to "give to everyone what [they] owe,"even paying taxes to the government (13:7). Accordingly, Paul's summary charge to "love your neighbor as yourself" (13:9; cf. Lev 19:18) — the believer's only inexpungible debt (13:8) — serves as much as a pattern for how

---

3.   See, e.g., the repeated mention of honor (12:10; 13:7), judgment (13:2; 14:10–13), and goodness (13:2; 15:2, 14).

they should relate to the state (13:1–7) as for how they should interact with other Christians (12:9–10; 14:15; 15:2). While believers are called to conduct themselves quite differently from unbelieving society ("not in carousing and drunkenness, not in sexual immorality and debauchery, not in dissension and jealousy,"13:13), they, though outsiders, must coexist within the state nonetheless, being ever mindful of the nearness of Christ's return (13:11–14). Precisely how, then, are believers to interact with the state?

Structuring Paul's Argument. Paul's remarks on relating to the state in Rom 13:1–7 are fairly straightforward. He begins with a general appeal (13:1a), supported by three paired arguments/warnings (13:1b–4b), a restatement of the general appeal (13:5–6), and a specific application (13:7). This is illustrated in the following outline.

Paul's Argument in Romans 13:1–7[4]

Verse	Rhetorical Function	Text
13:1a	General/Opening Appeal	Every person *must submit* to the governing authorities
13:1b	Argument 1	*For* every authority is from God
13:2	Warning 1	*Therefore* those who oppose authority oppose God and will incur judgment
13:3a	Argument 2	*For* rulers are a terror to those who do evil, not to those who do good
13:3b	Warning 2	*But* those who do evil will have reason to fear; those who do good will receive praise
13:4a	Argument 3	*For* God's servant in authority supports the good
13:4b	Warning 3	*But* the evil one will face the fear of the ruler's sword
13:5	Transition by Restated Appeal	*Therefore it is necessary to submit* on account of God's wrath and personal conscience
13:6	Practical Application	*For* this is why you pay taxes to God's servants
13:7	Specific/Final Appeal	*Pay* whatever you owe, whether taxes, fear, or honor

---

4. Cf. Mikael Tellbe, *Paul between Synagogue and State: Christians, Jews, and Civic Authorities in 1 Thessalonians, Romans, and Philippians* (ConBNT 43; Stockholm: Almqvist & Wiksell, 2001), 174–75.

A number of points stand out. Two imperatives bracket the passage, namely a general exhortation to submit to authorities (13:1) and a specific command to pay one's dues (13:7). Within this framework, the passage falls thematically into two sections. The first section (13:1–4) is structured by the interplay between three parties: (1) the governing authorities, (2) "everyone" who submits to the authorities, and (3) those who oppose the authorities. The appeal for everyone to be subject to rulers has two bases. The first is theological: God appoints the authorities, and resistance to them equates to opposition to God (13:1b–2). The second is practical: the authorities will punish "you" (singular) if you do evil (13:3–4).

The language of "good/right" and "evil/wrong" is key to the entire exhortative portion of the letter and roots this passage into that material. Romans 13:5 functions as a transitional hinge between the general argument of the passage and the particular issue raised in 13:6–7. It draws the argument to a head with the inferential conjunction "therefore" (13:5) and a restatement of the appeal "to submit to the authorities" as the basis for believers paying taxes (13:6). The opening phrase "This is also" (13:6) draws the practical application of the appeal, arguments, and warnings of 13:1–4 to a climax with the conclusion: "you [therefore] pay taxes." Romans 13:6 reiterates the first and third arguments—the authorities are God's servants and devote themselves to promoting good and restraining evil. The brief focus on relations to the state closes in 13:7 with both the second imperative ("give to everyone") and the specific appeal ("what you owe them")—which applies as much to taxes as to respect and honor.

Undifferentiated Authorities. In light of this, a number of important observations can be made. The first is elementary, but significant: Nowhere in the passage is Rome, the emperor, or any individual office ever mentioned—they are simply part of the undifferentiated "authorities" (13:1). These comprise imperial authorities, including the emperor, but Paul describes them as part of the undifferentiated, finite political powers that derive their existence from God.

God Authorizes Authorities. This leads to a second observation: It is God who sustains and authorizes the political authorities. While the emperor and his political subordinates go unnamed, God is mentioned six times. Political authorities may be feared and honored, but this is qualified by the fact that they are, according to Paul, servants of God (13:4). This is consistent with other perspectives within Jewish tradition, including that of Josephus. In fact, Paul's observation that "there is no authority except that which God has established" (13:1) parallels Josephus's declaration that "no one comes to rule apart from

God" (*J.W.* 2.140). In contrast to Josephus's lengthy commentary on the role of the Romans acting within God's purposes, Paul is decidedly minimalist in his description of how and why God establishes political authorities. Nonetheless, Paul's few words on governing authorities, when set against the likes of Josephus, fall within a common pattern of opinion. For both of them, and many fellow Jews, God is the primary agent in the universe, and it is by his power and for his purposes that kingdoms are established.

Inexhaustive Instructions. Third, the point of Paul's instructions is to shape conduct, not provide a theology of the state. Paul does not speculate about situations when rulers are unjust or what those under their authority should do in such cases. Rather, he reflects a common Jewish understanding of the limited but useful role of the state operating under authority appointed by God.

Honoring the Emperor. If Paul's opinion on God's providential oversight of political authority is in continuity with Josephus and other strands of Jewish tradition, it is not surprising that he reflects another aspect of this tradition when he encourages Roman Christians to give honor to governing authorities and to pay taxes. In particular, the payment of taxes was one of the few direct means of contact Christians living on the margins of Roman society had with the state. Thus, along with Josephus, there is nothing exceptional in Paul's exhortation, "Give to everyone what you owe them: If you owe taxes, pay taxes; if revenue, then revenue; if respect, then respect; if honor, then honor" (Rom 13:7). It is notable that while Paul makes no appeal for believers "to offer sacrifices for the welfare of Rome," as does Josephus (*J.W.* 2.197; cf. *Ag. Ap.* 2.75–78), neither does he mention offering prayers for the emperor or civic rulers (cf. 1 Tim 2:1–2). However, when it comes to relating to foreign overlords, both Josephus and Paul bring together the notions of taxation with respect and honor.

Both early Christians and post–AD 70 Jews knew that the "sword" of Rome had been meted out against objects at the center of their respective theological worlds: Roman soldiers tortured and crucified the believers' **Messiah**; Roman armies devastated Jerusalem and destroyed the Jewish temple. How did devout followers of Jesus and Torah-observant Jews reflect on the Roman state and their relationship to it? For Josephus, pagan rulers were significant in bringing about the punishing and purging of the Jewish nation for allowing a few rebels to bring them to a war that would destroy their sacred city and hallowed temple. Like his fellow Jew and near contemporary Josephus, Paul thought that governing authorities were appointed by divine providence and that even pagan ones were "servant[s] of God." He therefore instructed Roman Christians to offer respect and honor to these authorities and to maintain one of the few direct interactions they had with the state, namely, the payment of taxes.

These few verses on the state are rooted in Paul's broader vision for Christian ethics in Rom 12–15. The passage not only reiterates his emphasis on doing the "good" (12:21; 13:3–4), but connects, and even subjects, one's debt *to the state* to the believer's more important obligation in life: "the continuing debt to love *one another*" (13:8, italics added). It is more important because, for Paul, there is more to life than politics. In fact, the Christian community is not conceived within the primary context of the state. Rather, life within the church (13:8–10, picking up 12:1–13), in light of the coming salvation (13:11–14), is the primary context in which the state finds its place.

FOR FURTHER READING

Additional Ancient Texts

For the Jewish consensus that God gives political rulers their power, see Sirach 10:4; *Letter of Aristeas* 224; Wisdom of Solomon 6:3; Philo, *On the Embassy to Gaius* 280. For Paul on the authorities and citizenship, see 1 Cor 15:20–28; Phil 3:17–21; 1 Tim 2:1–2.

English Translations and Critical Editions

Josephus. Translated by H. St. J. Thackerary et al. 10 vols. LCL. Cambridge, MA: Harvard University Press, 1926–65.

Secondary Literature

Barclay, John M. G. "Why the Roman Empire Was Insignificant to Paul." Pages 363–87 in *Pauline Churches and Diaspora Jews*. WUNT 275. Tübingen: Mohr Siebeck, 2011.

Engberg-Pedersen, Troels. "Paul's Stoicizing Politics in Romans 12–13: The Role of 13.1–10 in the Argument." *JSNT* 29 (2006): 163–72.

Harrison, James R. *Paul and the Imperial Authorities at Thessalonica and Rome: A Study in the Conflict of Ideology.* WUNT 273. Tübingen: Mohr Siebeck, 2011.

Mason, Steve. *Josephus and the New Testament.* Peabody, MA: Hendrickson, 2003.

McKnight, Scot, and Joseph B. Modica, eds. *Jesus Is Lord, Caesar Is Not: Evaluating Empire in New Testament Studies.* Downers Grove, IL: IVP Academic, 2013.

CHAPTER 18

1 Maccabees and Romans 14:1–15:13: Embodying the Hospitable Kingdom Community

NIJAY K. GUPTA

Romans has long been hailed as one of Paul's most theological and even systematic letters. However, not everything in the letter is simply a timeless truth for every audience. Romans 14:1–15:13 appears in an extended set of teachings that inform the Christian life of obedience (Rom 12:1–15:13), and yet the passage is addressing tensions among the Christians specifically *in Rome*. Moreover, the issues at hand seem to concern religious purity. Now, modern Western believers are no strangers to church divisions and factional splits, but the central points of tension in Rome appear to relate to food preferences (14:2), observance of particular holy days (14:5), and perhaps also the use of wine (14:21). How does Paul set out to resolve the tension?

Paul separates the people involved into two groups: those who are "weak" in faith and those who are "strong" in faith. Paul does not represent either group as completely right or wrong, though he includes himself among the "strong" (15:1). His focus, instead, is on the attitude of "the strong" (see 14:1; 15:1), who have been treating "the weak" with contempt and judgment. With both sides in view, Paul urges each one to make choices regarding purity that lead to a clean conscience in their own reckoning and to foster unity and other-regard, with the example of Christ in mind (15:1–9).

Probably many informed readers of Romans will know that the OT law prohibits the consumption of unclean foods (e.g., pork; see Lev 11) and requires the observation of holy days (e.g., the Sabbath; see Lev 23). Many such readers will also remember that Jesus declared "all foods clean" (Mark 7:19; cf. Acts 10:1–16) and that the Sabbath was designed to serve humans, and not to restrict them (Mark 2:27). But the complexity of the ostensible situation in Rome seems to require contextual information beyond the above-mentioned assumptions. For example, why are *vegetables* singled out? And why is this provoking such judgmentalism and tension?

While we are not able to reconstruct, in detail, anything more about the *specific* situation among the Roman Christians, appeal to knowledge gained by 1 Maccabees (as well as other **Second Temple Jewish** texts) can help us to interpret Rom 14:1–15:13 in its sociohistorical context. By the account of many scholars, the events narrated in 1 Maccabees mark the beginning of a distinctive Jewish religious identity, and food habits are critically important in the demarcation of this identity.

1 Maccabees
"THEY CHOSE TO DIE RATHER THAN TO BE DEFILED BY FOOD"

In 1 Cor 8:8 Paul says, "Food does not bring us near to God." While most Protestant Christians today easily consent to this notion of the irrelevance of food choices to religious devotion, it was quite another thing for Jews in the first century. For most Jews, food was not merely stuff you put in your mouth for nourishment or enjoyment. Food choices (and limitations) were a matter of religious purity and distinctive of one's social and religious identity.

One can better understand the full weight of the seriousness of how Jews treated their commitment to God's commands about dietary purity by looking at the story of the Maccabees. First Maccabees, a text that appears in the OT **Apocrypha**, was written about a century before the birth of Christ and narrates, especially in the early chapters, the rule of a Greek tyrant named **Antiochus IV (Epiphanes)** who hated the Jews and their religion. We are told he plundered the Jerusalem temple (1:21–23), murdered Jews (1:24), set Jerusalem on fire (1:30), and imprisoned many of God's people (1:32). We do not know exactly why Antiochus despised Judaism as much as he did, but we are told he strove for uniformity in (Greek) culture and religion throughout his dominion (1:42). Out of fear, many Jews submitted to his demands and "adopted his religion; they sacrificed to idols and profaned the Sabbath" (1:43). Antiochus put an end to the Jews' sacrificial worship and even outlawed circumcision (1:48), with the hopes that "they would forget the Torah and change all the regulations" (1:49). There were those, however, who resisted. When the author of 1 Maccabees summarizes this resilience, he states: "But many in Israel stood strong and were resolved in their own minds not to eat what is impure. They chose to die rather than to be defiled by food or to desecrate the

holy **covenant**; and they did die" (1:62–63). It became clear in these events that
food became a social dividing line for devout Jews. The word "zeal" appears in
1 Maccabees as representative of Jewish passion for **covenantal** obedience, of
which food purity became distinctive (2:24, 26–27, 50, 54, 58).

In the second chapter of the book, an account is given of a Jew of priestly
descent named Mattathias, who lived in Modein, a stone's throw from Jerusalem. When Antiochus sent his officers to force pagan worship publicly in
Modein, Mattathias was singled out as a leader and brought forth to commit
apostasy (2:17). Not only did Mattathias refuse to acquiesce, but he killed a
fellow Jew who had given in to the demands of the Greek officers (2:23–24).
This incident incited a revolt against Antiochus that was initiated, in large part,
by Mattathias's sons, who were led by Judas Maccabeus.

Fourth Maccabees also records the persecution of Jews under Antiochus,
but this text's focus is on a Jewish philosophy of virtue. In chapter 5, Antiochus
engages with a Jewish leader, scribe, and priest named Eleazar. On the same
threat of execution we saw in 1 Maccabees, Eleazar takes the opportunity to
engage in philosophical debate. Antiochus encourages Eleazar to eat unclean
pork and save himself pain in his old age. He points out the weakness of the
Jewish philosophy and desires Eleazar to transcend to a more logical (Greek)
path (5:6–13).

Eleazar dared to parry Antiochus's first argument by explaining that
Jews trust the one true God, and that the food restrictions have their
rationale in his higher purposes. In this particular text, the rationale given
involves God's knowing what is proper to human nature and what is best
for their well-being (spiritual as well as physical): "These things which
are favorable to our souls, he has instructed us to eat; but those which are
troublesome to them he has forbidden" (5:26). He ends the first discourse
by saying, "Mouth! You will neither defile my old age, nor my long life of
obedience to the law. My fathers will welcome me as pure, not having shrunk
before your ultimatum, even to death. You may tyrannize the ungodly; but you
will not act as master over my thoughts about religion, either by your arguments or your actions" (5:36–38).

Much more could be said, but here we shall sum up what can be gleaned,
especially about food purity, from the above material.

Zeal. Because of the Jewish conflict with Antiochus IV, a clear dividing line
was drawn between those Jews who succumbed to **Hellenistic** assimilation
and those who maintained the traditions and covenant demands of the fore-
fathers. Thus, keeping the Torah's dietary regulations (and even stricter habits)
became a key indicator of true devotion to God. It was not that other aspects

of religious life were devalued, but that this one, in particular, was seen to be a mark of Jewish covenantal obedience, of zeal for God's law.

Identity. In large part due to the **Maccabean Crisis**, adherence to Jewish food laws became a signal of not only religious fidelity but also of in-group membership. Alongside circumcision and Sabbath keeping, maintaining a "holy diet" was a key way for Jews to strengthen their social identity.

Self-Control. Finally, the Jewish food laws were understood by many adherents as a prophylactic means of resisting indulgence and hedonism. Their ascetic consumption practices could be defended as a move toward self-mastery.

Romans 14:1–15:13

"NOTHING IS UNCLEAN IN ITSELF"

As we go back to Romans and inspect more closely the relationships among the house churches to which Paul wrote, we can gain a better sense of why dietary issues were such a big deal. Most scholars believe the original community of believers in Rome was founded by Jewish believers in Jesus. Over time, no doubt, Gentiles came to faith, and this would have led to differences in habits, traditions, and perspectives. It is quite possible that "the weak" in Rom 14:1–15:13 represent Jewish Christians who desired to maintain traditional practices related to meals and the Sabbath. "The strong," then, were primarily Gentile Christians who, like Paul, saw **the Christ event** as the beginning of a new era in which foods were no longer categorized according to purity.

Based on the above discussion of the Maccabean Crisis, we can see why Christians of Jewish descent would have found the idea of forsaking food traditions to be preposterous. First, they would have known obedience to dietary commands as a fundamental way of honoring God ("zeal"). Second, they would have seen food regulations as indicative of a unique social identity for God's people ("identity"). Third, many Jews would have seen the idea of dissolving food-purity expectations as a major step toward hedonism ("self-control").

Against the backdrop of the galvanization of a unique "Jewish identity" in the exilic and postexilic period, and in the context of ongoing ridicule and harassment from outsiders regarding their scrupulous dedication to particular rules, what stands out in Romans is Paul's counsel to the divided Christian community.[1] I now want to address how Paul handles, in Rom 14:1–15:13, the three areas regarding food and Jewish piety mentioned above.

---

1. See Richard N. Longenecker, *Introducing Romans: Critical Issues in Paul's Most Famous Letter* (Grand Rapids: Eerdmans, 2011).

Zeal in Christ. While first-century Jews considered strict devotion to food laws and traditions a major form of obedience to the one God, Paul makes a number of startling claims regarding true worship of God as revealed in the work of Jesus Christ. First, Paul boldly claims that "nothing is unclean in itself" (14:14; cf. 14:17, 20). This could have been perceived as a denial of Torah and perhaps even the rejection of Israel's God, but Paul is quick to establish that he has not succumbed to nihilism. Rather, each person is individually liable to God (14:4, 10–12), and it is not the food that matters, but the condition of one's heart (14:6–8).[2]

Purity is still a factor for Paul, but it comes down to the conviction of the conscience (14:5), not the recipe of the meal. Furthermore, Paul repeatedly affirms that God is most honored by zeal for respecting and loving the other (14:18). Indeed, the whole section ends with an extended focus on how Christ came to accept both Jew *and* Gentile *as they are* (15:6–13).

Identity. That takes us to our second concern. Many Second Temple Jews were concerned with safeguarding their social identity as *the people of God,* holy to the Lord. This concern with purity and holiness amounted (in many cases) to a theology of distinction—*we are other.* Without desiring to obliterate difference, Paul promotes a theology of *embrace.* That is, each group ("weak" or "strong") should take the focus away from being "right" and expend their energy on welcoming one another. This open-arms policy is not tolerance for the sake of tolerance, but a conscious reduplication of the hospitable character of God (14:3) and the all-embracing invitation of the cross (15:7).

What, then, makes Christians a distinct group? How can you tell them apart, if not by things like food habits? You will know them by their imitation of Christ (a symbol of discipleship), which demonstrates itself in unifying and upbuilding love (14:15, 19; cf. John 13:35).

Self-Control. But if you eat whatever you want, how does that not devolve into gluttony (a Jewish interlocutor might ask)? Paul does not directly engage that question, but, for Paul, "weakness" is not focused on the weak will regarding food, but on the "weakness" regarding a faith that has not assimilated the full implications of Christ's work in the new covenant (14:1). More importantly for the concern about self-mastery, though, is Paul's reinterpretation of the idea of "pleasure" and "pleasing." Paul agrees that one's aim should not be simply to please oneself (15:1).

---

2.   One can easily note echoes of Mark 7:18–19, where Jesus claims the focus should be on what comes out of the person (in righteous words and actions), not on the food that enters in.

The kind of food-based divisions that some were promoting, though, ended up fueling self-advocacy and hubris. Instead, Paul endorsed the kind of eating that aims to protect the consciences of others and to please *them*. Christ becomes the paramount model: "For even Christ did not please himself, but, as it is written:'The insults of those who insult you have fallen on me'" (15:3). Paul virtually transfers the concern over avoidance of hedonistic self-indulgence from the realm of food to the context of hospitality.

To conclude, some knowledge of Jewish-Gentile relationships in early Judaism aids the reader of Romans in better understanding why food was such a hot-button issue in the Roman community of believers. While first-century Jews used food rules to communicate devotional zeal, in-group identity, and the virtue of self-control, Paul saw divisions over meal practices to be disruptive to a hospitable community in Christ.

FOR FURTHER READING

Additional Ancient Texts

For further study of Jewish texts that demonstrate the important relationship of food, purity, and covenantal obedience, see Dan 1:1–21; *Jubilees* 22:16; Philo, *On the Life of Moses* 1.278; Philo, *On the Special Laws* 4.100–131; *Letter of Aristeas* 139, 142; Josephus, *Jewish Antiquities* 11.346; Tobit 1:10–12; Judith 12; *Joseph and Aseneth* 7:1; 8:5; cf. Diodorus Siculus, *Bibliotheca historica* 34.1–35.1.4

Other relevant Pauline texts include 1 Cor 8:1–13; Gal 2:11–21; Col 2:16–23.

English Translations and Critical Editions

NETS

Anderson, H. "4 Maccabees (First Century AD): A New Translation and Introduction."Pages 531–64 in vol. 2 of *The Old Testament Pseudepigrapha*. Edited by James H. Charlesworth. Garden City, NY: Doubleday, 1985.

Kappler, W. *Maccabaeorum liber I*. Septuaginta 9.1. Göttingen:Vandenhoeck & Ruprecht, 1967.

Secondary Literature

Barclay, John M. G. "'Do We Undermine the Law?': A Study of Romans 14.1–15.6."Pages 287–308 in *Paul and the Mosaic Law*. Edited by James D. G. Dunn. Grand Rapids: Eerdmans, 2001.

Bartlett, John R. *1 Maccabees*. GAP. Sheffield: Sheffield Academic, 1998.

Dunn, James D. G. *The Partings of the Ways: Between Christianity and Judaism and Their Significance for the Character of Christianity*. London: SCM, 1991.

Freidenreich, David M. "'They Kept Themselves Apart in the Matter of Food': The Nature and Significance of Hellenistic Jewish Food Practices." Pages 31–46 in *Foreigners and Their Food: Constructing Otherness in Jewish, Christian, and Islamic Law*. Berkeley: University of California Press, 2011.

MacDonald, Nathan. "You Are How You Eat: Food and Identity in the Postexilic Period." Pages 196–218 in *Not Bread Alone: The Uses of Food in the Old Testament*. Oxford: Oxford University Press, 2008.

Toney, Carl N. *Paul's Inclusive Ethic: Resolving Community Conflicts and Promoting Mission in Romans 14–15*. WUNT 2.252. Tübingen: Mohr Siebeck, 2008.

CHAPTER 19

Tobit and Romans 15:14–33: Jewish Almsgiving and the Collection

DAVID E. BRIONES

In Rom 15:14–33 Paul reflects on the completion of his apostolic ministry from Jerusalem to Illyricum (15:19) and maps out a future missionary endeavor westward toward Spain, requiring the assistance of the Christians in Rome (15:24, 28). Before that happens, however, he needs to complete an essential apostolic task: the collection for the Jerusalem believers (15:25–28), a theological and practical effort to take financial gifts collected from predominantly Gentile churches to distribute to poor Jewish Christians in Jerusalem. Undergirding, guiding, and even motivating this act of generosity, from Paul's perspective, is a rich theology of giving, one which includes God as a third party in the bestowal of gifts. In other words, the Jerusalem collection was not merely a two-way exchange between Gentile churches and destitute Jewish Christians. Paul sees God playing a critical role. Paul therefore configures the collection in Rom 15 as a three-way relationship, with God giving *to* the poor saints *through* the generous gifts of Paul's churches.

But this tripartite gift-giving dynamic is not unique to Paul, nor is it distinctively Christian. In early Judaism, those who participated in almsgiving—the practice of giving money or provisions to people in need—also envisioned God as playing a vital role in one's gifts to the poor. And this tangible display of generosity receives extensive treatment in the book of Tobit.[1] Some scholars have argued that Paul, rooted in his Jewish heritage, simply adopts the familiar method of almsgiving in his collection efforts. But a close comparison of almsgiving in Tobit and the collection in Rom 15—especially the gift-giving

---

1. For a general introduction to the book of Tobit, see chapter 15 (Goodrich).

dynamics and underlying theology attending each practice—will lead us to conclude that Paul's perspective on giving is *similar to and yet distinct from* Jewish almsgiving in Tobit.

Tobit

"ALMSGIVING DELIVERS FROM DEATH"

The term "almsgiving" appears at the beginning and end of Tobit, thus forming an **inclusio**. At the beginning of the story, the protagonist, Tobit, is described as a man who "walked in the ways of truth and righteousness all the days of [his] life" by performing "many acts of charity" (Tob 1:3). Then, at the story's end, Tobit delivers a final speech to his son, Tobias, encouraging him to "serve God faithfully and do what is pleasing in his sight," specifically by "giving alms" (14:8). Within this inclusio are three key texts that disclose the gift-giving dynamics and underlying theology of almsgiving:

> [5] All your days, my son, remember the Lord and do not desire to sin or to transgress his commandments. Live righteously all the days of your life, and do not proceed in the ways of unrighteousness, [6] because those who practice the truth will prosper in all their works. To all those who practice righteousness [7] give alms from your possessions, and do not let your eye begrudge the gift when you make it. Do not turn your face away from anyone who is poor, and the face of God will not be turned away from you. [8] If you have many possessions, give alms from them in proportion; if few, do not be afraid to give according to the little you have, [9] for you will be laying up a good treasure for yourself against the day of necessity, [10] because almsgiving delivers from death and prevents you from going into the Darkness. [11] For almsgiving, among all who practice it, is an excellent gift in the presence of the Most High.
>
> *TOBIT 4:5–11*

> [16] Give from your food supply to the hungry, and some of your clothing to the naked. Give from your abundance as alms, and do not let your eye begrudge your giving of alms. [17] Place your bread on the grave of those who are righteous, but give none to sinners.
>
> *TOBIT 4:16–17*

> [8] Prayer with fasting is good, but better than both is almsgiving with righteousness. A little with righteousness is better than wealth with

unrighteousness. It is better to give alms than to store up gold. [9] For almsgiving delivers from death and purges away every sin. Those who give alms will enjoy a full life, [10] but those who commit sin and do wrong are enemies of their own life.

TOBIT 12:8–10

Gift-Dynamics. Five gift-dynamics of Jewish almsgiving can be highlighted in these passages.

1. A person should not give begrudgingly (4:7), since, whether a person is rich or poor, gifts should be made according to their means (4:8), being drawn from their "surplus" (4:16).

2. Alms should only be given to "those who practice righteousness" (4:6), not "sinners" (4:17).

3. And yet the giving of alms is obligatory. Though subtle, linking almsgiving with the "commandments" (4:5), the forgiveness of sins (12:9), and the means of escaping "the day of necessity" and "Darkness" (4:10) shows how, for Tobit, almsgiving is mandatory for devout Jews.

4. Almsgiving is also likened to an "offering" in God's presence (4:11).

5. In fact, God—not the poor recipient of alms—is the one who gives a return to the almsgiver. He rewards charitable acts with forgiveness of sins (12:9), present prosperity (4:6; 12:9), and even eternal security (4:9), with the result that turning one's "face" from the poor will subsequently lead to God turning his "face" from that person (4:7; cf. 13:6; 14:10; Prov 19:17). Implicit in this gift-dynamic is the element of self-interest (4:6–7, 9–10; 12:8–9), but this self-interest is mutually advantageous rather than exploitative. The giver helps the needy and thereby honors God, while reaping a benefit for oneself.

Three-Way Relational Pattern. Together, these gift-dynamics reveal an embedded theological relational pattern, a three-way relationship between the giver, the beneficiary, and God, as illustrated in the following diagram:[2]

---

2. Every diagram in this chapter contains an arrow with a solid line, which represents the *initial* gift, and an arrow with a dotted line, which represents the *return* gift.

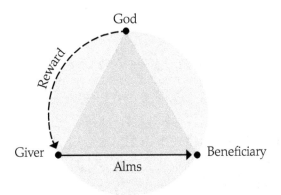

Interestingly, however, the beneficiary plays a minor role in the relationship. Gifts are indeed given to the poor beneficiary, but they do not bind the giver and beneficiary in a relationship of giving and receiving (i.e., reciprocity). God alone repays the almsgiver. Moreover, givers draw from their own "surplus" (4:16); they themselves are the source of their gifts. Ultimately, this gift-giving paradigm most likely stems from Tobit's underlying **Deuteronomic theology**, wherein Israelites are required to bestow gifts on the poor in *response* to what God has done for them in the exodus event (cf. Deut 10:17 – 19; 24:10 – 22).

Romans 15:14 – 33
"The Gentiles ... owe it to the Jews to share with them"

Before determining points of convergence and divergence between almsgiving and the collection, we need to set the context of Rom 15:14 – 33. Paul, in the preceding passage (14:1 – 15:13), attempts to reconcile two groups in the church whose differences prevent them from participating together in corporate worship. This prepares the groundwork for Paul's discussion in 15:14 – 33 on the Jerusalem collection, since this charitable project is an attempt to alleviate the relational tension between Jews and Gentiles by drawing them into corporate worship of God (cf. 2 Cor 9:11 – 15). Paul focuses on the collection in 15:25 – 28.

> [25] Now, however, I am on my way to Jerusalem in the service of the Lord's people there. [26] For Macedonia and Achaia were pleased to make a contribution for the poor among the Lord's people in Jerusalem. [27] They were pleased to do it, and indeed they owe it to them. For if the Gentiles have shared in the Jews' spiritual blessings, they owe it to the Jews to share with them their material blessings. [28] So after I have completed this task and have made sure that they have received this contribution, I will go to Spain and visit you on the way.

Gift-Dynamics. Five gift-dynamics in this text are almost identical to those in Jewish almsgiving.

1. Gifts should be given voluntarily, not begrudgingly; for the Macedonians and Achaians were "pleased" to contribute their finances (Rom 15:26–27 [2x]; cf. 2 Cor 8:3, 10–12; 9:5, 7).

2. The proper recipients are principally Jewish Christians (Rom 15:25–26, 31; cf. 1 Cor 16:1; 2 Cor 8:4; 9:1, 12).

3. Paul couches the collection in cultic language: "offering" (Rom 15:16), "share with" (Rom 15:27), "completed" (Rom 15:28; cf. 2 Cor 8:6, 11), "service of the Lord's people" (Rom 15:25; cf. 2 Cor 9:12).[3]

4. Against modern sensibilities of gift giving, Paul, like Tobit, perceives the collection as an obligation.

5. Indeed, the Gentiles "owe" the poor Jerusalem saints a *material* return for the *spiritual* riches they have received in Christ (Rom 15:27). This exchange unveils a central theological theme in Romans. The spiritual blessings—which are expressed in the single gift of grace in **the Christ event**—belong first to Jewish Christians, being a fulfillment of the promises made to Israel (1:16; 4:13–16; 11:17–24; 15:7–8). Gentiles, who share in these blessings (cf. 11:17–18), should therefore express their indebtedness and thanksgiving by reciprocating material gifts.

Three-Way Relational Pattern. There remains one final point of convergence: God is a vital third party in this exchange between Jews and Gentiles. This element, however, cannot be detected by merely reading Rom 15:25–28 in isolation from its wider literary context. In fact, the relational pattern emerging from this text alone would resemble the following diagram:[4]

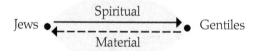

Nevertheless, God's crucial role in this exchange becomes apparent when 15:25–28 is read in conjunction with 15:15–19 (italics added):

---

3. For a close examination of the cultic language in Rom 15:14–32, see David J. Downs, *The Offering of the Gentiles* (WUNT 2.248; Tübingen: Mohr Siebeck, 2008), 146–60.
4. Every diagram in this chapter contains an arrow with a solid line, which represents the *initial* gift, and an arrow with a dotted line, which represents the *return* gift

¹⁵ Yet I have written you quite boldly on some points to remind you of them again, because of the grace God gave me ¹⁶ to be a minister of Christ Jesus to the Gentiles. He gave me the priestly duty of proclaiming the gospel of God, so that the Gentiles might become an *offering* acceptable to God, sanctified by the Holy Spirit.

¹⁷ Therefore I glory in Christ Jesus in my service to God. ¹⁸ I will not venture to speak of anything except what Christ has accomplished through me in leading the Gentiles to obey God by what I have said and done — ¹⁹ by the power of signs and wonders, through the power of the Spirit of God. So from Jerusalem all the way around to Illyricum, I have fully proclaimed the gospel of Christ.

Many interpreters neglect 15:15 – 19 when examining the Jerusalem collection, primarily because they understand the "offering" presented to God in 15:16 to be Paul's Gentile converts (as suggested by the NIV). However, it is better to translate the phrase as "the offering of/from the Gentiles" and to understand its referent as the Gentiles' gift to the poor Jerusalem saints rather than their own obedient lives.[5] Paul clearly values the obedience of the Gentiles, but not to the exclusion of their literal "offering" or "gift" to the poor. That said, 15:15 – 19 complements 15:25 – 28 insofar as the former passage presents a relational pattern assumed in the latter.

Beyond this, a tripartite relationship between God, Paul, and the Gentiles can be discerned in 15:15 – 19. "Grace" or "gift," which is none other than "the gospel of God" (15:16) and "gospel of Christ" (15:19), proceeds *from* God (15:15), *to* and *through* Paul (15:15, 18), and *reaches* the Gentiles (15:16). The gospel, then, with the help of the Spirit (15:16, 19), works in the hearts of the Gentiles to produce an "offering" *to* God (15:16). This can be diagrammed as follows:[6]

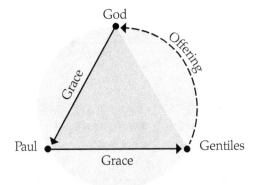

5.   See Downs, *Offering of the Gentiles*, 149–50.
6.   Every diagram in this chapter contains an arrow with a solid line, which represents the *initial* gift, and an arrow with a dotted line, which represents the *return* gift

One surprising element of this relational pattern is that the Gentiles' offering *to God* is simultaneously a gift *to the poor Jerusalem saints*. This is evident in 15:25–28, where one discovers the same relational dynamic. The churches in Macedonia and Achaia, according to Paul, were eager to contribute to the collection (15:26) since "the Gentiles"—not just the specific churches mentioned above—share in the "spiritual blessings" mediated *through* the Jews. In response, the Gentiles reciprocate by returning "material blessings" *to* the poor Jerusalem saints (15:27). Standing above both parties, however, is God, the ultimate giver of all gifts (cf. 11:36)—whether "spiritual" ("all are justified freely by his *grace*," 3:24, italics added) or "material" ("we want you to know about the *grace* that God has given the Macedonian churches ... [T]heir overflowing joy and their extreme poverty welled up in *rich generosity*," 2 Cor 8:1–2, italics added).

It follows, then, that God mediates material blessings *through* Paul *and* the Gentiles. Strikingly, Paul understands his agency as joined to that of the Gentiles in Rom 15:16–18, for the collection is Paul's "service" *to God* while, at the same time, the Gentiles' "offering" and "obedience" *to God*. Viewed together, their individual agencies form a united front to mediate material gifts to destitute saints, primarily because nothing is given *to God* that is not first received *from God*. Consequently, holding 15:15–19 and 15:25–28 together, the following relational pattern finally emerges:[7]

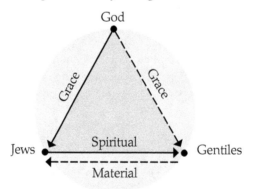

Points of Divergence. While there are many important differences between Paul and Tobit, two specific points of divergence should be noted. The first is that, unlike in Tobit, Paul suggests that God not only *rewards* human givers but also *provides the means* to give. It is he who grants Jews and Gentiles access to his surplus of goods rather than they who draw from their own resources. Following from this, the second point of divergence is that the inclusion of God as a vertical party

---

7.   Every diagram in this chapter contains an arrow with a solid line, which represents the *initial* gift, and an arrow with a dotted line, which represents the *return* gift

draws horizontal parties into a reciprocal, interdependent fellowship of gift and of need. In Tobit, the giving of alms did not establish relational ties between the giver and the poor recipient; reciprocal relations only existed between the giver and God. But, in Paul, God operates as the single, divine source in whom both Jews and Gentiles have a share. To illustrate this using Rom 11:17, just as the Gentiles became joint sharers with the Jewish people of the root of the olive tree, so too the Jews and Gentiles now equally share in and draw from a common source of grace. As such, the anticipated outcome of the collection, contrary to many, does not solely concern unity between Jews and Gentiles. Unity is merely the beginning of the more essential task of developing an intimate, mutually enhancing fellowship (cf. Rom 1:11 – 12; 12:1 – 21; 15:7; 2 Cor 1:3 – 11). In other words, unity is the means, but growing as an interdependent community "in Christ" is the ultimate goal.

For Further Reading

Additional Ancient Texts

On the importance of almsgiving, see Sirach 3:30 – 4:10; 7:10, 32 – 36; 12:1 – 7; 29:8 – 13; 35:17 – 26. For Pauline texts on giving, see 1 Cor 16:1 – 4; 2 Cor 8 – 9.

English Translations and Critical Editions

NETS

NRSV

Hanhart, Robert. *Tobit*. Septuaginta 8.5. Göttingen: Vandenhoeck & Ruprecht, 1983.

Weeks, Stuart, Simon Gathercole, and Loren Stuckenbruck, eds. *The Book of Tobit: Texts from the Principal Ancient and Medieval Traditions with Synopsis, Concordances, and Annotated Texts in Aramaic, Hebrew, Greek, Latin, and Syriac.* FSBP 3. Berlin: de Gruyter, 2004.

Secondary Literature

Apostle Paul: A Polite Bribe — An Apostle's Final Bid. DVD. Directed by Robert Orlando. The Nexus Project, 2014.

Briones, David E. *Paul's Financial Policy: A Socio-Theological Approach.* LNTS 494. London: T&T Clark, 2013.

Downs, David J. *The Offering of the Gentiles.* WUNT 2.248. Tübingen: Mohr Siebeck, 2008.

Fitzmyer, Joseph A. *Tobit.* CEJL. Berlin: de Gruyter, 2003.

Garrison, Roman. *Redemptive Almsgiving in Early Christianity.* JSNTSup 77. Sheffield: Sheffield Academic, 1993.

Orlando, Robert. *Apostle Paul: A Polite Bribe.* Eugene, OR: Cascade, 2014.

CHAPTER 20

Synagogue Inscriptions and Romans 16:1–27: Women and Christian Ministry

SUSAN MATHEW

Paul's letter closing in Rom 16 is unique among his letters in several ways. In Rom 16:1–16 not only does Paul instruct the church to greet an unusually large number of people (using the imperative "greet" sixteen times with reference to twenty-seven individuals); he also mentions most of them by name and provides a brief description of each.[1] What is more, no fewer than nine of these persons are women, and according to their descriptions, most were actively engaged in the ministry of the church. Thus, Paul refers to a certain Junia as one who is "outstanding among the apostles" (16:7), while recognizing Prisca, Mary, Tryphena, Tryphosa, and Persis for their "labor" in the Lord (16:3–4, 6, 12). He also acknowledges the hospitality of Rufus's mother (16:13), greets Julia and Nereus's sister (16:15), and commends Phoebe, the letter bearer from Cenchreae (16:1–2), a harbor town adjacent to Corinth.

What do these descriptive phrases tell us about the involvement of these women in the early church? And what does their inclusion alongside men, without any statements limiting their ministerial involvement, suggest about the apostle's posture toward women in church ministry and leadership? To help answer these questions, I will compare the roles and titles that Paul attributes to these Christian women with those that women possessed in other religious contexts in the Greco-Roman world, particularly in Judaism with a focus on synagogue inscriptions.

---

1. These descriptive phrases are employed with far greater frequency than in the closings of other Pauline letters and served to strengthen the bond between him and the Roman churches he soon hoped to visit.

Unlike literary texts, which have been the basis for comparison in the previous chapters of this book, inscriptions are often pithy, stand-alone statements or records inscribed on stone or bronze for the purpose of commemorating extraordinary people and events.[2] In **honor cultures** such as ancient Greece and Rome,[3] private groups, as well as entire cities, commonly utilized inscriptions to recognize publicly the acts and accomplishments of individuals, whether immediately following a noteworthy achievement (honorary inscriptions) or upon a person's death (funerary inscriptions). Such accounts often contain important biographical data, including the public roles an individual played and the titles they carried. This information makes inscriptions particularly illuminating in the study of Rom 16, where Paul recognizes the ministerial contributions of several of his female coworkers.

Synagogue Inscriptions
"Rufina, a Jewess and head of the synagogue"

It is widely recognized that the ancient Mediterranean world was comprised largely of patriarchal societies that often restricted the rights and roles of women in most social settings. Even so, it is important to realize that some women are known to have served publicly as leaders during both the **Hellenistic** and Roman periods. For example, Junia Theodora, a wealthy Lycian who resided in Corinth around the time of Paul's ministry there, was honored by the colony in five inscriptions for her numerous civic **benefactions**.[4] Moreover, Phile, the daughter of Apollonius and wife of Thessalus, was honored in a first-century BC inscription as "the first woman in Priene [western Asia Minor] to hold the office of magistrate" (*IPriene* 208).

Female Synagogue Benefactors. Numerous Jewish women from antiquity are also known to have served prominently in their primary socioreligious context, the synagogue.[5] Several women, for example, are attested in inscriptions as synagogue benefactors, having made generous donations to local

---

2. For an overview of the study of Greek inscriptions, see Bradley H. McLean, *An Introduction to Greek Epigraphy of the Hellenistic and Roman Periods from Alexander the Great Down to the Reign of Constantine (323 BC–AD 337)* (Ann Arbor: University of Michigan Press, 2002).
3. An honor culture is a social context in which acquiring and maintaining public recognition and respect are prioritized among its participants. Cf. David A. deSilva, *Honor, Patronage, Kinship and Purity: Unlocking New Testament Culture* (Downers Grove, IL: InterVarsity Press, 2000).
4. For texts on and discussion of Junia Theodora and other women in the public sphere, see Bruce W. Winter, *Roman Wives, Roman Widows: The Appearance of New Women and the Pauline Communities* (Grand Rapids: Eerdmans, 2003), 173–204.
5. Bernadette J. Brooten, *Women Leaders in the Ancient Synagogue: Inscriptional Evidence and Background Issues* (BJS 36; Chico, CA: Scholars Press, 1982).

synagogue building projects.[6] A third-century AD inscription from Phocaea in Ionia (western Asia Minor) honors a certain Tation for funding the construction of an entire synagogue.

> Tation, daughter of Straton, son of Empedon, having constructed the building and the enclosure of the open courtyard with her own funds, gave them to the Jews. [Therefore] the synagogue of the Jews honored Tation, daughter of Straton, son of Empedon, with a golden crown and the seat of honor. (CII 738)[7]

Tation must have had considerable wealth to have independently paid the expense for the synagogue building. Moreover, the seat of honor she received for her generosity, though probably entirely honorific rather than being a functional position, plainly shows that Tation, as Paul Trebilco concludes, "was an important and respected person in the community."[8]

Female Synagogue Leaders. A sample of inscriptions from the second century BC to the sixth century AD also shows that certain women held important synagogue offices. Five inscriptions attest to women bearing the title "mother of the synagogue" (CII 496; CII 166; CII 523; CII 639; CII 606), which most likely indicates their active involvement in administration and leadership. An inscription of unknown date from Thessaly (northern Greece) mentions a certain Peristeria and refers to her as a "leader" (CII 696b). Moreover, Beronikene (CII 581) from Apulia (Italy) and a certain Rebeka (CII 692) from Thrace (north of the Black Sea), together with several other ancient Jewish women, are given the title council "elder" on their tombs, which suggests they were highly respected and considered to be leaders.

Importantly, three women from Asia Minor are also attested as "head of the synagogue"—the title borne by the person who, according to Trebilco, was "the spiritual and intellectual leader of the synagogue and responsible for its spiritual direction and regulation, including at times teaching the community and on other occasions inviting someone else to preach."[9] A funerary inscription from Smyrna (western Asia Minor), dated to the second or third century AD, recognizes a certain "Rufina, a Jewess and head of the synagogue," who had "built this tomb for her freed slaves and the slaves

---

6. Paul R. Trebilco records that four out of fifty-three inscriptions regarding donations mention that they were provided by women alone and another fifteen were from women and their husbands (*Jewish Communities in Asia Minor* [Cambridge: Cambridge University Press, 1991], 112).
7. Trebilco, *Jewish Communities*, 110.
8. Ibid.
9. Ibid., 104–5.

raised in her house" (*CII* 741). A fourth- or fifth-century AD inscription from Crete mentions a certain "Sophia of Gortyn, elder and head of the synagogue of Kisamos" (*CII* 731c). A final attestation from Caria (western Asia Minor), dated to the fourth or fifth century AD, recognizes one "Theopempte, head of the synagogue" (*CII* 756). Some scholars believe the roles attributed to these women were entirely honorific, having been granted due to the prominence of their husbands; the positions they occupied, it is therefore suggested, carried no responsibility. However, because their husbands are not mentioned in the inscriptions, it is best to assume the roles these women filled were the same as their male counterparts, who "were active in administration and exhortation."[10] This is perhaps most true of Rufina, whose administrative competence is apparent from the fact that she managed numerous slaves and freedmen. It is quite plausible, then, for her to have served as a synagogue leader.

This brief survey shows that certain women, despite the patriarchy of ancient Mediterranean societies, were afforded the opportunity to serve in prominent positions in various public contexts, including Jewish synagogues. Some Jewish women bore the same titles as men, being identified as synagogue heads, elders, leaders, and mothers. Most of the references examined were not from the first century AD. However, by cautiously using this evidence it could be postulated that first-century Jewish culture was not opposed to, and in fact occasionally celebrated, women serving in leadership roles, a historical phenomenon that has significant implications for our reading of Romans.

Romans 16:1 – 27

"PHOEBE, A DEACON OF THE CHURCH ... THE BENEFACTOR OF MANY"

The leadership positions held by the Jewish women mentioned above find close parallels in the roles occupied by the women mentioned in Rom 16. I will focus here on Phoebe, who holds a special place in the letter and is a fitting representative of the others.

Paul begins the letter closing by introducing and commending Phoebe, the person commissioned by Paul to deliver the epistle to the Roman believers: "I commend to you our sister Phoebe, a deacon of the church in Cenchreae. I ask you to receive her in the Lord in a way worthy of his people and to give her any help she may need from you, for she has been the benefactor of many people, including me" (16:1 – 2). Paul is eager to mention

---

10. Brooten, *Women Leaders*, 30; cf. Trebilco, *Jewish Communities*, 106.

the ways Phoebe has served both him (as benefactor) and the local church in Cenchreae (as deacon), for her contributions speak to her credibility and deservingness to be welcomed by the believers in Rome. But what do Paul's descriptions of Phoebe suggest about her role in local church ministry?

Phoebe as a Church Leader. The Greek concrete noun translated "deacon" in Rom 16:1 probably refers to a position of prominence in the local church, though the original nature of the role is not clearly explained anywhere in the NT. Paul uses the term, which can also be translated "servant," to refer to various functions in the context of the church. It is noteworthy, however, that the role often involves teaching (e.g., 1 Cor 3:5–6; Eph 3:7; Col 1:7, 23–25; 4:7). Paul also uses the related abstract noun, normally translated "ministry" or "service," in a range of contexts and in relation to a variety of individuals, including himself (Rom 11:13; 15:31; 2 Cor 4:1; 5:18; 6:3; 11:8), Archippus (Col 4:17), Stephanas and his household (1 Cor 16:15), and other Christians (Rom 12:7; 1 Cor 12:5; Eph 4:12). Most importantly, in Phil 1:1 Paul addresses "deacons" together with "overseers," the latter being local church leaders (1 Tim 3:2; Titus 1:7; cf. Acts 20:28; 1 Pet 5:2), which suggests that both there and in Rom 16:1 the term translated "deacon" refers to a prominent position in the church.

Some interpreters, however, assume that the deacon position to which Paul refers in Rom 16:1 is the same office of deaconess attested in the third- and fourth-century church. That later office was mainly responsible for caring for the sick, the poor, and other women.[11] If this were the case for Phoebe, then her leadership and ministerial responsibilities would have been quite limited compared to her male counterparts. But the term translated "deacon" in Rom 16:1 is no different from the titles given to men, so it would be illegitimate to assume that Phoebe filled a less prominent role than a male deacon simply because of her gender. As its appearance in Phil 1:1 suggests, Phoebe's title indicates she was a leader in the church of Cenchreae, even if no rigid ecclesial hierarchy existed in the mid-first century AD. Thus, the rendering *"minister* of the church in Cenchreae" is perhaps most suitable.

Phoebe as a Church Benefactor. It is also likely that Phoebe's influence in Cenchreae was due in part to her wealth, for in addition to the title "deacon," Paul refers to her as a "benefactor of many people, including me" (Rom 16:2). The term Paul uses for benefactor, though not appearing elsewhere in the NT, occurs in numerous ancient inscriptions referring to female patrons

---

11. For interaction with this view, see Caroline F. Whelan, "Amica Pauli: The Role of Phoebe in the Early Church," *JSNT* 15 (1993): 67–85, at 67.

of various socioreligious groups, including synagogues and private guilds.[12] The implications of the title are wide-ranging. In the light of its non-Christian occurrences, Paul's use of the term suggests that Phoebe was an influential figure with some socioeconomic standing who utilized her wealth and status for the benefit of Paul and others, probably even hosting visitors and church meetings in her home. And the recipients of her generosity, according to Paul, were "many," implying that those who benefited from her patronage were not easily counted.

A Ministry of Mutuality. It is because of Phoebe's generosity, then, that Paul asks the Romans to welcome her warmly; indeed, he requests they "give her any help she may need" (16:2), an astonishingly open-ended request. In so doing, Paul desires that Phoebe be reciprocated for the benefits he and others received from her. In other words, the Roman Christians to whom Paul is writing and to whom Phoebe is to deliver the letter should offer her hospitality, not only "in a way worthy of his people," but in a way similar to how she herself sacrificially served and hosted the believers in Cenchreae (16:2). Paul's pattern of ministry and leadership, then, is one of mutuality: the beneficiaries of gifts and favors should give back to, or pay forward on behalf of, those from whom they have received. As Paul writes elsewhere, "Your plenty will supply what they need, so that in turn their plenty will supply what you need. The goal is equality" (2 Cor 8:14). Thus, whatever Phoebe's help looked like, the Romans are expected to reciprocate.

Paul's description of Phoebe, therefore, gives us an insight into Paul's attitude toward women in leadership. By referring to Phoebe as a "deacon" and "benefactor," Paul implies that she is a full participant with him in church ministry and leadership. In fact, her leadership is acknowledged alongside that of men and without apology or qualification. Moreover, the reciprocity Paul demands on her behalf is irrespective of gender: he inserts her into a social matrix that includes himself, his churches, and the Romans, and thereby mandates that honor and favors be mutually exchanged between all parties. And Paul does similarly with Prisca, Mary, Junia, Tryphena, Tryphosa, Persis, Julia, Rufus's mother, and Nereus's sister, whom we have not discussed, but whom Paul honors by offering salutations and acknowledging their Christian service. It is my belief that by recognizing these women and attributing to them the roles and titles that he does, Paul goes as far as, if not beyond, other Jewish communities by allowing and even encouraging women to serve in leadership positions.

---

12. Trebilco, *Jewish Communities*, 109.

FOR FURTHER READING

Additional Ancient Texts

On the prominence of women in Israel, see Judg 4–5 (Deborah), Esther, and Judith. For other Pauline texts, see particularly 1 Cor 11:2–16; 14:34–35; 1 Tim 2:9–15.

English Translations and Critical Editions

Frey, Jean-Baptiste, ed. *Corpus inscriptionum iudaicarum*. 2 vols. Rome: Pontifico Istituto di Archaeologia Cristiana, 1936–1952.

Secondary Literature

Brooten, Bernadette J. *Women Leaders in the Ancient Synagogue: Inscriptional Evidence and Background Issues*. BJS 36. Chico, CA: Scholars Press, 1982.

Campbell, Joan Cecelia. *Phoebe: Patron and Emissary*. Paul's Social Network. Collegeville, MN: Liturgical Press, 2009

Cohick, Lynn H. *Women in the World of the Earliest Christians: Illuminating Ancient Ways of Life*. Grand Rapids: Baker Academic, 2009..

Mathew, Susan. *Women in the Greetings of Romans 16.1–16: A Study of Mutuality and Women's Ministry in the Letter to the Romans*. LNTS 471. London: T&T Clark, 2013.

Payne, Philip Barton. *Man and Woman, One in Christ: An Exegetical and Theological Study of Paul's Letters*. Grand Rapids: Zondervan, 2009.

Some definitions in this glossary are adapted from Mark L. Strauss, *Four Portraits, One Jesus: A Survey of Jesus and the Gospels* (Grand Rapids: Zondervan, 2007).

Allegory, allegorical: An interpretive method that goes beyond the literal meaning of a text by highlighting connections to other ideas or events.

Already/not yet: See *Inaugurated eschatology.*

Ancient Near East: The phrase describes the peoples who lived in Egypt, Palestine, Syria, Asia Minor, Mesopotamia, Persia, and Arabia from the beginning of recorded history up to the conquest of Alexander the Great (c. 333 BC), though some also informally use this phrase to refer up to the first century AD.

Antiochus IV Epiphanes (c. 215–164 BC): A ruler of the Seleucid Kingdom (175–164), the Hellenistic state in Syria partitioned from Alexander the Great's vast empire. Antiochus provoked the Maccabean conflict by trying to Hellenize Jews.

Anthropology, anthropological: Literally "the study of humans." This includes topics such as human composition (e.g., body, soul), human ability (e.g., free will), and ethnic diversity (e.g., Jew, Gentile).

Apocrypha, apocryphal (also known as the deuterocanonical books): A collection of Jewish texts written after the OT period and which are combined with a Greek translation of the OT to form the Septuagint. These were considered authoritative by patristic Christians and therefore accepted by Roman Catholic and Orthodox Christians as canonical but are rejected by Protestants as Scripture. In nonacademic settings, "apocryphal" is often used as a description of stories that sound true but are not.

Apocalyptic, apocalyptic tradition: An "apocalypse" is literally a "revelation" of previously hidden things. These terms are most associated with the revelation of God and of heavenly realities through visions and dreams, and the revelation of divine actions to establish God's (future) rule among his covenant people and the whole world to help explain the problem of evil. Thus, there is often focus on spatial (heaven/earth) and temporal (present/future) dualisms.

Benefaction: A social arrangement in which patrons (those of greater means) give gifts of support to those of lesser means (clients) or to their local communities, often with the expectation of receiving services, respect, or loyalty in return.

Canonical: Texts are considered canonical when they are included in a collection of texts considered to be inspired and authoritative Scripture. The OT and NT are indisputably part of the Christian canon, whereas different Christian traditions dispute the inclusion of the Apocrypha. See *Apocrypha*.

Christ event, the: A phrase referring to the life and work of Jesus as the Christ/Messiah.

Christology, christological: More generally, this term describes the person and work of Jesus. Specifically, the term relates to Jesus' role as the Christ. "Christ" (*christos*) is Greek for "anointed one," and it often served as the direct translation of the Hebrew term "messiah." See *Messiah*.

Covenant, covenantal: An agreement between two parties that places obligations on each party. Important covenants in the Bible include the Abrahamic covenant (Gen 15; 17), the Mosaic covenant (Exodus; Leviticus; Deuteronomy), the Davidic covenant (2 Sam 7); and the new covenant (Jer 31; Ezek 34–37).

Covenant community: Jewish groups who believed they were faithful to God's covenants with Israel considered themselves to be a "covenant community." This conceptuality is sometimes used by groups (like those at Qumran) to distinguish themselves from other Jews who are not considered faithful to the covenants. See *Dead Sea Scrolls*.

Covenantal nomism: A description, coined by E. P. Sanders, of the way Second Temple Jews viewed the interplay of grace, election, and obedience to the law. Sanders argued that Jews understood their election as members of the covenant people of God to be by grace (getting in) and that they maintained their position in the covenant by obedience to the law. (Law is *nomos* in Greek). This position is often associated with the New Perspective on Paul.

Dead Sea Scrolls: A collect of texts discovered in caves near the Dead Sea in 1947 and likely associated with the first-century Jewish community at Qumran. The scrolls include copies of biblical and other Jewish literature, as well as sectarian texts arising from the Qumran community. See *Sectarian*.

Deuterocanonical: See *Apocrypha*.

Deuteronomic theology (or pattern): A theological view, expressed most fully in Deuteronomy, whereby God issues to his people material blessing and protection for covenant obedience, and cursing and suffering for disobedience.

Diatribe: A rhetorical technique that may include asking questions to fictional conversation partners.

Didactic: A description of a text or speech that is focused on teaching, often through the means of propositional arguments.

Eschatology, eschatological: Literally, "the study of the end times." The term indicates any event or idea that is associated with the final days. In Jewish and Pauline studies, though, the term "eschatology" does not refer simply or only to the end times, but to God's action to restore his rule through key agents or events.

Eschaton: The final state after God brings resolution to history. See *Eschatology*.

Hasmoneans (167–63 BC): The Jewish family that ruled a semi-autonomous and later fully autonomous kingdom as the Jews secured independence from the Seleucids. As a result of infighting among the family, the Jews lost their independence to the Romans in 63 BC. See *Maccabean Revolt*; *Seleucids*.

Hellenism, Hellenistic, Hellenize, Hellenization: The spread and influence of Greek language and culture in the ancient world, particularly after the military conquest of Alexander the Great (336–323 BC).

Honor culture: A culture whose social dynamic is determined by the struggle for honor as the basis for social status. Varying levels of honor mark one's position on the social ladder and thus determine how one can and should relate to others with higher, similar, or lower social standing.

Inclusio: A literary practice of showing the limits of a section of text by repeating key terms and ideas at the beginning and the ending of the passage.

Inaugurated eschatology ("already/not yet"): The belief that the "end times" have already begun but have not yet reached their fulfillment. In Paul's theology, God's first advent through Christ and the Spirit marks the beginning of the end times, but God's kingdom will not be fully consummated until the return of Christ and his ultimate restoration of God's rule. See *Eschatology*.

Josephus (AD 37–c. 100): Once a Jewish Pharisee and military leader, Josephus was taken captive during the Jerusalem War against Rome and eventually made a Roman citizen and dependent of Emperor Vespasian. His four extant works are very important for our understanding of the history and culture of Second Temple Judaism: a history of the Jewish people (*Jewish Antiquities*), an account of the Jerusalem War (*Jewish War*), a work in defense of Judaism and the Jewish way of life (*Against Apion*), and an autobiography (*The Life*).

LXX: The abbreviation for the Septuagint. See *Septuagint*.

Maccabean Revolt (or Crisis/Conflict): The Jewish rebellion against Seleucid rule in 175–164 BC. The conflict is titled after "the Maccabees" (Hebrew for "hammer"), which was a name given to Judas and his brothers, who led Israel during this period.

Masada: A Jewish fortress destroyed by the Romans (along with the second temple) during the first-century Jewish revolt (AD 66–70).

Messiah, messianic: A transliteration of a Hebrew word meaning "anointed one" and which is translated into Greek as "Christ." There was no single Jewish view about the Messiah, though all views envision this person as God's agent who will deliver his people.

Ontology: Literally, "the study of being." This term describes the nature of being or existence and is often used in contexts related to what constitutes humans or God, but it can refer to any person or object's state of being.

Personification: The attribution of human characteristics to any inanimate object, abstract concept, or impersonal being. Personifications can be as simple as a common idiom (e.g., "time marches on") or complex enough to be associated with a divine power (e.g., Wisdom in Proverbs).

Philo (c. 20 BC–AD 50): A Diaspora Jew influenced by Platonism from Alexandria, Egypt. He authored numerous philosophical treatises and exegetical studies on the Pentateuch. See *Plato*.

Plato, Platonism: Plato is a famous Greek philosopher who lived in Athens (c. 428–347 BC). He wrote a number of philosophical treatises on ethics, physics, creation, logic, and rhetoric, among other things. There are various forms of Platonism that draw in differing ways from Plato's thought, but a primary aspect was a dualism based on a distinction between the realm of conceptual realities (immaterial and unchangeable) and the realm of concrete realities (material and changeable).

Pseudepigrapha, pseudepigraphic: Literally, "falsely ascribed writings." A pseudepigraphic text is a text written under the name of another (often centuries earlier) person. The Pseudepigrapha specifically refers to Jewish pseudepigraphic texts not included in the Apocrypha, but since this was a common practice for Second Temple Jews, the term pseudepigrapha has generally become a catchall for all Jewish texts not included in another specific category, such as the Apocrypha or Dead Sea Scrolls, or authored by specific writers, such as Josephus and Philo.

Qumran: A site located near the Dead Sea and close to the caves in which the Dead Sea Scrolls were found. The common view is that the community that lived there during the Second Temple Period were Essenes and the ones responsible for producing the Dead Sea Scrolls.

Second Temple Period, Second Temple Judaism, Second Temple Jewish (c. 516 BC – AD 70): The period in Jewish history roughly from the return from exile (about 516 BC) until the destruction of the temple by the Romans in AD 70. Other phrases used for all or part of this time period are Early Judaism, Middle Judaism, and the Intertestamental Period.

Sectarian: That which pertains to a particular religious group, notably the texts composed by and for the Dead Sea Scroll community. See *Dead Sea Scrolls*.

Seleucids, Seleucid Kingdom (312–115 BC): A kingdom in the region of Syria that was formed after Alexander the Great's kingdom was subdivided after his death. Judea was eventually ruled by the Seleucids, who attempted to force the Jews to assimilate to Hellenism. See *Hellenism; Maccabean Revolt*.

Septuagint (LXX): A collection of authoritative Jewish texts in Greek that includes the Greek translation of the Hebrew Bible, as well as other Jewish writings. The abbreviation LXX is the Roman numeral for 70 and is based on the tradition that 70 (or 72) men translated the Hebrew Pentateuch into Greek.

Stoicism: One of the main Greco-Roman philosophical traditions during the Hellenistic era. Founded by Zeno (335–263 BC), it is known for its emphasis on fate, reason, and inner self-mastery to achieve the primary goal of a virtuous life.

Two-ways paradigm: A theological view in which humans are presented with the options of good or evil and can determine for themselves which path to follow. This perspective is rooted in Deuteronomic theology. See *Deuteronomic theology*.

Theodicy: A defense or explanation of how God is just, even though evil exists, especially with regard to the righteous who suffer unjustly at the hands of the wicked.

Contributors

Ben C. Blackwell (PhD, University of Durham) is assistant professor of Christianity at Houston Baptist University and is a former research assistant for N. T. Wright and John Barclay. He is the author of *Christosis: Pauline Soteriology in Light of Deification in Irenaeus and Cyril* (WUNT 2.314; Tübingen: Mohr Siebeck, 2011).

David E. Briones (PhD, University of Durham) is professor of New Testament at Reformation Bible College, Florida, and author of *Paul's Financial Policy: A Socio-Theological Approach* (LNTS; London: T&T Clark, 2013).

Joseph R. Dodson (PhD, University of Aberdeen) is assistant professor of biblical studies at Ouachita Baptist University, Arkansas, and author of *The 'Powers' of Personification: Rhetorical Purpose in the 'Book of Wisdom' and the Letter to the Romans* (BZNW 161; Berlin: de Gruyter, 2008).

Ben C. Dunson (PhD, University of Durham) is professor of New Testament at Reformation Bible College, Florida, and author of *Individual and Community in Paul's Letter to the Romans* (WUNT 2.332; Tübingen: Mohr Siebeck, 2012).

John K. Goodrich (PhD, University of Durham) is chair and assistant professor of Bible at Moody Bible Institute, Chicago, and author of *Paul as an Administrator of God in 1 Corinthians* (SNTSMS 152; Cambridge: Cambridge University Press, 2012).

Nijay K. Gupta (PhD, University of Durham) is assistant professor of New Testament at George Fox Evangelical Seminary, Oregon, and author of *Worship That Makes Sense to Paul: A New Approach to the Theology and Ethics of Paul's Cultic Metaphors* (BZNW 175; Berlin: de Gruyter, 2010) and *Colossians* (SHBC; Macon, GA: Smyth & Helwys, 2013).

Wesley Hill (PhD, University of Durham) is assistant professor of biblical studies at Trinity School for Ministry, Pennsylvania, and author of *Paul and the Triune Divine Identity* (Grand Rapids: Eerdmans, 2015).

Mariam J. Kamell (PhD, University of St. Andrews) is assistant professor of New Testament at Regent College, Vancouver, and coauthor (with Craig Blomberg) of *James* (ZECNT; Grand Rapids: Zondervan, 2008).

David Lincicum (DPhil, University of Oxford) is university lecturer in New Testament studies at the University of Oxford, UK, and author of *Paul and the Early Jewish Encounter with Deuteronomy* (WUNT 2.284; Tübingen: Mohr Siebeck, 2010; repr., Grand Rapids: Baker Academic, 2013) and co-editor (with Markus Bockmuehl) of Graham Stanton's *Studies in Matthew and Early Christianity* (WUNT 309; Tübingen: Mohr Siebeck, 2013).

Jonathan A. Linebaugh (PhD, University of Durham) is associate professor of New Testament at Knox Theological Seminary, Florida, and author of *God, Grace, and Righteousness: Wisdom of Solomon and Paul's Letter to the Romans in Conversation* (NovTSup 152; Leiden: Brill, 2013).

Jason Maston (PhD, University of Durham) is assistant professor of theology, chair of the department of theology at Houston Baptist University, author of *Divine and Human Agency in Second Temple Judaism and Paul: A Comparative Approach* (WUNT 2.297; Tübingen: Mohr Siebeck, 2010), and contributor to and co-editor (with Michael F. Bird) of *Earliest Christian History: History, Literature and Theology; Essays from the Tyndale Fellowship in Honor of Martin Hengel* (WUNT 2.320; Tübingen: Mohr Siebeck, 2012).

Susan Mathew (PhD, University of Durham) is assistant professor of New Testament at Faith Theological Seminary, Kerala (India), and author of *Women in the Greetings of Rom 16.1–16: A Study of Mutuality and Women's Ministry in the Letter to the Romans* (LNTS 471; London: T&T Clark, 2013).

Mark D. Mathews (PhD, University of Durham) is pastor of Bethany Presbyterian Church, Oxford, Pennsylvania, and author of *Riches, Poverty, and the Faithful: Perspectives on Wealth in the Second Temple Period and the Apocalypse of John* (SNTSMS 154; Cambridge: Cambridge University Press, 2013).

Orrey McFarland (PhD, University of Durham) is an ordinand in the North American Lutheran Church and the author of numerous articles, including "Whose Abraham, Which Promise? Genesis 15.6 in Philo's *De Virtutibus* and Romans 4," *JSNT* 35 (2012): 107–29, and "'The One Who Calls in Grace': Paul's Rhetorical and Theological Identification with the Galatians," *Horizons in Biblical Theology* 35 (2013): 151–65.

Dean Pinter (PhD, University of Durham) is rector of St. Aidan Anglican Church, Saskatchewan, and author of "The Gospel of Luke and the Roman Empire," in *Jesus Is Lord, Caesar Is Not: Evaluating Empire in New Testament Studies* (ed. S. McKnight and J. B. Modica; Downers Grove, IL: IVP Academic, 2013), 101–15, and *Acts* (The Story of God Bible Commentary; Grand Rapids: Zondervan, forthcoming).

Aaron Sherwood (PhD, University of Durham) is assistant professor of New Testament at Alliance Theological Seminary, New York, and author of *Paul and the Restoration of Humanity in Light of Ancient Jewish Traditions* (AJEC 82; Leiden: Brill, 2013).

Kyle B. Wells (PhD, University of Durham) is pastor of Christ Presbyterian Church, Santa Barbara, California, adjunct professor at Westmont College, and author of *Grace and Agency in Paul and Second Temple Judaism: Interpreting the Transformation of the Heart* (NovTSup 157; Leiden: Brill, 2014).

Sarah Whittle (PhD, University of Manchester) is lecturer in biblical studies at Nazarene Theological College, Manchester, UK, and author of *Covenant Renewal and the Consecration of the Gentiles in Romans* (SNTSMS 161; Cambridge: Cambridge University Press, 2014).

Jonathan Worthington (PhD, University of Durham) is lecturer in New Testament at Belfast Bible College, UK, and author of *Creation in Paul and Philo: The Beginning and Before* (WUNT 2.317; Tübingen: Mohr Siebeck, 2011).

Passage Index

Subject Index

Adam, 43–44, 80–85, 87, 89, 91, 101, 104, 108–13

Abraham, 22, 50, 54, 66–72, 80, 119–120, 131, 133

almsgiving, 158–60, 162

anthropology, 39, 44, 64, 92, 94, 113

Christ, 17–18, 31–33, 36, 38, 46, 49–50, 57, 59, 62–64, 66–67, 71, 73–74, 77–78, 85, 87, 89–93, 98, 100, 105–6, 108, 111–15, 120, 122, 126–28, 136, 140–41, 143, 147, 151–52, 154–56, 162–163, 165

circumcision, 46–50, 56, 66, 68–71, 152, 154

collection, the, 158, 161–65

creation/re-creation, 14, 26, 41, 43, 47–48, 87–88, 90, 96, 108–13, 138–39

death, 17, 36, 42–44, 59, 61–64, 77–78, 80–85, 87–98, 100, 102–5, 109–13, 120, 137–38, 140, 153, 159–60, 167

eschatology (including already/not yet, eschaton), 32–34, 39, 49–50, 60–61, 73, 76, 94, 102–3, 106, 111, 130–34

ethnic(ity), 17, 46–50, 119–21

faith, 32–36, 42, 50, 52, 56–57, 63–64, 66–67, 69–78, 102, 106, 115–16, 119–23, 126–30, 132–34, 136–37, 141, 151, 154–55, 159

glory, 23, 43, 67, 73, 77–78, 89–90, 103, 108–13, 115, 131, 140, 143, 163

grace, 31, 36, 40, 59, 64–65, 73, 76–78, 80–81, 85, 87–92, 115, 120, 129, 134, 136, 162–65

Israel, 22–26, 31–36, 39–44, 48–50, 53–54, 66–67, 71, 75, 95, 101–5, 115, 119–27, 129–35, 145, 152, 155, 161–62

justification, 17, 48, 52–57, 62–64, 66, 70, 73, 77, 80, 85, 108

law, works of law, Mosaic law, Torah, 17, 22–23, 27, 32, 46–50, 52–57, 59, 62–64, 66–74, 85, 90, 93–98, 100–6, 115–116, 122–28, 136–41, 149, 151–55

life, 21–27, 32–36, 40, 43, 67–71, 73–74, 76, 78, 80–82, 85, 87–92, 94–98, 100–6, 108–12, 118, 122–24, 127, 130, 136–41, 144, 150–54, 159–60

mercy, 40, 42, 81–83, 103, 115, 119–21, 129–30, 132–34, 136, 139

Platonism, 27, 82, 84, 123

providence, 143–45, 149

reason, 35, 41–43, 48, 56–57, 71, 75, 78, 82, 89–91, 102, 104, 115–19, 129, 136–140, 147

righteousness, 14, 33, 36, 38–43, 46, 48, 50, 52–64, 66, 68–71, 74–76, 78–79, 85, 87–91, 101–3, 105–06, 109–10, 112, 115–18, 122–27, 129, 131, 136, 159–60

salvation, 14, 38, 42, 55–57, 73, 76–77, 92, 102, 106, 112, 129–34, 150

Author Index

Printed in the USA
CPSIA information can be obtained
at www.ICGtesting.com
LVHW020708050824
787165LV00009B/59